$\mathscr{P}$ROFILES IN AMERICAN HISTORY

Significant Events and the People

Who Shaped Them

Volume 3: *Indian Removal to the Abolition Movement*

Indian Removal
John Ross, Black Hawk, Winfield Scott
Industrialization
Samuel Slater, Eli Whitney, Harriet Hanson Robinson
Women and Reform
Sarah and Angelina Grimké, Susan B. Anthony, Amelia Bloomer
Slave Controversies
Denmark Vesey, Nat Turner, John Quincy Adams
Plantation System
James Henry Hammond, Harriet A. Jacobs, Mary Chesnut
Antislavery Movement
David Walker, William Lloyd Garrison, Frederick Douglass, Sojourner
Truth, Harriet Beecher Stowe

Volume 4: *Westward Expansion to the Civil War*

Westward Expansion
Stephen Austin, Sam Houston, Marcus and Narcissa Whitman
Mexican War
Zachary Taylor, Jessie and John Frémont
Economic Growth
Christopher "Kit" Carson, John Sutter
Transcendental and Romantic Movements
Henry David Thoreau, Nathaniel Hawthorne, Margaret Fuller
Pre-Civil War Controversies
Dred Scott, Stephen Douglas, John Brown
Civil War
Robert E. Lee, Abraham Lincoln, Martin Delany, William Tecumseh
Sherman, Anna Carroll, Mathew Brady, Walt Whitman

PROFILES IN AMERICAN HISTORY

Constitutional Convention to the War of 1812

1786-1787
▼
Shays' Rebellion occurs over farmers' debts.

1787
▼
Assembly of state representatives writes the United States Constitution.

1791
▼
The states ratify ten amendments to the Constitution, adopting the Bill of Rights.

1790
▼
Rhode Island becomes last of the original thirteen states to ratify the Constitution.

1789
▼
Twelve states ratify the Constitution. George Washington elected President.

1791
▼
Robert Gray sails to the Pacific Northwest and "discovers" the Columbia River.

1803
▼
President Thomas Jefferson purchases the Louisiana Territory.

1804-1806
▼
Lewis and Clark journey across the United States.

1828
▼
Noah Webster prints *The American Dictionary of the English Language.*

1815
▼
United States Congress ratifies Treaty of Ghent, which ends war.

1812-1814
▼
Advance of whites onto frontier erupts in War of 1812, fought between the British and their allies and the United States.

PROFILES IN AMERICAN HISTORY

Significant Events and the People

Who Shaped Them

2

Constitutional Convention to the War of 1812

JOYCE MOSS

and

GEORGE WILSON

AN IMPRINT OF GALE RESEARCH INC.

3 9075 02902301 4

PROFILES IN AMERICAN HISTORY:
Significant Events and the People Who Shaped Them

VOLUME 2: CONTINENTAL CONVENTION TO THE WAR OF 1812

Joyce Moss and George Wilson

Staff

Carol DeKane Nagel, *U•X•L Developmental Editor*
Thomas L. Romig, *U•X•L Publisher*

Christine Nasso, *Acquisitions Editor*

Shanna P. Heilveil, *Production Assistant*
Evi Seoud, *Assistant Production Manager*
Mary Beth Trimper, *Production Director*

Mary Krzewinski, *Cover and Page Designer*
Cynthia Baldwin, *Art Director*

The Graphix Group, *Typesetting*

Library of Congress Cataloging-in-Publication Data

Profiles in American history : significant events and the people who shaped them.

Includes bibliographical references and index.

Contents: v. 2. Continental convention to the war of 1812.

1. United States—History—Juvenile literature. 2. United States—Biography—Juvenile literature. 3. United States—History. [JUV] 4. United States—Biography. [JUV] I. Moss, Joyce, 1951- . II. Wilson, George, 1920- .

E178.M897 1994 920.073 94-6677

ISBN 0-8103-9207-0 (set : acid-free paper)
ISBN 0-8103-9209-7 (v. 2 : acid-free paper)

∞™ This book is printed on acid-free paper that meets the minimum requirements of American National Standard for Information Sciences—Permanence Paper for Printed Library Materials, ANSI Z39.48-1984.

Printed in the United States of America

Published simultaneously in the United Kingdom by Gale Research International Limited (An affiliated company of Gale Research Inc.)

I(T)P™ U·X·L is an imprint of Gale Research Inc.,
an International Thomson Publishing Company.
ITP logo is a trademark under license.

Contents

Reader's Guide

The many noteworthy individuals who shaped U.S. history from the exploration of the continent to the present day cannot all be profiled in one eight-volume work. But those whose stories are told in *Profiles in American History* meet one or more of the following criteria. The individuals:

- Directly affected the outcome of a major event in U.S. history
- Represent viewpoints or groups involved in that event
- Exemplify a role played by common citizens in that event
- Highlight an aspect of that event not covered in other entries

Format

Volumes of *Profiles in American History* are arranged by chapter. Each chapter focuses on one particular event and opens with an overview and detailed time line of the event that places it in historical context. Following are biographical profiles of two to seven diverse individuals who played active roles in the event.

Each biographical profile is divided into four sections:

- **Personal Background** provides details that predate and anticipate the individual's involvement in the event
- **Participation** describes the role played by the individual in the event and its impact on his or her life
- **Aftermath** discusses effects of the individual's actions and subsequent relevant events in his or her life
- **For More Information** provides sources for further reading on the individual

Additionally, sidebars containing interesting details about the events and individuals profiled, ranging from numbers of war casualties to famous quotes to family trees, are sprinkled throughout the text.

Additional Features

Maps are provided to assist readers in traveling back through time to an America arranged differently from today. Portraits and illustrations of individuals and events as well as excerpts from primary source materials are also included to help bring history to life. Sources of all quoted material are cited parenthetically within the text, and complete bibliographic information is listed at the end of the entry. A full bibliography of scholarly sources consulted in preparing the volume appear in the book's back matter.

Cross references are made in the entries, directing readers to other entries in the volume that elaborate on individuals connected in some way to the person under scrutiny. In addition, a comprehensive subject index provides easy access to people and events mentioned throughout the volume.

Comments and Suggestions

We welcome your comments on this work as well as your suggestions for individuals to be featured in future editions of *Profiles in American History*. Please write: Editors, *Profiles in American History,* U·X·L, 835 Penobscot Bldg., Detroit, Michigan 48226-4094; call toll-free: 1-800-877-4253; or fax: 313-961-6348.

Preface

"There is properly no History; only Biography," wrote great American poet and scholar Ralph Waldo Emerson. *Profiles in American History* explores U.S. history through biography. Beginning with the first contact between Native Americans and the Vikings and continuing to the present day, this series offers a unique alternative to traditional texts by emphasizing the roles played by significant individuals, including many women and minorities, in historical events.

Profiles in American History presents the human story of American events, not the exclusively European or African or Indian or Asian story. But the guiding principle in compiling this series has been to achieve balance not only in gender and ethnic background but in viewpoint. Thus the circumstances surrounding an historical event are told from individuals holding opposing views, and even opposing positions. Slaves and slaveowners, business tycoons and workers, advocates of peace and proponents of war all are heard. American authors whose works reflect the times—from James Fenimore Cooper to John Steinbeck—are also featured.

The biographical profiles are arranged in groups, clustered around one major event in American history, though each individual profile is complete in itself. But it is the interplay of these profiles—the juxtaposition of alternative views and experiences within a grouping—that broadens the readers' perspective on the event as a whole and on the participants' roles in particular. It is what makes it possible for *Profiles in American History* to impart a larger, human understanding of events in American history.

Acknowledgments

For their guidance on the choice of events and personalities, the editors are grateful to:

Jonathan Betz-Zall, Children's Librarian, Sno-Isle Regional Library System, Washington

Janet Sarratt, Library Media Specialist, John E. Ewing Junior High School, Gaffney, South Carolina

Michael Salman, Assistant Professor of American History, University of California at Los Angeles

Appreciation is extended to Professor Salman for his careful review of chapter overviews and his guidance on key sources of information about the personalities and events.

For insights into specific personalities, the editors are grateful to Robert Sumpter, History Department Chairman at Mira Costa High School, Manhatten Beach, California.

Deep appreciation is extended to the writers who compiled data and contributed the biographical profiles for this volume of *Profiles in American History:*

Diane Ahrens
Erica Heet
Dana Huebler
Colin Wells

The editors also thank artist Robert Bates for his research and rendering of maps and illustrations and Paulette Petrimoulx for her careful copy editing.

Introduction

A period of confusion followed the Revolutionary War as Americans struggled to create a nation. Never before had a republic—which placed power not in a monarch but in the hands of the people—been attempted on such a grand scale. It was a daring experiment, one that fostered heated debate. In 1776 and 1777 each state wrote its own constitution, dividing power among the governor, legislature, and courts to guard against possible dictatorship. Meanwhile, a committee from different states wrote a document of union, the Articles of Confederation. Not approved by all the states until 1781, this document formed a central government, creating the United States of America.

Shaping the Republic

Political and social disagreements erupted during the early decades of the new republic. The Articles of Confederation proved too weak to bind the states together, and a convention to strengthen the document produced the United States Constitution. After reforming the central government, leaders struggled over issues such as how to raise money and what specific powers Congress and the Supreme Court would hold.

Disputes within the government spilled over into society, where interest groups began taking root. Poor farmers protested the government's collecting taxes or taking away lands. Slaves who were newly freed (primarily in the North) faced discrimination, leading to struggles for social equality. And women began demanding more freedom as well, voicing their opinions and claiming their right to be educated.

Expanding the Republic and Establishing an Identity

The new government leaders faced the problem of how to keep members of society on an equal footing. Thomas Jefferson was firmly convinced that democracy could survive if enough land were made available for all citizens to earn a living. When France offered to sell to the United States all the territory between the Mississippi River and the Rocky Mountains, Jefferson purchased it. This windfall doubled the size of the nation and dramatically increased, according to Jefferson's theory, its chances of survival and success. This acquiring of the Louisiana Territory was followed by the Lewis and Clark Expedition across it, which led to frontier settlement.

Made up of untamed stretches of land sparsely occupied by Native Americans, the frontier became an important element in the shaping of a separate national identity. In the early 1800s American writers first began to define this identity through literature. They developed an American version of the English language and spun tales that drew on uniquely American people, settings, and events. A distinctly American character was created, one with a personality informed by experiences of the frontier.

Confirming Independence

But the Americans continued to be challenged by foreign powers, particularly the British. The British dismissed the Americans as less than equal, even though they had won the Revolution, and interfered with American shipping. In the early 1800s British sea captains impressed about 10,000 American sailors to serve in the Royal Navy. British soldiers also refused to abandon their forts in the American Northwest, which they had promised to do after the Revolution. Indian nations remained in contact with these British soldiers, joining forces with them in the War of 1812 to defend their tribal homelands.

In the end neither the British nor the Americans won any material gains in this deadly war. The British were soundly defeated by the Americans in a final battle, however, and with this victory came the growth of a national spirit. U.S. citizens began to view the whole war as a success, or at least felt that the United States had confirmed its independence from Great Britain. But other Americans held a drastically different view of this war. The Indian peoples of the Northwest who had waged and lost a battle to retain their homelands found their dream of a separate Indian state smashed and their tribal powers broken. This saga would continue over the next two decades, and would move south in the tug-of-war for territory.

Picture Credits

The photographs and illustrations appearing in *Profiles in American History: Significant Events and the People Who Shaped Them,* Volume 2: *Constitutional Convention to the War of 1812* were received from the following sources:

On the cover: **Courtesy of The National Portrait Gallery:** Richard Allen, James Fenimore Cooper; **bequest of Winslow Warren, courtesy of The Museum of Fine Arts, Boston:** Mercy Otis Warren.

Courtesy of The Smithsonian Institution: pages 5, 73, 223; **courtesy of The National Portrait Gallery:** pages 15, 25, 49, 61, 85, 97, 127, 149, 169, 181, 195, 209, 229, 251; **bequest of Winslow Warren, courtesy of The Museum of Fine Arts, Boston:** page 35; **courtesy of The Library of Congress:** pages 117, 237; **courtesy of The Denver Public Library:** page 139; **The Bettmann Archive:** page 245.

Constitutional Convention

1774 ▼
First Continental Congress.

1775-1776 ▼
Second Continental Congress declares independence and hires George Washington to lead army.

1783 ▼
Americans win War for Independence.

1781 ▼
Articles of Confederation are ratified.

1777 ▼
Need for a stronger union results in conference, which prepares Articles of Confederation.

1787 ▼
Convention is held to improve Articles of Confederation; delegates, led by **James Madison,** write Constitution.

1787 ▼
Majority approves final draft of Constitution. **Elbridge Gerry** refuses to sign, despite a plea from **Benjamin Franklin.**

1787-1788 ▼
Mercy Otis Warren writes pamphlet that criticizes Constitution for having no bill of rights.

1791 ▼
The states ratify ten amendments to the Constitution, adopting the Bill of Rights.

1790 ▼
Rhode Island becomes last of the original thirteen states to ratify the Constitution.

1789 ▼
Eleven states ratify Constitution. George Washington elected President. North Carolina ratifies Constitution.

CONSTITUTIONAL CONVENTION

Held in Philadelphia from May to September 1787, the Constitutional Convention was the assembly of state representatives who wrote the United States Constitution.

The Articles of Confederation, the first constitution in use after the Revolution, had been adopted in 1781. It linked the states together only loosely in what has been described as merely a series of treaties. For the most part, the states acted independently of one another, printing their own money, raising their own taxes, and passing laws that protected their own trade at the expense of neighboring states. Problems resulted, prompting Alexander Hamilton, George Washington, and others to call for a meeting of state representatives to address the Articles' shortcomings. These Revolutionary War heroes hoped to create a stronger central government, with enough power to act decisively.

Several other heroes of 1776—such as Samuel Adams and Patrick Henry—hated the idea of a strong central government. Like many in the general public, they feared such a government might trample on states' rights, threaten the freedom of individuals, or fall under the control of one power-hungry man. Years of British rule had added to their distrust of strong central government. Many feared it would be as bad as a return to colonial days. Yet even they accepted that the Articles needed improvement.

The convention was called for the sole purpose of revising the Articles of Confederation. In other words, the delegates were only supposed to fix the old constitution, not—as they in fact ended up doing—to create a new one. The summer turned out to be even hotter than usual. For more than three sweltering months, from late May to mid-September, the delegates met daily at Philadelphia's State House (now Independence Hall). Among them were representatives from all of the original thirteen states except Rhode Island, which refused to participate because of its opposition to a strong national government. Like Washington and Hamilton, some of the representatives were champions of a strong federal government. Others, like Adams and Henry, favored strong states' rights and a weak central government.

Groups at the Convention— What They Wanted

Federalists: Strong executive branch, weak states' rights, representation in legislature according to population.

Antifederalists: Weak executive branch, strong states' rights.

Small-state men: Weak executive branch, equal representation in legislature for all states regardless of population.

In the end, the delegates replaced the Articles of Confederation with a new document, the Constitution. It, in turn, replaced Congress—which was the only branch of government under the Articles—with three divisions: a legislative branch (the new Congress), made up of two houses; an executive branch to carry out laws; and a judicial branch to interpret the laws. The three branches were given much broader powers than the old Congress, but these powers were divided so that no single branch could dominate the others.

The Constitution put into practice some new and untried ideas about government. For example, two theories of the day, separation of powers and the idea that the branches would provide checks and balances, appear in the writings of the French philosopher Montesquieu (1689-1755). These ideas had never been put into practice in a working constitution for a large government. Also evident in the new Constitution were the ideas of English writer John Locke (1632-1704), who declared that any sound government must rely on the "consent of the governed." In other words, the government should follow the will of the people, not the other way around. This was revolutionary thinking at the time. Never in history had a large nation attempted to be governed entirely by the will of the people. It was a grand experiment.

Largely through the efforts of **James Madison,** these ideas would be combined into a new system of government suitable for and agreeable to a large population. Even so, many of his proposals were changed during the long months of debate. Small-state men (delegates from the less-populated states) raised objections, for example. Madison wanted the Congress to be proportionately elected, with each state represented according to its population. But small-state men wanted Congress to have an equal number of representatives from each state. Robert Sherman proposed a compromise that was finally accepted. Congress would consist of two houses, one proportional (the House of Representatives) and the other with equal representation (the Senate).

Despite all the compromises, as well as the urging of **Benjamin Franklin,** three men refused to sign the final version of the Constitution. Among them was **Elbridge Gerry.** There were Americans who, like these three representatives, would oppose the Constitution once it was presented to them. These opponents came to be known as Antifederalists. Those who supported the Constitution called themselves Federalists.

As states held their own conventions to decide whether to ratify the document, the greatest objection raised was that it lacked a "Bill of Rights." Such a bill was needed, some thought, to spell out in clear and plain language the freedoms of citizens. It was because of the protests of Gerry, **Mercy Otis Warren,** and others that a Bill of Rights was finally added as the first ten amendments to the Constitution. Today, the Bill of Rights is perhaps the best known part of the document. Fifteen other amendments have been added over time. In providing for such amendments, the Constitution makers managed to create a document that could be adjusted to fit the needs of a changing society, yet still hold true to the ideas expressed within its original framework.

James Madison

1751-1836

Personal Background

James Madison, Jr., was born on March 16, 1751, in his grandparents' home in King George County, Virginia. His parents, James and Nelly, immediately brought him to their home (which he would later call Montpelier) in the rolling, forested hills of western Virginia's Orange County. Three generations earlier, in 1716, his great-grandfather James Taylor had helped explore and map Orange County when it was still unsettled by Europeans.

Frontier tales. By the time Madison was born, Orange County was no longer on the frontier. In the 1750s the frontier lay farther west, over the Blue Ridge Mountains that ran between Virginia and the fabled land of Kentucky. During James's childhood, stories of frontier battles between Indians and white settlers captured his imagination and sparked his lifelong interest in the West.

Growing up. Small in size and the oldest son of seven children, Madison did not especially enjoy the outdoor pastimes popular among the other children of Virginia's "upland." Instead of riding or shooting, he preferred to read. His earliest schooling took place at home, and at around the age of twelve, he was sent to the school of Donald Robertson, a well-known teacher who had been educated in Scotland. There he learned Greek, Latin, French, and mathematics, and read famous works of literature. At age seventeen

▲ James Madison

Event: Constitutional Convention.

Role: For his role in the Convention and in shaping the document it finally approved, Madison is often called "the Father of the Constitution." His energy and political skill also played a large part in getting the new Constitution approved, or ratified, by the states.

he returned home to study under a tutor, the Reverend Thomas Martin. In the five years he had been away, events began to occur that would lead to the colonies rebelling against control by Great Britain.

North to Princeton. Martin, who lived with the Madisons, had attended college at Princeton, in the northern colony of New Jersey. Although most young Virginian men went off to William and Mary College in the Virginia capital of Williamsburg, Martin spoke highly of Princeton and advised James to go there instead. Under the leadership of Dr. John Witherspoon, Princeton had won a reputation for independent thinking that would make it a breeding ground for Revolutionary leaders. As protests in the colonies increased against British policies, students kept up a lively interest in what was occurring. Like many of his schoolmates, Madison favored strong actions against the British. He studied tirelessly, and finished the four-year program in two years, from 1769 to 1771.

Virginia politics. Madison's relentless work habits at school had affected his health, and he went home to rest after graduating. He remained there for several years, following political developments and reading constantly. In 1774 he served on the Orange County Committee of Safety; in 1776 he was elected to the Virginia convention. Meeting in Williamsburg, the convention delegates declared Virginia's independence from Britain and wrote the state's new constitution. Foreshadowing his later work on the national constitution, Madison's contribution to the Virginia constitution broadened the idea of religious "toleration" to absolute "liberty of conscience for all." During the early part of the Revolutionary War, he served on the governor's council, living in Williamsburg and assisting governors Patrick Henry and Thomas Jefferson. In 1780 Madison was elected to represent Virginia in Congress at Philadelphia.

Participation: Constitutional Convention

"Half a piece of soap." At twenty-nine, Madison was Congress's youngest member. Small but neatly built, with blue eyes and a rosy complexion, he almost always wore simple black. Sometimes he brushed his already thinning hair forward; at other times he wore the stiff, powdered wig fashionable in his day. His step was light and quick, giving the impression of boundless energy. His size made him look even younger than he was. One observer described him as "no bigger than half a piece of soap" (Peterson, p. 121). Madison complained often about his health and suffered from a constant list of minor ailments. Despite his worries, however, he would enjoy a long, healthy life marked by periods of intense effort. He seemed to thrive on such periods, after which he usually needed time to recover. He spoke softly, even when addressing Congress. His friends called him Jemmy.

Broken heart. Madison spent nearly four years in Congress, attending every session except for two short breaks (a record that still has been rarely matched). He rented rooms from the aptly named Mrs. House, about a block-and-a-half away from the State House, where Congress met. A delegate from New York, William Floyd, also lived at Mrs. House's with his beautiful and charming sixteen-year-old daughter, Kitty. Madison, though twice Kitty's age, fell deeply in love with her. She agreed at first to marry him but later changed her mind. It would not be until his forties that Madison would think of marrying again.

Congress. Madison's work in Congress helped take his mind off the broken engagement. He became the leader of a group calling for stronger powers for the United States government. Under the Articles of Confederation, the states had more power than the Congress, the central government at that time. In fact, each state had so many powers that the new nation acted more like a collection of independent states than a team of united ones. Each state had very different interests; southern planters had little in common with middle states farmers or New England fishermen. Therefore the states passed laws that protected their citizens and hurt the trade of their neighbors. Additionally, they raised taxes for their own needs but often refused to pay taxes to the Congress. As a result, the central government had no money and little respect at home or abroad.

Madison, along with Alexander Hamilton and George Washington, had begun arguing for a convention that would further define the central government's powers. They felt that such a convention might strengthen the central government in the way that was necessary for the young country to prosper. At the time, the imperial nations of Spain and Britain, eager to expand their influence in America's North, West, and South, posed a serious threat to the separate territories of the United States. They would have to pull together to meet the threat, or even to survive.

Readings in political theory. After his term in Congress, Madison spent three years continuing to push for a convention, as well as preparing himself for such a meeting. His close friend Thomas Jefferson sent him boxes of books from Paris, France, where Jefferson represented the U.S. government. Madison read works by authors such as Voltaire and John Locke, who believed that government should take its powers from the people, that powers should be shared between local and national governments, and that all men should receive equal treatment before the law. These basic principles came out of the "Age of Enlightenment," the movement among European thinkers that influenced the formation of American democracy.

Opposing views. Although American statesmen Patrick Henry said, "United we stand, divided we fall," he, like Samuel Adams, rejected a stronger central government because he feared it would threaten the freedom of individuals. Though the two men would not take part in the convention, their views were supported by delegates from small states, such as those from Maryland and Delaware. These delegates feared that larger, more populous states such as Virginia and Pennsylvania would win control of a national government.

Virginia Plan. As troubles among the states mounted during the 1780s, it became clear that something needed to be done. Largely owing to the efforts of Madison and Hamilton, a convention was finally called, requesting that delegates meet in Philadelphia in May 1787. (Rhode Island did not participate.) Madison, a delegate from Virginia, had prepared a plan that he hoped would replace the Articles of Confederation. Known as the Virginia Plan, it called for three separate branches of government (executive, legislative, and judicial), each with well-defined powers that would guard against any one branch becoming dominant. The national government would possess broad "general powers," while "local powers" would remain with the states. With its three governmental branches and built-in "checks and balances," Madison's Virginia Plan eventually became the basis for the Constitution.

Philadelphia, May 1787. Madison, coming from Virginia, had rented out his old rooms at Mrs. House's several weeks before most of the representatives appeared. Delegates began arriving in Philadelphia on May 13, though bad weather postponed the convention's opening until May 25. George Washington was elected the convention's president. Washington, who as commander-in-chief had suffered from Congress's inability to collect taxes to pay his army, was a firm supporter of a strong national government. Another supporter was Benjamin Franklin, the famous Philadelphian and Pennsylvania delegate (see **Benjamin Franklin**).

Washington and Franklin only rarely joined the debate, however. Madison's most effective support came from Pennsylvania delegate James Wilson, also a Philadelphian. Called the unsung hero of the convention, Wilson argued coolly and logically in favor of a "single executive." This office, at first frighteningly similar to that of a king, eventually would be held by the "president." The idea of approving such a position and a strong central government upset many Americans of the time, who had just thrown off the tyranny of a strong English king and parliament. Massachusetts delegate Elbridge Gerry, for example, who helped inspire the Revolution, was one opponent of a strong government (see **Elbridge Gerry**), in contrast to Madison. Such different viewpoints promised a summer full of heated arguments on the structure and powers of the government.

The convention, ordered by Congress only to improve the Articles of Confederation, ignored its instructions to act mildly from the start. On May 29 Madison's fellow Virginia delegate Edmund Randolph (also the state's governor) introduced the Virginia Plan, which served as a starting point for further debate.

New Jersey Plan. Madison's preparation proved important, for it took his opponents three weeks of loud and often bitter argument on the convention floor to come up with an alternative. Put forward by William Paterson of New Jersey on June 15, the "New Jersey Plan" proposed patching up the Articles of Confederation to meet the needs of the day while safeguarding the rights of the states. Madison delivered a stinging attack against the plan on June 19, and the delegates voted against it. While much debate lay ahead, the three branches of government in the Virginia Plan had begun to seem less frightening after three weeks of consideration.

Madison takes minutes. For Madison the convention represented another period of almost superhuman effort. Not only was he active in the debates (he gave more than 200 speeches), but he kept a virtually complete record of the entire convention. Writing tirelessly, he took notes in shorthand all day long, then recopied them out at night. Because of this achievement, history has a nearly perfect account, which Thomas Jefferson called the ablest work of its kind ever yet carried out. "The whole of everything said and done there," Jefferson continued, "was taken down by Mr. Madison, with a labor and exactness beyond comprehension" (Bowen, p. 30). Later Madison said that the effort nearly killed him.

Madison Takes Notes

"I chose a seat in front of the presiding member [Washington], with the other members on my right and left hand. In this favorable position for hearing all that passed, I noted ... what was read from the Chair or spoken by the members; and losing not a moment unnecessarily between the adjournment and reassembling of the Convention I was enabled to write out my daily notes ... I was not absent a single day, nor more than a casual fraction of an hour in any day, so that I could not have lost a single speech, unless a very short one." (Bowen, p. 30)

Great Compromise. Despite overcoming Paterson's New Jersey Plan, Madison was unable to win the convention over to his ideas completely. Madison strongly believed that the government should represent the people, not the individual states. He thus advocated a legislature that was directly elected, with each state represented according to its population. This issue provoked one of the biggest disagreements among delegates; the small states feared that they would be unfairly outweighed by the large ones. Roger Sherman of Connecticut offered a compromise. He proposed a legislature consisting of two houses, one in which each state would be represented according to population, and one in which each state would have equal representation. This "Great Compromise" was finally accepted by both sides and became the basis for today's Congress. Though Sherman convinced them of the need for a single president (rather than an executive council), he was unable to persuade the delegates that the president should be elected directly by the people. The electoral college system resulted from another compromise, in which chosen electors would vote for the new president.

Concerns for the future. On one issue, Madison and his supporters carried the day: how future states were to join the Union.

Elbridge Gerry and others argued that the original thirteen states should remain in control of the government. Madison, always thinking of the West and the future, said that new states "neither would nor ought to submit to a Union which degraded them from an equal rank with other states" (Bowen, p. 180). Another influential Virginian, George Mason, agreed. "If the Western States are to be admitted into the Union as they arise, they must—I will repeat—they must be treated as equals" (Bowen, p. 180). At first in a minority, such views soon swayed the other delegates, and a provision for equal admission of new states was written into the final document.

Signing. On September 17, 1787, the final draft of the Constitution was approved. Despite a plea from Franklin, though, three delegates, including Gerry, refused to sign. The convention could still claim "unanimous consent of the states present," however, because at least one delegate from each state still at the convention signed the document. Many had gone home to escape the city's exhausting summer heat.

> ## From Madison's Record of the Convention
>
> In his notes, Madison spoke of himself the same way as others, taking pains to be objective in his reporting:
>
> > "Mr. Madison, reminded Mr. Patterson that his doctrine of Representation which was in its principle the genuine one, must for ever silence the pretensions [claims] of the small states to an equality of votes with the larger ones." (Madison, p. 259)
>
> Mr. Patterson's name was actually Paterson; Madison paid more attention to arguments than to spelling.

Aftermath

Ratification. Under the Constitution's terms, nine out of the thirteen states needed to approve it in order for it to become law. Popularly elected conventions in each state would vote on ratification. Madison knew that all his efforts came down to whether the states would approve the new Constitution, and it was his idea to set up the state conventions. He wanted the people to choose the delegates who would vote on the Constitution directly, rather than leaving ratification up to the state legislatures (which would have to vote on whether to give up much of their own power). Without a pause, he swung into action to win public support for the Constitution.

Virginia vote. Madison and other supporters of the Constitution became known as "Federalists," because the document defined a federal relationship in which each state gave up sovereignty, or self-rule, in order to win certain benefits. One of Madison's arguments was that this arrangement was similar to a citizen's loss of sovereignty in society, where he or she enjoys the benefits of laws that also limit his or her behavior. Such arguments served Madison well in campaigns throughout the states, as one by one, states ratified the Constitution. Eight states had ratified when the Virginia convention met in June 1788, so one more state was needed to tip the balance. Madison faced the opposition of Patrick Henry, a fiery speaker who scorned the Constitution's "chain-rattling ridiculous ideal checks and contrivances" (Peterson, p. 157). In his own quiet style, Madison spoke calmly and logically in favor of ratification. The convention approved, by only ten votes (eighty-nine for, seventy-nine against). Unknown to the Virginia delegates, New Hampshire had in the meantime become the ninth state to ratify.

Federalist Papers. While the Constitution had safely passed its worst trial, the large state of New York had yet to vote. Madison wanted to win it over as well, and he succeeded. As part of his campaign to win New York, he wrote a series of essays with Alexander Hamilton and John Jay, both leaders of the Federalists in that state. Though they probably did not change the course of ratification, the *Federalist Papers,* as they are called, stand as the most forceful expression of the Federalists' case. Madison wrote twenty-nine essays in all, sometimes several in one week. This high level of productivity came as he organized campaigns in various states. The *Federalist Papers,* originally published in New York newspapers, remain available in book form today. Interestingly, Hamilton and Madison later opposed each other, with Hamilton in favor of a far stronger central government than Madison. A new party formed, the Democratic-Republicans, and Madison and Jefferson were two of its leading members.

Presidency. Madison continued on to a brilliant political career, serving as secretary of state under President Thomas Jefferson (1800-1808) and then as president (1808-1816).

During his presidency, he pursued the policies of Jefferson, his longtime friend and mentor. The two Virginians complemented each other: Madison was as methodical and practical as Jefferson was bold and speculative. Their friendship and political alliance lasted fifty years. As Jefferson's secretary of state, Madison oversaw the Louisiana Purchase, and as president, he led the nation in fighting the War of 1812. His wife, Dolley, a vibrant and attractive widow whom he married in 1794, was considered Washington's most fashionable and popular woman (see **Dolley Payne Madison**).

Retirement. Madison retired to Montpelier after his second term as president. He afterward took part in Virginia politics from time to time and advised his successor, President James Monroe. Beginning in the 1830s, however, Madison's health gradually grew worse, and he died on June 28, 1836. The nation mourned Jemmy Madison as the last of the founding fathers.

For More Information

Bowen, Catherine Drinker. *Miracle at Philadelphia: The Story of the Constitutional Convention—May to September, 1787.* New York: Little, Brown & Co., 1966.

Madison, James. *Notes of Debates in the Federal Convention of 1787, Reported by James Madison.* New York: W.W. Norton & Co., 1987.

Peterson, Merrill D. *James Madison: A Biography in His Own Words.* New York: Newsweek, 1974.

Rutland, Robert A. *James Madison: The Founding Father.* New York: Macmillan, 1987.

Benjamin Franklin

1706-1790

Personal Background

Benjamin Franklin was born in Boston, Massachusetts on January 17, 1706. His father, Josiah Franklin, was a candlemaker who had come to Boston from southern England in 1683. After his first wife died in childbirth he married Abiah Folger, who had been born on the Massachusetts island of Nantucket. Together they had ten children, of which Benjamin was the eighth. A very religious man, Benjamin's father held strict Puritan views, believing that people should be serious and hardworking. He planned for Benjamin to become a minister.

High spirits. The boy's personality, however, was not suited for the life his father planned. Benjamin enjoyed games, athletics, getting into fights, and swimming, which he mastered at an early age. He also liked to invent devices to improve his performance. For example, he wore special paddles on his hands to swim faster. Once he even towed himself across a lake by lying on his back and flying a kite. His inventive, skeptical mind did not allow him to accept religious teachings with the kind of unquestioning faith expected of a boy who was going to become a minister. Once, after his father gave a lengthy dinner blessing, Benjamin (so the story goes) suggested he save time by blessing the family's whole food supply at one time. Wisely, Josiah Franklin took his son out of religious school and arranged lessons for him in the writing and arithmetic necessary to

▲ Benjamin Franklin

Event: Constitutional Convention.

Role: An old man (and a national hero) by the time of the convention, Franklin encouraged cooperation and compromise among the younger men who were debating their bold ideas. Disagreeing with some of its parts, he nonetheless accepted the proposed Constitution and helped persuade others to do the same.

become a craftsman. Soon, however, his schooling had to end so that he could help his father in the candle shop for a time.

Printer's apprentice. Benjamin's older brother James had become a printer, and when Benjamin was twelve he went to work for James as an apprentice. Already fond of books, Benjamin thereafter would consider printing his profession, despite the many other areas—from politics to science—in which he achieved fame. The printing business brought him into contact with a wider range of books, which he read hungrily. As he later wrote, he would sometimes "borrow a small one, which I was careful to return soon and clean. Often I sat up in my Room reading the greatest Part of the Night" (Clark, pp. 16-17). Equally important was the mechanical side of printing, which gave him practical skills he would later use to build scientific instruments and tools.

Silence Dogood. When Benjamin was in his teens, he became interested in writing. At first he wrote mostly short, entertaining poems, which his brother published. Then at sixteen Benjamin wrote an essay of a few pages. In it he pretended to be a bossy and stern middle-aged Puritan widow, Silence Dogood, who gave advice to readers. Afraid that his brother would refuse to publish it if he knew who wrote it, Benjamin waited until the middle of the night and slipped it under the door of the printing office. At work the next day he listened as his brother and his friends discussed the piece, praising it and trying to guess the author. His brother assumed the writer must be a man of great learning and reputation who wished to remain anonymous.

James Franklin published the essay in his newspaper, *The New England Courant,* printing a request for more pieces by the same author and promising that "no Questions shall be asked" about the mysterious writer's identity (Clark, p. 20). Benjamin went on to write thirteen more "Silence Dogood" pieces. The clever and popular essays, poking fun at the Puritans' stern morality, revealed the wit and talent of their young author (though his authorship was not known for another century) and showed how far apart he had grown from his father's strict religion.

Philadelphia and London. When James was sent to jail for a month for publishing criticism of the Massachusetts government,

Benjamin ran the paper until his brother was released. James returned, and Benjamin stepped back into his old position. He had grown accustomed to being in charge, however, and grew impatient under his brother's domination. In 1723, at age seventeen, Benjamin ran away from Boston to Philadelphia, Pennsylvania, where his skill and energy quickly brought him printing work. A year later he went to London, England, and worked there as a master printer.

Franklin spent two valuable years in London, sharpening his printing skills, meeting people, and learning the ways of a more sophisticated city than America had to offer. He returned to Philadelphia in 1726, an athletic, well-built, twenty-year-old young man, ambitious and eager to get ahead. He soon set up his own printing shop and began building it into a profitable business.

Gazette and Almanack. Franklin's earliest profits came from winning public contracts (such as those for printing money), and within a few years he was publishing his own newspaper, the *Pennsylvania Gazette.* In 1732 he began writing and publishing *Poor Richard's Almanack,* a yearly collection of miscellaneous information and homespun wisdom. Soon found in every well-stocked colonial library—or as the only book in the homes of poorer folk—the *Almanack* would become a lasting success. Franklin also served as clerk of the Pennsylvania Assembly and as Philadelphia's postmaster. As his wealth grew, he invested in print shops in other colonies, as well as in Canada and the West Indies.

Home life. In 1730 Franklin married a young widow named Deborah Read. She helped him run his printing shop and a second business, which sold stationery supplies and general goods as well as books and newspapers. Thrifty and hardworking, Deborah lived up to the homespun ideals that her husband put forward in his *Almanack.* A son, William, is thought to have been born in 1731, although there is some doubt about whether Deborah was in fact his mother. (Charges of involvement with other women fol-

> ## Poor Richard's Almanack
>
> Franklin created the character Poor Richard, but he did not write all of the sayings in *Poor Richard's Almanack.* In most cases, he only reworded them to be more pleasing to the ear. They are guides to living that contain a type of folk wisdom.
>
> - Early to Bed, and early to rise, makes a Man healthy, wealthy and wise.
> - There are no Gains, without Pains.
> - Success has ruined many a man.
> - Laziness travels so slowly that Poverty soon overtakes him.

▲ **Scenes from Franklin's life**

lowed Franklin for most of his life.) Whatever the facts of William's birth, Deborah, warm and affectionate, gave him a mother's love and support. Another son, Francis, was born in 1732, only to die of smallpox at the age of four. Sally, the couple's only other surviving child, was born seven years later. Both children would be an important source of strength for Franklin throughout his life.

Public interests. Franklin was very active in public affairs. In 1731, he founded the Junto, a group of civic-minded businessmen who worked to improve city services in Philadelphia. Led by Franklin, the Junto established the city's first lending library (1731) and fire company (1736). In 1743 Franklin founded the American Philosophical Society, a leading academic association that still flourishes today. In 1748, at the age of forty-two, Franklin had enough money to leave a partner in charge of the shop and retire from printing. After his retirement, he was able to devote more time to his many projects. He and the Junto established a college, which later became the University of Pennsylvania (1749), an insurance company, and a hospital (1751). In the 1750s, during the French and Indian War, Franklin organized and helped lead the Pennsylvania militia in defending frontier settlements from Indian attacks.

Engineer, scientist. Franklin also pursued his scientific interests after quitting the printing shop. It was as a scientist and an inventor that his fame first spread beyond Philadelphia itself. The wood-burning Franklin stove, which improved the heating in colonial homes, was used throughout the North. Franklin's work with electricity in the 1750s made his name well known in Europe too. Through his famous kite experiment, he was the first to establish for certain that the energy in lightning begins with electricity. Out of this discovery came the idea for the lightning rod, which he also invented. Afterward, the rod was widely used to protect buildings around the world from lightning.

Statesman. Beginning in the 1750s, Franklin played an important role in local and then national politics. Elected to the Pennsylvania Assembly in 1751, he quickly rose to lead the Quaker-dominated party that supported the interests of the people against the Penns, the family that owned the colony. During the late 1760s to the mid-1780s, as the colonies struggled toward independence, Franklin acted as agent, first in England for the colonies and then in France for the young United States government. He enjoyed living abroad and was popular in both countries. Still, he missed Pennsylvania and wrote home for packages of his favorite foods. "Pray remember to make me as happy as you can," he wrote in one letter to Deborah, "by sending some Pippins [apples] for my self and friends, some of your small Hams, and some Cranberries" (Clark, p. 147).

He did not live abroad for all of this time, but returned to America for periods of up to a few years (for example, in 1775 and 1776, as the Revolution began). Meanwhile, tragedy struck in Franklin's personal life. Deborah died in 1774. Added to this grief was his son William's support for the English cause. William (who had been Franklin's companion in England) remained a Loyalist, moving to England after the Revolution.

Sage of America. Franklin returned home to a hero's welcome in 1785, after nearly a decade of serving his country's interests in France. His simple ways, lively humor, and scientific achievements had won him great popularity in France. The seventy-nine-year-old, suffering from painful bladder stones and having returned "to die in my own country," promptly accepted election as Pennsylvania's president (Clark, p. 394). He also devoted time to issues such as the abolition of slavery, which he had advocated for years, and completed his *Autobiography,* which has become a classic of its kind. The unequaled scope of his achievements, along with his age, experience, and personality, had cast him into the role of America's sage, or wise man.

Participation: Constitutional Convention

Convention in Philadelphia. Beginning in 1781, when the new nation was still fighting to defeat the British, the powers of the United States government had been defined by the Articles of Confederation. After independence from Britain was won in 1783, the most serious question facing national leaders was how to balance power between the states and the national government. Under the Articles, the states had nearly all the power. They acted almost like separate countries. The national government, however, had very little power and was unable to enforce its own laws.

As the states fought among themselves over questions of foreign policy and trade, it became clear that they were not really "united" at all. Finally, they agreed on one thing: that a convention should be called to improve the Articles of Confederation. Each state (except Rhode Island, which refused to participate) elected delegates to the convention, which was to be held in Philadelphia during the summer of 1787. It was natural that America's sage, Benjamin Franklin, was chosen as one of Pennsylvania's delegates.

George Washington slept here. On May 13 delegates began arriving in Philadelphia, one day before the convention was to begin. George Washington, escorted into the city by the crisply uniformed soldiers of the City Troop, made his way straight to Franklin's house, where he spent the night. (Franklin opened a special cask of wine for the occasion.) A delegate from Virginia and a firm believer in strong central government, Washington would be elected president of the convention. Like Franklin, he would rarely join in the debates to come. His presence alone would have a strong influence in controlling the often bitter disagreements. Thomas Jefferson was not at the convention (he was in France at the time), but had served in the Continental Congress with Franklin and in the Virginia legislature with Washington. He later said that he "never heard either of them speak for ten minutes at a time, nor to any but the main point which was to decide the question. They laid their shoulders to the great points, knowing that the little ones would follow" (Bowen, p. 29).

Stormy weather. Heavy rains slowed the arrival of the delegates, and it was not until May 25, a Friday, that enough had appeared to begin meeting. The bad weather kept Franklin away from the State House (where the convention met) until Monday the 28th. Aside from two days during the Fourth of July holiday and ten days while a special committee was meeting, the first Friday was the only day Franklin missed. Given his age and poor health, his attendance shows how important the convention's outcome was to him.

Unique transportation. Because of his bladder stones, Franklin traveled to the convention each day in his special "sedan chair," an enclosed seat supported on two long poles. This was the only transportation that did not bump him painfully. Carried by four large prisoners from the nearby Walnut Street Jail, the chair was a well-known sight in the city. It had glass windows on both sides, from behind which the good-natured Franklin could smile and wave at the people on the street. On that Monday, as on most other days that hot and fateful summer, the prisoners brought their famous cargo carefully up the State House steps and into the east room, where Franklin was helped out and assisted to a comfortable armchair at the Pennsylvania delegates' table.

Reminder of destiny. From his armchair, Franklin followed the heated arguments as the convention threatened to split up over its thorniest problem: if the central government was to be strengthened, how were the interests of the small states to be balanced against those of the larger states? Delegates from small states like Delaware and Maryland resisted the idea of proportional representation in the new Congress. Proportional representation, which meant that each state would be represented according to the size of its population, raised the possibility that small states could be overwhelmed by large ones, like Pennsylvania and Virginia. By late June all hope of agreement seemed gone.

From his armchair, peering over his famous bifocals (eyeglasses with two lenses built in, which he had invented), Franklin sought to calm the delegates. He reminded them that during the darkest days of the Revolution—in the very room in which they now sat—Congress had met to decide the nation's fate. The meetings had been opened with prayers for God's help. Franklin proposed opening the convention's meetings with similar prayers to remind the delegates that their obligations went beyond the disagreements of the day to the interests of generations to come. The suggestion was rejected (probably because of lack of money to pay a clergyman to give the prayers), but it had the desired effect. A calmer atmosphere settled over the meetings.

Voice of compromise. Those who believed in a strong central government (see **James Madison**) supported proportional representation. How else, they argued, could the government represent the people, rather than merely the states. States' rights supporters, such as Maryland's Luther Martin, wanted each state to have equal representation in the legislature. Roger Sherman of Connecticut had three times put forward a compromise in which the new Congress would consist of two houses, one proportional and one equal. Each time, his proposal was rejected. Two days after speaking in favor of prayer, Franklin again addressed the convention. "When a broad table is to be made," he said, "and the edges of the planks do not fit, the artist takes a little from both, and makes a good joint. In like manner here both sides must part with some of their demands, in order that they may join" (Bowen, p. 130). The delegates finally accepted Sherman's compromise, solving the convention's most difficult problem and deciding the shape of the Congress as we know it today.

Unanimous consent. By September 17 the new Constitution was finished and ready for signing. Some of the delegates, especially the states' rights men, still did not want to sign it, however. Once again, Franklin rose. But he was too weak to speak, and gave his speech to James Wilson to read out loud. Franklin agreed that the Constitution was not perfect, but argued that it was the best one possible. All the delegates should sign it, he said, because it was important that the convention be unanimous. In the end, three delegates refused to sign, yet the Constitution still won the approval of all participating states. So the document was signed "by the unanimous consent of the States present" (Bowen, p. 256).

Rising sun. As the last delegates were signing, Franklin looked toward George Washington's chair. Behind the chair was a painting of a rising sun. According to James Madison's notes, Franklin observed "that painters found it difficult in their art to distinguish a rising from a setting sun.... I have, said he, often ... looked at that behind the President without being able to tell whether it was rising or setting: But now at length I have the happiness to know that it is a rising and not a setting sun" (Bowen, p. 262).

Aftermath

Ratification. Franklin had one service left to perform for his country. In the long struggle to have the new Constitution ratified, or approved by the states, he helped as much as he was able. But he could do little more than throw the weight of his name and popularity behind it. Weakness and old age were finally catching up with him.

Death and taxes. By 1789 he was confined to his bed, where he reflected on the new government. He was happy that the new Constitution seemed to be one that would last, but, he added to a friend "in this world nothing can be said to be certain, except death and taxes" (Clark, p. 413). Death came peacefully to Franklin on April 17, 1790.

For More Information

Bowen, Catherine Drinker. *Miracle at Philadelphia: The Story of the Constitutional Convention—May to September, 1787.* New York: Little, Brown & Co., 1966.

Clark, Ronald W. *Benjamin Franklin: A Biography.* New York: Random House, 1983.

Franklin, Benjamin. *Poor Richard: An Almanack.* New York: David McKay Co., 1976.

Elbridge Gerry

1744-1814

Personal Background

Elbridge Gerry (pronounced "gary") was born on July 17, 1744, in Marblehead, Massachusetts. His father, Thomas Gerry, had immigrated from England in 1730 and settled in Marblehead, a sleepy fishing village north of Boston situated on a rocky peninsula jutting into the stormy Atlantic. In 1734 he married Elizabeth Greenleaf, the only daughter of a village craftsman. Thomas Gerry's arrival occurred at the same time as new prosperity for Marblehead. For years, fishing had been the town's livelihood, but the catch always had been exported by merchants from Boston or Salem, who kept the profits. Thomas Gerry was one of a number of locals who bought their own ships to carry the cod to foreign customers. The valuable fish were "split" and sun-dried in Marblehead, then shipped to Europe or the Caribbean. The Gerrys were soon one of Marblehead's wealthiest families, part of a merchant class that was called "the codfish aristocracy."

Strict attitudes. Thomas and Elizabeth had eleven children, but only five survived into adulthood: Thomas, John, Elbridge, Elizabeth, and Samuel Russell. Though wealthy, the Gerrys lived simply. The children were raised according to their father's strict views about religion and society. In religion, Thomas was closer to the Puritan immigrants of a century earlier than to some of his neighbors, whose "Vanities" and "Balls" he complained about in a letter to

▲ Elbridge Gerry

Event: Debates on the Constitution; Bill of Rights.

Role: Elbridge Gerry, fearing the effects of a strong central government, opposed many aspects of the Constitution. He was one of three delegates who refused to sign the final document.

an English friend (Billias, p. 5). Thomas Gerry's political ideas also showed his stern character. He disliked the colonial way of holding frequent town meetings, believing that too much political participation by the common people would "naturally have a bad effect" (Billias, p. 5). These attitudes, passed on to his children, continued to influence Elbridge Gerry throughout his life.

Harvard. Little is known of Gerry's early education, but at fourteen (the usual age for college in those days) he entered Harvard. He was the only child in his family to attend college. At Harvard, Gerry was interested in the history of the ancient Greek democratic city-states and the Roman Republic. He read Greek and Latin works by ancient writers such as Plato, Pliny, and Cicero. These writers discussed issues of government, raising basic questions: What was the relationship between the people and the government? What kind of government was best? Who should be in charge of it? Gerry was especially interested in the decline of the Roman Republic, which had been governed by leading citizens only to fall under the power of a single man and become the Roman Empire.

Family business. Though he had a genius for the scholar's life, after finishing at Harvard Gerry decided to join the family business. His education gave him a leading role, and he often acted as attorney for the company. By the late 1760s, when he was in his early twenties, his older brothers and even his father often relied on Gerry's leadership. It was also a time of political trouble, as Britain began passing laws that taxed American merchants like the Gerrys. As Massachusetts merchants became more closely involved in politics, questions like those Gerry had studied at Harvard (such as why the Roman Empire collapsed) took on a strong importance in his life.

Revolutionary leader. By 1772 Gerry had become well known locally for his opposition to the British policies. Marblehead, second only to Boston in the Massachusetts economy, emerged as second to that city in revolutionary activity as well. Gerry was elected to the Massachusetts General Court in 1772, which lifted him from local leadership to a role in colonial government. He became friends with Samuel Adams, Boston's fiery revolutionary leader. Twenty-two years younger than Adams, Gerry worked closely with the Boston rebel in organizing revolutionary activity. He became a familiar figure among Massachusetts patriots. A slender man of medium height, Gerry had strong, sharp features that made him look a little like a bird—a stern and angry bird when he gave speeches about the rights of Americans to govern themselves. His quick gestures and a certain way of squinting, along with a stutter, completed the image.

Lexington and Concord. Elected to the Massachusetts legislature in 1774, Gerry played a leading role in putting the colony on a wartime footing. He was selected to serve on the legislature's Committee of Safety and grew increasingly busy gathering supplies and arms for Massachusetts militiamen. On April 18, 1775, Gerry, Samuel Adams, John Hancock, and others on the committee were meeting at the Black Horse Tavern outside of Boston. The tavern lay on the road to the nearby town of Concord, where one of several supplies of arms had been hidden. At the afternoon meeting, the committee decided to issue orders to shift the various hiding places in case the British tried to find the weapons and powder. Unknown to them, British troops under General Thomas Gage had already marched from Boston to do just that.

After the meeting, Adams and Hancock rode off to nearby Lexington, where they were to spend the night. Gerry and two others stayed at the tavern, where they awoke in the night to the sound of British soldiers filing by on the road outside. Several soldiers broke away and headed toward the tavern. The story has it that Gerry was about to go out, possibly to confront them, when the innkeeper warned, "For God's sake, don't open that door!" (Billias, p. 52). The three escaped out the back, where they hid in a cornfield until the danger was over. The night was so cold that one of the men, Jeremiah Lee, suffered from exposure and later died. The next day these same troops clashed with local militia at Concord; other troops, sent to round up Adams and Hancock, fought with militia at nearby Lexington. It was the opening of war with Britain.

Signer of the Declaration of Independence. Gerry was among the first to support the nomination of George Washington to command the American forces. He was elected to the Continental Congress in 1776, and continued to play a major role in assembling arms and supplies, this time on a national scale. One of his proudest accomplishments as a member of Congress was his signing of the Declaration of Independence. One famous story at the time reported that tension was high as the members lined up to sign. The men were committing themselves to an act that, if the war should be lost, would mean death at the hands of the British. Next to Gerry stood Benjamin Harrison, the heavy-set representative from Virginia. Turning to the birdlike Gerry, whom he dwarfed, Harrison made a grim joke to lighten the atmosphere. "I shall have a great advantage over you, Mr. Gerry, when we are all hung for what we are doing. From the size and weight of my body I shall die in a few minutes but from the lightness of your body you shall dance in the air an hour or two before you are dead" (Billias, p. 345).

Participation: Constitutional Convention

Years in Congress. Gerry served in Congress on and off for nearly a decade after his 1776 election. While a member, he signed the Articles of Confederation, which were later approved, or ratified, in 1781 to become the first constitution of the United States government. Before ratification, however, Gerry felt that the rights of the states were already being worn down by the central government, so he resigned from Congress in 1780. He returned to Congress in 1783, serving until 1785, when he again resigned. During the 1780s it became clear that the Articles had not given the central government, which was essentially Congress, enough power. Despite his earlier misgivings, Gerry eventually agreed with this view. Yet he and others (like his old friend Samuel Adams) feared the effects of giving too much power to a national government and not enough to the separate states. At the urging of leaders like James Madison (see **James Madison**) and Alexander Hamilton (see **Alexander Hamilton**), who wanted a strong central government, Congress agreed that a convention should be held that would discuss ways to improve the Articles.

Shays' Rebellion. The most important reason behind Gerry's decision to support a convention was a national crisis that occurred in Massachusetts itself. Beginning in the fall of 1786, a group of Massachusetts farmers, including Revolutionary War veteran Daniel Shays (see **Daniel Shays**), led a revolt against the state government. Protesting taxes so high that many could not pay them and so were losing their land, they took over Massachusetts' courthouses. The rebellion eventually had to be put down with the help of federal troops sent especially by Congress. Like other Massachusetts politicians, Gerry was alarmed by these events. Before he had feared the tyranny of a powerful government; now he began to fear the power of an angry mob and to think that a stronger central government might be needed to control such outbursts.

Friends, marriage. Not everyone reacted as strongly as Gerry to Shays' Rebellion. Thomas Jefferson, Shays friend from Revolutionary War days, wrote to Abigail Adams: "I like a little rebellion now and then" (Bowen, p. 46). Gerry had met John and Abigail Adams (see **Abigail Adams**) during his service in Congress with John, who was Samuel Adam's cousin. As Samuel was Gerry's closest political ally in his early years, so would John prove to be in the second half of his career. Normally rather cold, John wrote letters to Gerry that show an intimacy that he shared with few others. Gerry's friendship with Abigail began with a mistake that later became a joke between them. John gave Gerry a package of tea to pass along to Abigail, but Gerry delivered the tea to the wrong "Mrs. Adams," giving it instead to Samuel's wife. After they became friends, Abigail played matchmaker, trying to find a wife for Gerry, who jokingly kept up a "Defense of Batchelors" in his letters to her (Billias, p. 141).

Gerry's other close Massachusetts friends were the married couple James and Mercy Otis Warren. Both had been part of the exciting events of the 1770s, and Mercy's brother James Otis had, before Samuel Adams, served as leader of the Massachusetts rebels. Intelligent and accomplished, Mercy wrote plays in the 1770s that supported the cause of American liberty from Britain. She, like Gerry, would later oppose the Constitution (see **Mercy Otis Warren**).

In 1786, the year before the convention, Gerry married the young and beautiful Ann Thompson, the daughter of a wealthy and socially prominent New York merchant. Gerry's simple bachelor life became a thing of the past, and the couple moved from Marblehead to stylish Cambridge, near Boston. There they lived in a luxurious house called Elmwood, surrounded by servants and comforts.

Delegate to Philadelphia. From Elmwood, Gerry set off to Philadelphia in May 1787, as one of Massachusetts' delegates to the convention. (Each state sent as many delegates as it chose—except for Rhode Island, which did not attend.) He left behind not only his wife, but a young daughter, Catherine, who had been born in March. He arrived on May 29, four days after the convention had been called to order. On his arrival at the Pennsylvania State House—the same building in which he had signed the Declaration of Independence more than a decade earlier—he could see the other political leaders. Along with James Madison, whose ideas formed the basis for the final document, Benjamin Franklin (see **Benjamin Franklin**) was there, as was George Washington, already chosen as the convention's president. For the next three-and-a-half months, debate often would become heated, and Gerry would be as argumentative as anyone. In fact, he became the sixth most talkative speaker, giving more than 150 speeches in all.

Small states, large states. The greatest disagreement came over the question of how much power the central government would have in relation to the state governments. Would it be able to overrule their laws? If so, why have state governments at all? If not, why bother with a central government? Furthermore, how were the states to be represented in the legislature? Equally, with each state having the same number of representatives? Or according to population, giving larger states more representatives—and therefore more power—than smaller ones?

On one side were supporters of a strong national government, including Madison, Washington, Hamilton, and James Wilson of Philadelphia. They favored representation by population, to make the government represent the people rather than the states. On the other side were supporters of states' rights, among them Luther Martin of Maryland, and "small-state men" like William Paterson of New Jersey, who wanted equal representation in the legislature.

"Excess of democracy." One reason that men like Gerry wanted to balance national power with the power of the states was that, to a certain extent, they distrusted the judgment of the people. Shays' Rebellion was still fresh in their memories, and the prospect of mob rule seemed very real. "The evils we experience flow from an excess of democracy," Gerry declared. "The people," he felt, were not always able to judge properly, and were easily fooled by "pretended patriots" (Bowen, p. 45). For this reason, Gerry opposed election of the president by popular vote. He believed that instead the president should be chosen by the state governors. (The system of the electoral college that was finally adopted—and still exists—came into being for similar reasons.)

Compromise. Although Gerry wanted to change the balance of power between the states and the national government, he thought the nationalists wanted too much power for the central government. He strongly opposed them, favoring instead a "middle of the road" approach. Opposed to giving either side too much power, Gerry had a hand in encouraging an atmosphere of compromise. The nationalists, for example, wanted the Congress to be able to overturn the laws of the states. The small-state men argued against this. Gerry instead argued in some cases the central government should have this authority, but that unlimited power to veto state laws would "enslave the States" (Billias, p. 166). Partly owing to his arguments, the nationalists failed to win for Congress an unlimited veto over state laws, though the Supreme Court was, in the end, given the power to declare state laws unconstitutional. Although the Constitution ended up being a compromise for both sides, Gerry refused to sign it.

Standing army. Gerry's greatest fear was of giving the central government control over an army. Military force, he thought, might be used unfairly if a few crooked or power-hungry men were in charge. He was not alone among the founding fathers or among the people as a whole in his suspicions of a "standing" or permanent army. Traditionally, American citizen-militias were called up as the need arose. Gerry wanted a prohibition in the Constitution against a standing army in peacetime, or at least a limit of 2,000 to 3,000 soldiers in it. Washington's sarcastic response was that there should be another provision making it unconstitutional for any enemy to invade the United States with an army larger than that.

Refusal to sign. On its completion in mid-September, the Constitution was written out ("engrossed") and presented to the delegates for signing. Of the delegates present, only Gerry and two others refused to sign. Gerry had presented his arguments against it in a list of eleven points, many of which concerned details such as the length of Congressional terms and Congress's power to choose voting places and set their own wages. Gerry also had deeper reasons for his refusal to sign. First, he had called for a Bill of Rights, such as many states had added to their own constitutions to define the freedoms of the individual. Nationalists such as Hamilton and Madison argued that this was unnecessary. Though the demand was defeated by a vote of ten states to none, a Bill of Rights was, in fact, added after ratification. For many today, the Bill of Rights—securing freedom of speech, freedom of the press, and more—makes up the most important part of the Constitution. Gerry correctly saw that people would demand to have their rights guaranteed in plain language in the Constitution.

Even more important, Gerry feared that the proposed Constitution would allow a dangerous concentration of power in the hands of a few men, or even one man. For Gerry, this was as strong a fear as the fear of mob rule. Such fears seem farfetched to people today. Yet before the last state had ratified the Constitution, events that illustrated Gerry's worst fears had begun unfolding in another country. The French Revolution of 1789 was based on many of the same ideas that shaped America's young democracy. In France, however, the high ideals of the revolution gave way to years of bloody mob rule, followed by one man, the Emperor Napoleon, seizing total power. That the United States escaped such a fate may be due as much to the honorable thoughts and actions of leaders like Gerry as to the genius of men like Madison.

Aftermath

Opposition and service. Though Gerry helped lead the fight against ratifying the Constitution, once it went into effect he became a strong supporter of the new government. Representing Massachusetts in Congress from 1789 to 1793, he usually backed the policies of President George Washington. He took an active part in the debate over the Bill of Rights, which was adopted in 1791. It was Gerry, for example, who proposed the Fourth Amendment: "the right of the people to be secure ... against unreasonable searches and seizures."

XYZ Affair. In 1797 Gerry's old friend John Adams, now president, appointed Gerry as one of three men sent to conduct delicate negotiations with France. When a French minister demanded a large bribe before meeting with the Americans, they refused. The other two left France, but Gerry stayed, wishing to avoid a diplomatic break that might lead to war. The resulting scandal, called the XYZ Affair, led to public criticism of Gerry for not leaving with his colleagues. Adams, however, praised Gerry and stood by his old friend.

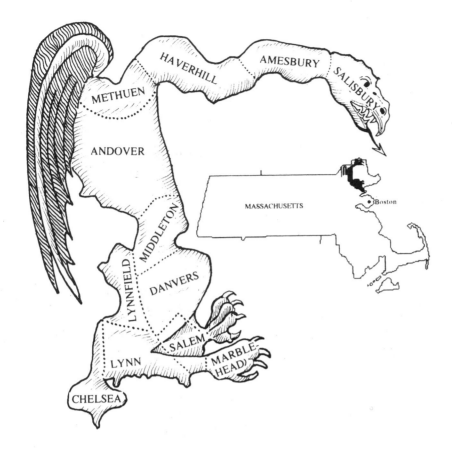

▲ Gerry's "Gerrymander"

Governor and vice-president. Elected governor of Massachusetts in 1810, Gerry was defeated in 1812 after supporting a bill that manipulated the boundaries of election districts in order to keep his party in power. One district created by the bill had such an odd shape that it was compared to a salamander. A critic called it a "gerrymander," a word that has since entered the American political vocabulary. Gerry was elected vice-president in 1812, serving under his old rival James Madison, the winning candidate for president. Elbridge Gerry died in Washington, D.C. while in office, on November 23, 1814.

For More Information

Billias, George Athan. *Elbridge Gerry*. New York: McGraw-Hill, 1976.

Bowen, Catherine Drinker. *Miracle at Philadelphia: The Story of the Constitutional Convention—May to September, 1787*. Boston: Little, Brown & Co., 1966.

Mercy Otis Warren

1728-1814

Personal Background

Mercy Otis was born on September 25, 1728, in her family's home in Barnstable, Massachusetts, on Cape Cod about twenty-five miles southeast of Plymouth. The Otises had moved to Massachusetts from England in 1635. Mercy's father, James, was a successful businessman and local political leader. His wife, Mary Allyne Otis, was a descendant of *Mayflower* Pilgrims; Mercy's great-great-grandfather had signed the historic Mayflower Compact. She had two older brothers, James (called Jemmy) and John, as well as four younger brothers and sisters.

Her brothers' footsteps. Mercy's father was well respected in the community. The self-educated son of a farmer, he was always a bit embarrassed about his lack of schooling. Therefore, he wanted his sons to have the best education possible. In those days girls were not expected to pursue "book learning." Mercy enjoyed being with her brothers, however, and followed them when they took their books to the kitchen table after supper. She especially worshiped Jemmy, her oldest brother, whose liveliness and unpredictability contrasted with her own personality. A serious, quiet girl, Mercy soon became interested in books. By the time she was ten or eleven, when Jemmy went off to study at Harvard, Mercy had become an eager student. It was probably about then that she discovered one of her favorite books, Sir Walter Raleigh's *History of the*

▲ Mercy Otis Warren

Event: Debate over the Constitution.
Role: An opponent of the Constitution, Mercy Warren shared her feelings about the document in her frequent letters to powerful friends such as Elbridge Gerry and Abigail Adams. The letters, along with her many other writings, offer an excellent summary of the opinions that led many to oppose the new system of government.

World. She loved the drama and color of stories from history. Her father did not object to her studies. Though her interest in books and learning went against the fashion of the day, he was proud of her accomplishments. Still, as the oldest daughter, Mercy was expected to take on a large part of her mother's housework.

Jemmy at Harvard. During Mercy's teens, Jemmy shared with her many of the new ideas he was learning at Harvard. Also at Harvard was Samuel Adams, three years older than Jemmy. Both boys studied the political works of writers like Englishman John Locke (1632-1704), who believed that government should be based on the consent of the people. Such ideas were important in shaping political opinions of colonists such as Samuel Adams and James and Mercy Otis. All three were destined to play large parts in the revolution that grew out of the ideas that appeared in Locke's writings.

Courtship and marriage. Another Harvard boy was James Warren of nearby Plymouth, a year younger than Jemmy. Handsome and sandy-haired, James also came from one of the original *Mayflower* Pilgrim families. His sense of fun, while quieter than Jemmy's, had led to a friendship between the two boys. Mercy probably met James at her brother's graduation in the summer of 1743, when she was fifteen. Their courtship began seven years later, and in November of 1754, Mercy and James married. Twenty-six was an old age for a woman to marry then, yet there is no evidence that Mercy had been in any hurry. And like Mercy, James was patient, preferring caution to careless romance. (In typical style, Jemmy, on the other hand, married hastily soon after his sister, but the match ended later in a bitter divorce.)

Starting a family. After the wedding, Mercy and James moved to the Warren family home. A few miles south of Plymouth, the 400-acre farm sat on the banks of the twisty Eel River. The couple lived there for three years, during which Mercy helped her sister-in-law Sally run the household and James helped his father run the farm and the family business. When the fine Plymouth home of a General Winslow became available, James and Mercy bought it and moved there. They started a family, and had five sons over the next decade: James, Jr. (born in 1757); Winslow (1759); Charles (1762); Henry (1764); and George (1766).

James Otis the Patriot. While Mercy was raising her family, her brother Jemmy was pursuing a political career that would eventually win him fame as America's first patriot. Aided by Samuel Adams, Jemmy organized the very earliest opposition to the British. The fun-loving boy had become a fiery and brilliant speaker, and he encouraged Massachusetts leaders to resist the increasing attempts by the British to impose new taxes. His opponent was Thomas Hutchinson, the lieutenant-governor of the Massachusetts colony.

In 1760 a group of Boston merchants hired Jemmy, who practiced law in the city, to make their case in court against "writs of assistance." The writs allowed customs officers to break into private property in search of illegal (untaxed) cargoes. Among the judges sat Thomas Hutchinson, at that time chief justice as well as lieutenant-governor of the colony. Jemmy spoke for four hours, defending the colonists' rights as Englishmen. His arguments were based on time-honored English laws as well as on the more recent principles put forward by John Locke.

Unwritten constitution. "The freedom of one's house is an essential branch of English liberty. A man's house is his castle; and while he is quiet, he is as well guarded as his prince," Jemmy declared (Fritz, p. 42). In other words, as long as someone obeys the law, his privacy should be as respected as that of the king. Furthermore, he claimed, the writs went against England's unwritten constitution, which was stronger even than the right of Parliament to pass laws: "No act of Parliament can establish such a writ ... for every act against the constitution is void [without rightful power]" (Fritz, p. 43).

Jemmy's words put Hutchinson in a difficult spot. If Hutchinson disagreed with him and supported the writs, he would have to explain why, and he couldn't find a weakness in Jemmy's argument. If he decided in Jemmy's favor, on the other hand, he risked being disloyal to Britain. Finally, he turned the whole matter over to the British courts, which of course decided in favor of the writs. Because of his action, Hutchinson was viewed as a tool of the British and a betrayer of American rights. During the next decade, as the resistance to British rule became more and more violent, the public would regard James Otis as the chief defender of those rights.

Family and friends. As the conflict built, Mercy followed her brother's deeds closely. The history she had always read about in books was now happening around her, and she and Jemmy were right in the middle of it. Her husband, James, too had a part to play, having been elected to the Massachusetts legislature.

While much of her life centered around her children—especially handsome, light-hearted Winslow—Mercy had many friends, and often traveled to Barnstable or Boston, or received guests at home in Plymouth. During the late 1760s, one guest who began coming frequently was John Adams, Samuel's younger cousin, a skillful young lawyer with political ambitions. By the early 1770s, John and his wife Abigail had become close friends with both Mercy and James Warren.

Political concerns. Tragedy struck in the early 1770s too. Jemmy—now known throughout the colonies as "James Otis the Patriot"—became mentally ill, perhaps from a blow to the head he had received from a Tory during an alehouse brawl. Always slightly unstable even in his brilliance, Jemmy was insane for a time, and never again took a leading part in politics. Mercy, however, became increasingly involved in the growing movement for independence from Britain. Her friendships with people like John and Abigail Adams were based on their shared political views, and while women were not supposed to be politically active in those days, neither she nor Abigail hesitated to express their opinions. Their letters to each other combined political observations with everyday household news. Unlike Abigail, however, Mercy was not satisfied to confine her thoughts to private letters or conversation.

"First Lady of the Revolution." With John Adams's encouragement, Mercy began writing works of political satire, plays that put the local political scene into a mythical Roman setting. Thomas Hutchinson, for example, became the villain, "Rapatio," who was killed off in each play only to return in the next. Jemmy was "Brutus," the Roman who had given his honor and life to preserve democracy. And when fighting broke out in 1775, Mercy decided to write a history of the American Revolution and began taking notes for the work right away. For her writings more than for her friendships with revolutionary leaders, Mercy Otis Warren became known as "the First Lady of the Revolution."

Participation: Debate Over the Constitution

New political issues. As the war for independence seemed to be drawing to a successful end in the early 1780s, Mercy began to work seriously on her book about the Revolution. At the same time, Americans began to wrestle with the problems of establishing a system of government that was both efficient and fair. These problems replaced independence as the central political issue of the day. Leaders like James Warren and Samuel Adams believed that, with independence won, the Congress (the national ruling body) should take a back seat to the legislatures of the separate states. George Washington and others (see **James Madison**) thought that only a powerful central government could ensure the new nation's prosperity. The Articles of Confederation, adopted as the first constitution in 1781, made Congress the only branch of the national government and strictly limited its powers over the states. Under this system, the states were only loosely joined together. It rapidly became clear that they would not get along well enough for Congress to be effective.

Convention in Philadelphia. Accordingly, all the states except Rhode Island agreed to send delegates to a convention that would attempt to improve the Articles. Held in Philadelphia, Pennsylvania, in the summer of 1787, the convention was dominated by the "Federalists," men like Madison and Washington who wanted to discard the Articles completely and start over. Their opponents were the "Antifederalists," who accepted the need for greater central authority, but feared that a strong government might endanger the rights and freedoms they had fought so hard to win. Mercy expressed these fears in a letter to an English friend:

> Our situation is truly delicate and critical. On the one hand we stand in need of a strong federal government founded on principles that support the prosperity and union of the colonies. On the other, we have struggled for liberty ... and there are still many among us [who love liberty too much to give up] the rights of man for a dignity of government. (Fritz, p. 243)

"Silence and secrecy." All summer, from May to September, the delegates hammered out the document that would become the new Constitution. Mercy remained in Massachusetts, tensely awaiting the results. Since the convention's proceedings were kept secret, no one had any idea of what was happening behind the large doors of Philadelphia's State House. This secrecy made Mercy suspicious. She wrote a letter, questioning her friend Elbridge Gerry, one of the delegates from Massachusetts. Eighteen years younger than Mercy, Gerry had worked closely with Samuel Adams, who rose to replace James Otis in the early 1770s as leader of the Massachusetts rebels. Like Mercy and Adams, Gerry feared a strong central government (see **Elbridge Gerry**). He was perhaps the only man at the convention whose political views Mercy trusted absolutely. Has anything been decided, Mercy wondered, "or is all yet locked up in silence and secrecy" (Fritz, p. 244)? The final document was ready in late September. Mercy must have felt that she had worried for good reason when she heard that Gerry had refused to sign it.

"Observations." Now began the battle over ratification, the approval that the states had to give the Constitution in order to make it law. Massachusetts would meet to accept or reject it January 9, 1788. Beforehand Mercy, who had not written a political work since the Revolution, contributed one of the most important pieces to the Antifederalist cause: the nineteen-page pamphlet, *Observations on the New Constitution*. Published without her name on it, the pamphlet was mistakenly thought to have been written by Elbridge Gerry. Mercy expressed in her pamphlet several key objections to the Constitution. It had no bill of rights, for example, to guarantee specific freedoms for citizens. Nor did it guarantee the right to trial by jury in civil courts, or guard against the president's staying in office for life. All of these safeguards were eventually added in later amendments. Mercy's other objections, such as that against a permanent army, failed to prompt an amendment.

Personal battles. The Warrens' objections to the Constitution affected their friendship with John and Abigail Adams. Although they were in England during the convention, the Adamses had followed events in America closely and, of course, had been kept up to date by letters from friends. On their return to America in 1788, they both strongly supported the Constitution. As the public battle between the two sides grew more bitter, the Adamses were as disappointed with the Warrens as the Warrens were with them. Since political agreement had helped form the friendship, political disagreement threatened to end it. Added to this, Mercy was devastated in 1791 by the death of her beloved son, Winslow, killed in battle against Indians while serving in the army.

Aftermath

Lingering suspicions. Despite the adoption of a Bill of Rights, Mercy's doubts about the government continued. She stopped making public objections to it, however. She was now in her sixties, and she still mourned her son's death. She continued work on her history project and published a small book of poetry and other short works. Gradually she regained her enthusiasm. James's health, poor for several years, improved noticeably, and Henry, her second-youngest son, had a baby girl (born on Mercy's

> ### Major Works of Mercy Otis Warren
> **Plays:**
> The Adulateur (1773)
> The Defeat (1773)
> The Group (1775)
>
> **History:**
> History of the Rise, Progress and Termination of the American Revolution (1806)

birthday) whom he named after his mother. Yet in the political world, the divisions between Federalists and Antifederalists continued, except that now the two parties were called Hamiltonians and Jeffersonians. The Constitution, it seemed, had settled little. With many disputes still unresolved, Mercy felt unable to complete her history, which was supposed to be the story of the Revolution. As long as the Hamiltonians (whom she called "monarchists") were in power, she thought, the Revolution itself was in danger.

Adams's presidency. John Adams, having served as George Washington's vice president, won the presidency in 1796. As president, Adams pursued a number of policies that alarmed the Warrens and many other Americans. Foremost among them was the Sedition Act of 1798, which outlawed writing or saying anything that was intended to stir up opposition against the government. Many felt that this contradicted the first amendment's guarantee of free speech. For James and Mercy, this was exactly the sort of limitation they had feared might happen under the new Constitution.

Completing the *History*. In 1800 Thomas Jefferson defeated Adams in the presidential election and repealed measures such as the Sedition Act. With Jefferson in power, Mercy finally felt that the time had come to write the last chapters of her history. In them, she admitted that the Constitution seemed to have turned out to be as good a "form of government that could have been devised by the wisdom of man" (Fritz, p. 296). After she finished writing, there were three years of work left to do—finding printers, investors and so forth. By 1806 all three volumes were finally printed. Mercy was seventy-seven years old.

In the fashion of the day, the book carried a long title: *The History of the Rise, Progress and Termination of the American Revolution, Interspersed with Biographical, Political and Moral Observations.* Before the break in their friendship, John Adams had joked, "I dread her history" (Fritz, p. 296). Now, indeed, her account of his presidency wounded him and widened the gulf between the two old friends. While she praised his actions in the earlier years, she accused him of later having "forgotten the principles of the American Revolution" (Fritz, p. 297).

Mending broken friendships. While Mercy and Abigail had made up shortly before John became president and had continued to keep in touch, they had kept their conversations and letters limited to nonpolitical subjects. Even after James Warren's death in 1807, John remained cool to Mercy, despite attempts by mutual friends such as Elbridge Gerry to bring the two together. Finally in 1813, Abigail sent Mercy a lock of her own hair, set with pearls in a small piece of jewelry. "I forward to you," she wrote, "a token of love and friendship. I hope it will not be the less valuable to you for combining, with a lock of my own hair, that of your ancient friend's, at his request" (Fritz, p. 315). The "ancient friend," of course, was John. Soon after, the two old patriots were corresponding regularly again, as warmly as

---

Mercy Otis Warren on the Role of Women

Going against the customs of her time, Mercy Otis Warren rejected the idea that "all political attentions lay out of the road of female life" (Fritz, p. 153). Yet she appeared sensitive to the opinions of others on the proper role for women. When John Adams, for example, wrote her a letter that avoided any political topics, she took it to mean that he wished her to "stay away from anything so far beyond the line of my sex" (Fritz, p. 153). Despite such concern for the views of her society, Mercy pressed ahead.

before. Mercy, by this time a frail old woman in her eighties, had to dictate the letters to her son James, Jr. After a happy year in which her old friends had come back to her, she died on October 13, 1814.

For More Information

Anthony, Katherine. *First Lady of the Revolution: The Life of Mercy Otis Warren.* Port Washington, New York: Kennikat Press, 1958.

Fritz, Jean. *Cast for a Revolution.* Boston: Houghton Mifflin Co., 1972.

Domestic Disputes

1776
▼
As new government is formed by men, **Abigail Adams** reminds husband, John Adams, to "remember the ladies."

1783
▼
Depression in America. Government and farmers in debt.

1791
▼
Money and government: **Alexander Hamilton** opens national bank and issues national money.

1787
▼
Richard Allen opens a Methodist church for African Americans.

1786-1787
▼
Shays' rebellion occurs over farmers' debts. **Daniel Shays** is one of its strongest leaders.

1794
▼
Whiskey Rebellion by farmers against government tax on whiskey.

1794-1795
▼
Indian confederacy defeated at Fallen Timbers. Treaty of Greenville sets boundary between Indian lands and those open to settlement.

1816
▼
Richard Allen founds the African Methodist Episcopal Church.

1801
▼
Marbury v. Madison: the Supreme Court, under Chief Justice **John Marshall,** begins to define federal and states' rights.

1800
▼
Political parties form: Adams vs. Jefferson party system.

DOMESTIC DISPUTES

Disputes among residents of the United States have been part of its heritage since the country's beginning. Early disagreements ranged from the politics of setting up national and state governments, to economic questions such as how to raise money, to social differences over, for example, who was entitled to an education in the new republic.

The Revolutionary War had left the government penniless. It was in debt from the beginning, unable to pay soldiers for their military service in the war. By 1783 farmers were in debt as well. Britain and the British West Indies, major buyers of American products, had closed their markets to the American rebels. Exports dropped and there was a temporary depression. Meanwhile, state governments levied taxes that their citizens were unable to pay. A struggle began in Massachusetts, casting the state government against the farmers. The government moved to take over the farmland of citizens who failed to pay their taxes. In 1786 **Daniel Shays,** a farmer and an unpaid Revolutionary War veteran, helped lead an armed rebellion against the state government.

The uprising, called Shays' Rebellion, lent support to the arguments of **Alexander Hamilton** and others for a stronger central government that could maintain order. Hamilton also proposed establishing a national bank and system of money as a way out of the government's financial troubles. Some states viewed this as a threat. They already had their own money systems. A few years later another rebellion, this time in Pennsylvania against a whiskey tax, was put down by several thousand militiamen. Hamilton used this uprising as further proof of the need for a strong central government. His opponents, however, accused him of making the situation, called the Whiskey Rebellion, seem more serious than it was just to win support for his ideas.

Whiskey Rebellion

In the summer of 1794 about 500 armed men surrounded a tax collector's house outside Pittsburgh. They exchanged rifle fire with soldiers inside for several hours, allowing them to surrender before burning down the house. A month later Alexander Hamilton arrived with 1,300 soldiers. The rebels fled at the sight of the approaching army. Later, Thomas Jefferson, who, unlike Hamilton, was against having a strong central government, laughed at the overreaction. He joked that an insurrection was announced and armed against, but could never be found. As Jefferson saw it, Hamilton was, as always, simply out to strengthen the federal government.

After the Constitution went into effect, presidents and judges rushed to define the roles of the players in government. President John Adams stacked the courts with his own appointees shortly before he left office, establishing a practice later presidents would follow. Chief Justice **John Marshall,** for example, was a last-minute appointee. Like Adams, he was in favor of a strong federal government. Marshall led the fight to define the roles of the executive, federal, and legislative branches under the new Constitution. He served during the administration of President Thomas Jefferson, who, unlike Marshall, favored independent rights for the states rather than a strong federal government.

Most of the American population had accepted slavery as the natural order of society before the Revolution. There were even then, however, some colonists who questioned the treatment of African Americans and the justice of slavery. Such questioning increased as the Revolution made clear a contradiction between Americans who had struggled for liberty from England yet kept slaves in bondage. At the same time black freemen started to challenge the white-dominated system. In 1787 **Richard Allen** organized the first African American Methodist church, beginning to declare independence through religion. Such actions constituted the first steps toward demanding equality for all races in the new democracy.

Women, like African Americans, began breaking through the bounds placed on them in early American society. While **Abigail**

Adams accepted the belief of her times that women and men had different roles to play in society, she insisted that both were equally important and pushed for women's right to an education. She continually shared her political opinions with her husband, John Adams. He, in turn, shared public and private concerns with her, much as President James Madison would with his wife, Dolley. In both cases, the First Ladies' opinions were highly valued. Abigail Adams shared her opinions with other major politicians of her day as well. She directly urged her husband while he was helping shape the government to "remember the ladies," becoming one of the first champions of rights for the women in the democratic republic.

Population growth soared in the 1780s, leading to westward movement and conflict with native Americans for territory. Indians of the Northwest resisted white movement onto their lands but, after being defeated in the Battle of Fallen Timbers, then had to forfeit much of the Ohio territory in the Treaty of Greenville. The government had by this time recognized the rights of native Americans to the land. Aiming to obtain as much of it as possible, officials decided that transfers of ownership could be best achieved in treaties. They recognized the Indians as the original occupants and owners of the land. Henry Knox, the first secretary of war under President George Washington, announced government policy. There were only two lawful ways for whites to get hold of Indian lands: A tribe could either give them up of its own free will or lose them to the victors in war. Treaties would conclude the transfer of territory in either case. They became the official document of conquest in America's formative years of decisions and disputes.

Richard Allen

1760-1831

Personal Background

Born to slavery. Richard Allen was probably born on February 14, 1760. His exact birth date is uncertain since records of births and deaths of black slaves in the early days of the United States were poorly kept. It is known that he was born in the house of Benjamin Chew, where Allen's parents worked as domestic slaves. As his slave families grew, Chew, a lawyer in Philadelphia, Pennsylvania, found it increasingly difficult to support them. By the time Allen was seven, his owner was forced to consider selling some of his slaves. Perhaps unusual for his time, Chew was not willing to break up the slave families by selling members to different owners, nor would he sell his slaves to southern owners. Opportunity came in the form of a Mr. Stockley, owner of a plantation near Dover, Delaware. The Allen family were all sold to become farm workers on the Stockley plantation.

Owning and caring for slaves, however, became a financial burden for Stockley during the depression of the 1780s. When the Allens had more children, Stockley decided to sell the parents and younger siblings to another owner. He kept Richard Allen, his brother, and a sister, who were all old enough to work. Allen, a teenager at the time, would never again see his mother and father. His mother's last words to him encouraged the young man never to abandon the Methodist religion.

▲ Richard Allen

Event Establishment of black churches in America.
Role: Richard Allen, once a slave and later a free man, established the first black Christian church in America and was a leader in the fight to discourage the resettlement of free blacks in Liberia.

In spite of Stockley's decision to separate the family, Allen felt that Stockley was "a good master. More like a father to his slaves than anything else" (Allen, p. 16). Stockley encouraged his slaves to learn to read and write, and allowed them time to listen to the many traveling preachers passing through Dover. During this time, Allen managed to study religion. In 1777, at the age of seventeen, he joined the Methodist Episcopal Church, one of the two major Methodist factions in America. It was a decision that would have special significance for young Allen.

Methodism. Francis Asbury served as bishop of the Methodists in America during this time. He had begun his work in 1784 when there were about 400 Methodists in the whole country. The bishop had founded the Methodist Episcopal wing of the church and was energetically recruiting members (when he died in 1815 there would be 214,000 members of the church). Asbury was the first Methodist bishop in America and, as the leader of the church, had a great influence on the young Allen.

Freedom. Freeborn Garrettson was one of the traveling ministers who passed through Dover. Garrettson had once heard Asbury speak on equality, and had also heard Daniel Buff preach about the evils of slavery. If anyone could shake Stockley into giving the Allens their freedom, Garrettson could. Allen persuaded Stockley to listen to the traveling minister preach. Garrettson spoke in the Stockley living room about the evils of slavery and accused the owner of being found wanting in the eyes of God. His message was effective. A few days after the sermon, Stockley called in the Allen boys and offered to sell them their freedom. They could contract with him to pay sixty pounds in British money, or 2,000 dollars in Continental money. At the age of twenty, Allen accepted the challenge and agreed to buy his own freedom. He would pay Stockley 2,000 dollars within three years. At twenty-three, Allen became a free man.

Black freemen. Once freed, Allen set out to make his living in a white society. It was a difficult time for blacks in America. While black slaves were subjected to confining and miserable positions, free blacks often had no position at all. Black slaves were fed and housed by their owners and bound in service to them. Black freemen, newly liberated from a situation that afforded them no opportunity for education or job training, received little help from a white community that did not understand or care about their plight. Rather, black freemen were a threat to the white citizens and were as carefully isolated and segregated as slaves. They were left on their own to make their way in a society they themselves did not understand. As early as 1770 a Reverend Sam Hopkins of Newport had recognized this dilemma and suggested a solution. His idea was to send willing free blacks to Africa or some other part of the world where they could establish their own society. Those blacks who were slaves, of course, would remain in the colonies, bound to their masters.

Allen worked for a time as a traveling farmhand in New Jersey and Delaware, then chose to try to make his way in the larger and busier environment of Philadelphia. Here he found work in a brick-yard, earning fifty dollars a month. He continued to preach about Methodism, as he had done since the age of twenty-two.

In Philadelphia, Allen married and became a respected family head. He and his wife had six children, lived in a large house, and shared a comfortable life together.

Participation: Founding the African Methodist Episcopal Church

St. George's Church. Allen joined St. George's Methodist Episcopal Church in Philadelphia and attended the Sunday evening meetings for blacks. Soon he preached at these five o'clock meetings, becoming a leader among the black Methodists in the city. Allen was an able preacher and felt that the church's message should be open to everyone. It disturbed him that these early Sunday evening services were restricted to people of color. After a year Allen was so unhappy he withdrew his membership from St. George's.

St. George's Church had grown with a membership that included both blacks and whites. However, it had not grown equally in racial tolerance. When the mixed congregation exceeded the church's limits, blacks were asked to leave the pews and to line up along the walls of the church to listen to the services. Then a new

51

and larger facility was built; blacks were asked to sit in the balcony. It was here that Allen and a friend, Absalom Jones (who had become the first black Methodist priest in 1804), experienced something that changed Allen's life.

The two were kneeling in the balcony to pray when a trustee of the church grabbed Jones and asked him and Allen to leave. Apparently, the part of the balcony where they were praying was not for blacks. When Jones asked permission to finish his prayers, the trustee insisted that he leave. Allen and Jones continued their worship, however, until the trustee summoned other trustees to force the two to move. Allen, Jones, and some friends promptly left the church and never returned. With his own money, Allen bought a lot at Sixth and Lombard Streets and moved an old blacksmith shop onto the site. This he remodeled and in 1787 opened as the first black Christian church in America, called Bethel. Those who frequented the church to hear Allen's preaching became known as Allenites. Allen, however, continued to work within the framework of the Methodist Episcopal Church.

Allen's Words to Free Blacks

"Much depends upon us for the help of our color—more than many are aware. If we are lazy and idle, the enemies of freedom plead it as a cause why we ought not to be free, and say we are better in a state of servitude, and that giving us our liberty would be an injury to us; and by such conduct we strengthen the bands of oppression and keep many in bondage who are more worthy than ourselves." (Allen, p. 93)

Blacks and the yellow fever epidemic. A terrible epidemic struck Philadelphia in 1793, which resulted in the deaths of 4,000 citizens before year's end. Possibly because they were segregated from the white population, blacks in Philadelphia did not seem to contract the disease as readily as the whites. When the epidemic spread, the medical facilities and funeral homes of the city were overwhelmed.

Many people panicked and tried to shut themselves off from the sick. They refused to bury their own dead. One black volunteer happened to pass a house when a sick woman was being thrown out the front door to be left to die in the street. It was a scene that would reoccur in many places in the city.

An appeal was made in the newspaper for blacks to come to the aid of the city, and Allen and his longtime friend Absalom Jones responded. From their congregation they recruited black workers, including a Doctor Rush and his student, Edward Fisher. Under the direction of these two men, the blacks of Bethel and others who joined the effort took medicine to the sick, bled them as instructed, and carried many to their graves. With their own resources, they constructed coffins for the dead.

For their services, Allen demanded no pay except for contributions volunteered by grateful families of the ill. But as conditions worsened, the black community did not have the people or resources to carry the burden themselves. They were forced to hire some people to help carry off the dead. When the worst of the epidemic was over, newspaper accounts in the white community accused blacks of taking advantage of the sick by overcharging for aid. Allen was upset by this turn of events:

> We feel ourselves sensibly aggrieved by the censorious epithets of many who did not render the least assistance in the time of necessity, yet are liberal of their censure for us, for the prices paid for our services.... all the money we received for burying and for coffins, which we ourselves purchased and procured, has not defrayed [made up for] the expense of wages which we had to pay those whom we employed to assist us. (Allen, p. 50)

Allen's Statement of Bethel's Costs in the Epidemic	
Costs in English money, or pounds:	
Cash paid for coffins	33
For the hire of 5 men, three for 79 days and the other two for 63 days	378
	411
Cash received, for burying dead ... and beds	233
Debt due us, for which we expect but little	110
From this statement ... we are out of pocket	178
(Adapted from Allen, p. 51)	

When they were more fully exposed to the yellow fever, black immunity to the disease turned out to be less than was earlier thought. Several black people contracted and died from yellow fever while caring for or burying those afflicted. Still the black church continued its aid throughout the crisis, establishing a reputation for community service that would continue into the 1900s.

A church for blacks. Allen was acutely aware of the plight of free black people, whom he felt had been separated from their African origins through generations of slavery. They now had only

American traditions to guide them, though they were not fully allowed to participate in these traditions. His sensitivity to their needs drew free blacks of Philadelphia to his church. His congregation grew so much that in seven years he was able to build a new church, also called Bethel. Allen opened the doors of the church in 1794. Over protests from some of the white clergy of the state, he secured a charter from the Pennsylvania legislature to operate the church. In 1799 Allen was ordained a minister in the Methodist Episcopal Church, the first black minister in that denomination.

The African Methodist Episcopal Church. There was a great deal of white support for reducing or abolishing slavery in the new United States. Many of those who favored abolition, however, still did not want to associate with blacks. Nor did they care to help newly freed slaves fit into the economic and social setting of free American society. To Allen's dismay, this attitude resulted in second-class treatment of blacks within the Protestant churches.

These were not the only experiences that persuaded Allen of the need to establish a church that would support blacks in their struggles for recognition and equality. In the early 1800s Allen was captured by a slave hunter and falsely accused of having run away from his master. This happened after he had been a resident of Philadelphia for twenty years and had gained the respect of both black and white citizens. When witnesses testified to Allen's status as a free man, the slave hunter was fined and imprisoned. The incident was upsetting, but the minister believed in forgiveness and acted in keeping with his beliefs. Allen later pleaded for and won a reduced prison term for the slave hunter.

In 1816 Reverend Allen gathered a few black Christians in his own home for the purpose of organizing a new offshoot of Methodism. In that same year, the new church held a first General Conference in Philadelphia. Fifteen black men gathered at this conference and organized the new church. Allen was elected church leader and given the title of bishop. Significantly, he was to be the bishop of the African Methodist Church rather than a bishop of the Methodist Episcopal Church. Richard Allen thus became a symbol of black independence in America. One year later Allen would again break new ground by allowing a woman to preach at Bethel in spite of the

Methodist policy of not calling women preachers. Society in those days strictly confined women to certain roles (see **Abigail Adams**).

In his capacity as bishop, Allen toured the New England states, rallying free blacks to the Methodist church. He was, however, not allowed in the southern states, where suggestions to free the black slaves were beginning to upset slaveowners. A few organizers were encouraging black slaves to stop working for their masters until their freedom was arranged and salaries provided.

The African Methodist Church was an immediate success among black Americans. Within ten years, it formed two separate conferences headed by two bishops, supported seventeen preachers, sent ministers to five missions, and built a membership of nearly 8,000.

Two years after the African Methodist Church was founded, Allen began a church publishing department. In 1817 he had published a book about discipline and, in 1818, a church hymnal. Allen was the first book steward (head publisher) of the church. Beyond these two publications, however, the new publishing department did not flourish for nearly twenty-five years. Most of the membership of the church came from slave states or the District of Columbia. These places, for the most part, did not allow blacks to attend school, so few learned to read and write.

The issue of Liberia. In the same year that Allen organized the new church, a group of whites founded the Colonization Society. Based on the ideas proposed by Hopkins in 1770, the society offered to finance support of any free blacks who wished to leave America. They would be relocated to Africa, where they would be given land and the tools to work it. Allen was very much opposed to the idea, arguing that it was unrealistic to believe that people removed from their native cultures and brought up in a society that did not allow them an education could return to the now unfamiliar continent of Africa and succeed.

In the midst of this divisive turmoil over this issue, a man named David Walker emerged as spokesperson for black Americans. He was a North Carolina-born son of a free woman and a slave and had escaped the South to set up a clothing store in Boston, Massachusetts. Now, in 1829, he wrote one of the most powerful rallying documents against slavery. *Walker's Appeal in Four Articles: Together with a Preamble, to the Coloured Citizens of the World, But in Particular, and very Expressly to Those of the United States of America* made a strong case for humane treatment of southern slaves, but an even stronger case for blacks to strike for freedom:

> Fear not the number and education of our enemies, against whom we shall have to contend for our lawful right; guaranteed to us by our Makers; for why should we be afraid, when God is, and will continue to be on our side? (Mathews, p. 122)

Allen knew of Walker and respected him, but was not a champion of his proposal, which suggested the need for violence. Allen was probably surprised to find that Walker praised him and used a letter written by him as support in the *Appeal*. In the letter Allen had spoken of his concerns about a colony in Africa and also described the status of blacks in the early 1800s:

> There have always been and still remain great and insurmountable objections against the scheme. We are an unlettered people, brought up in ignorance, not one in a hundred can read or write, not one in a thousand has a liberal education; is there any fitness for such to be sent into a far country, among heathens, to convert or civilize them, when they themselves are neither civilized or christianized?... It is said by the Southern slave holders, that the more ignorant they can bring up the Africans, the better slaves they make. Is there any fitness for such people to be colonized in a far country...? (Ducas, p. 92)

His prediction of absolute failure for such a scheme was nearly correct. Some free blacks did take advantage of the society's offer and sailed for Africa, where land was bought for them from the local tribal chiefs (chiefs of the same tribes that had been active in gathering slaves from nearby groups and selling them to be sent to America). Many of the settlers soon abandoned hope and returned to the United States. One determined black man, Elijah Johnson, persisted and finally organized a government, and, with much help from European countries, succeeded in founding the nation known today as Liberia.

A convention for blacks. In 1830 Allen received a letter from black community leader Hezakiah Grice, suggesting that some prominent blacks get together and plan a Negro Convention. It was an idea that appealed to the bishop because of recent events that followed the wide circulation of *Walker's Appeal,* and because of the man who sent it. Grice had been apprenticed to a farmer in Virginia, but, when he was whipped by the farmer's wife, had run away to become a black leader in Baltimore, Maryland.

At the same time southern legislatures were demanding that Walker be arrested and imprisoned for publishing the *Appeal.* The concern over this publication had spread to Cincinnati, Ohio, where the city management tried to enforce an old law that required blacks to register and post a bond of 500 dollars. Many could not afford this and others did not want to put up with it, so a group was sent to Canada to see if blacks would be accepted there. When Canadians assured them of equal treatment, more than 1,000 blacks left Cincinnati for Canada.

Allen felt that showing black solidarity through a convention was necessary in the tension-filled atmosphere. He and Grice gathered a group of five men who put out a call for a Negro Convention to open in Philadelphia, September 15, 1830. The organizers were the only ones initially present when the convention was finally held at Bethel Church. Soon, however, other African Americans came to ask how these five men could pretend to represent the country's black people. Some of them were made honorary members of the convention. Others, representatives of the Zion Methodist Church, were given full membership. Soon more than forty representatives from nine states were present to discuss the ideas of the American Colonization Society and emigration to Canada. The Convention opposed the idea of the society, but recommended that some blacks consider migration to Canada. It was the beginning of even larger conventions of blacks, who were meanwhile becoming aware of the politics of a young Illinois lawyer, Abraham Lincoln, and his hatred of the practice of lynching.

Aftermath

Final years. Allen died in 1831, having devoted much of his life to the African Methodist Church. The Church lived on and grew more influential after his death. In the opinion of one present-day historian "the African Methodist Episcopal Church of America has exerted a wider and better influence upon the Negro race than any other organization created and managed by Negroes" (Williams, p. 452).

Activities of the church ranged from religion to education to social welfare. In 1841 the publishing department that Allen had started began to publish a quarterly magazine. When that proved successful, a weekly journal, the *Christian Herald,* began in 1848. By 1852 this successful journal had been expanded to become the *Christian Recorder,* which is still published today and has more than 50,000 subscribers.

In 1856 members of the Cincinnati Conference of the Church decided to establish a university for young black people. The result was Wilberforce University, dedicated in October of that year. In 1881 representatives of the church joined the Ecumenical Council of the Methodists in London, presenting papers and lectures at this gathering.

Under the direction of Allen, the African Methodists had begun missionary work in 1827, extending aid and ministry first to the people of Haiti and then the Dominican Republic. A missionary society was organized in 1844; it began aiding blacks in Liberia and South Africa in 1887 and 1889. In the twentieth century, America's African Methodist church has expanded so that there is now a bishop of Africa.

Through the years, Allen's African Methodist Episcopal Church has continued to serve black communities as it did under its creator. For example, the First African Methodist Episcopal Church of Los Angeles (the name shortened to A.M.E. Church in the media) took a leading role in aiding those stricken in the 1992 riot in that city by opening the church building to those who sought to calm the rioters and begin to rebuild the inner city.

For More Information

Allen, Richard. *The Life Experience and Gospel Labors of the Right Reverend Richard Allen.* Nashville: Abingdon Press, 1960.

Ducas, George, ed. *Great Documents in Black American History.* New York: Praeger Publishers, 1970.

Mathews, Marcia M. *Richard Allen.* Baltimore: Helicon, 1963.

Williams, George Washington. *A History of the Negro Race in America.* Vol. 2. New York: Bergman Publishers, 1983.

Daniel Shays

1747-1825

Personal Background

Family and community life. For all his reluctance to become involved in the affairs of state, Daniel Shays was an unusual man for his day. Born in 1747 at Hopkinton, Massachusetts, he grew up in the large family of Patrick Shays (who sometimes spelled his name in the Irish way, *Sheas*) and Margaret Dempsey. His was an Irish family of poor dirt farmers, which usually meant the whole family worked to earn enough to survive. Daniel's parents, however, insisted on education for their children. Though he was needed as a worker, they made sure that young Daniel attended school at least for a year or two, long enough to count him among those who could read, write, and sign their names with other than a mark.

Daniel grew into a respected young man in his community. Though he did not own a farm of his own, he proved a responsible and capable worker. His work on the farms around his home in Brookfield earned him high regard from his neighbors and registration in the town records as "gentleman," a title usually reserved for those who owned land.

Revolutionary soldier. Shays was twenty-nine years old when the War for Independence erupted. Immediately he joined the army, where his ability to read and write, along with his good reputation, was put to use. Before the war it had not been unusual in the

▲ Daniel Shays

Event: Shays' Rebellion.
Role: A former army officer, Daniel Shays entered into a rebellion over taxation and representation in Massachusetts after the Revolutionary War. Drawn somewhat reluctantly into the rebellion, he became one of its strongest leaders. Shays earned fame for his exploits against superior forces in confrontations at Springfield.

Massachusetts militia for a man to earn the rank of an officer by recruiting soldiers who would follow him. Shays used his reputation in the community to recruit soldiers for the war and thus became a second lieutenant in the Massachusetts Regiment. He led his men into battle in some of the most important events of the war: Lexington-Concord, Bunker Hill (where he was cited for his gallantry), Saratoga, and Stony Point. A second successful recruiting excursion, along with his distinguished record in the early battles of the revolution, earned him a promotion. Shays became a captain in the Fifth Massachusetts Regiment in January 1777. Although he was not trained for the military as some of his fellow officers had been, he proved a fairly good soldier.

During the war, Shays served under the beloved French officer, the Marquis de Lafayette. It was Lafayette's practice to reward his officers for work well done, and he gave to Shays a sword from France. Many of the officers used their own funds to support their troops, but Shays had no money of his own. Therefore, when Shays could no longer afford to feed and house his troops, he decided to sell the sword to pay for the expenses. This became the subject of much ridicule among other officers, who felt the award of the sword too great an honor to handle in such a way. Their scoffing and the difficulty he had getting his rank of captain confirmed (it finally became official in 1779) eventually led Shays to resign his commission and leave the army in 1780.

Marriage and farming. After his service at Lexington, Shays had returned home long enough to marry Abigail Gilbert. Now the young couple moved to the Scotch-Irish settlement of Pelham, a town spread across two hills in central Massachusetts. They settled into farm life, and Shays became an active member of the community. He took on the assignment of drilling the town militia.

Conditions for farmers after the war were difficult. They had lost a major market for their goods because England was cut off from trade with the colonies. Also, the new state governments had no funds. Some of them tried printing paper money and encouraging bankers and merchants to accept it. While a few had success with the new currency, the experiment encountered problems in nearby Rhode Island, so Massachusetts leaders were reluctant to try it. Without a market to sell products to, with no gold for buying goods or paying off loans, and with new governments levying new taxes to support themselves, many farmers were so deeply in debt that they could not climb out from it. (Even George Washington was considerably behind in paying his taxes.) Massachusetts had debtors laws to punish those who could not pay their debts and a Court of Common Pleas to enforce the laws.

Taxes. At that time, Massachusetts had been divided into counties, and it was the custom for the Court of Common Pleas to travel from county seat to county seat, setting up court and making judgments about civil cases. (Criminal cases were settled by another court.) By 1787 the Court of Common Pleas would regularly ride into town, set up court, decree that some farmers were behind on taxes, and rule that their goods—household items, cattle, farm equipment—be sold to pay the amount owed. Almost everywhere in Massachusetts, farmers were losing their farm equipment and even their farms.

Something had to be done about the situation. Petitions were sent to the General Court (Massachusetts' legislature) in Boston, asking that paper money be created as a means of exchange and that there be some relief from the collection of taxes to protect the farmers. Those petitions, however, fell on deaf ears in Boston, where little farming took place. Rumors flew about the colony: The government leaders were collecting extraordinarily high salaries. Meanwhile, this farmer and that one were the next to be called by the Court of Common Pleas. Some farmers were plotting to upset the confederation and rejoin England. As the rumors and news about the court mounted, hostilities between the rural farmers and the Bostonians also grew. In the minds of farmers west and north of Boston, something had to be done. They felt that their only defense against the heavy tax burdens was to close the Court of Common Pleas and to call for more county conventions in order to send the message more firmly to Boston that the courts, in their minds, had to treat debtors less harshly.

In August 1787 the Court of Common Pleas met in Northampton and Concord. Already, farmers from Massachusetts, among them Adam Wheeler of Hubbardston, Luke Day of Northampton, Abraham and Henry Gale of Princeton, and Job Shattuck of Middlesex, were urging their neighbors to join together to prevent the

▲ Virginia currency

court from acting in their communities. It was rumored that Day had formed a militia of 500 men to block the court. Furthermore, some of the men whom Shays trained at Pelham had already left to join forces with others from Northampton and Concord. Shays, however, did not agree with interfering with the courts; a good government, he felt, would pay attention to the petitions of the people in city meetings.

Rebellion brews. Shays believed in the new state government even though, as designed by John and Samuel Adams, it did not allow everyone to participate in the election process. Only property owners could vote or hold office. In addition, people interested in running for office were required to take a religious oath that excluded, among others, Catholics. Several communities, Hampshire and Bristol among them, had demanded that the new government act immediately to correct this inequality, but the General Court took no action. On August 29 the farmers, led by Day, gathered in force to block the opening of the Court of Common Pleas in Northampton. Successfully preventing the court from opening there, the uprising moved to Worcester to block the court that was planning to open September 5. Meanwhile, Wheeler, a Revolutionary War veteran, was making plans at Hubbardston to take away some of the court's powers there.

Because the Court of Common Pleas dealt with debtors, it was the focus of the rebellion. Determination to close this hated court spread across Massachusetts. Shays, however, continued to object to the farmers' use of force.

Shays' first move. There were other circulating courts in the state. The Supreme Judicial Court heard criminal cases and, like the Court of Common Pleas, moved from town to town. None of the leaders of the rebellion cared about this court; after all, they were good, hard-working citizens, not criminals. So when the Supreme Judicial Court met September 19 in Worcester, no move was made to block it. In its meeting, however, the Supreme Judicial Court called the leaders of the rebellion "criminals" and put out warrants for the arrest of Wheeler and Abraham and Henry Gale. In Boston people were demanding that the "criminals" be subjected to "condign" punishment, which most of the rebels took to mean "capital" punishment. When Shays heard of this, he was moved to action. These friends in a common cause were not criminals in his view. Shays gathered those of his Pelham militia who had not already joined the fray and headed for Springfield, the next town in which the Court of Common Pleas was to hear cases.

Participation: Shays' Rebellion

Showdown at Springfield. Springfield was an important location from the point of view of the government. During the Revolutionary War, a large arsenal had been built there and was still the storehouse for large amounts of war weapons and gunpowder. Springfield was defended by the state militia under Major General William Shepard, and Shepard had prepared to defend the town by recruiting 200 additional local men who were sympathetic to the government. Altogether he commanded more than 900 men. Against this force, Shays led a ragged band of 700 who had come from all over the farm country to join his Pelham troops. Probably fewer than 200 of these had weapons other than clubs. When Shays' group arrived at the courthouse, they found Shepard and his army standing guard with a cannon.

Shays swung into action, demonstrating the leadership ability that had made him so popular. He halted his troops some distance from the courthouse and began to organize them. It was not an easy task to make this group look like a unified fighting force. A few wore their old Revolutionary War uniforms, but most were dressed in ragged homespun clothes. To give them something of a uniform appearance, Shays declared that every man should wear a sprig of hemlock in his cap. Shepard's men responded by adding a piece of white paper to their own caps.

Shays knew that he had no chance to win a fight with the state militia. Still, he lined his men in columns and marched toward the courthouse. At the square, he stopped once more and rode forward to tell the general his purpose; his men wanted to parade and requested permission to do so on the square in front of the courthouse. Shepard saw no harm in a simple parade since he obviously had the superior force. So Shays marched his men up and down the square in front of the militia. It was a strange affair. Men on the other side, in the militia, watched as their brothers and friends marched with the rebels. Some militia traded their white paper for a sprig of hemlock and joined the parade. Others fell into the ranks as the parade continued. As his numbers grew, Shays appointed a committee to ask that the judges not hold court. The judges, committed to carrying out their responsibility, refused to grant the request. At this point, Shays and the other rebel leaders were hard-pressed to restrain their forces. Nothing happened, however. The judges finally decided it was not a good idea to convene court, and the rebels went away satisfied that they had won the day.

The government reacts. The "attack" on Springfield had aroused the state government. Now Samuel Adams, who had won a reputation as a revolutionary only a few years earlier, pressed for new laws to contain the rebellion. He and others urged the General Court to abolish the rule of habeas corpus, making it easier to cap-

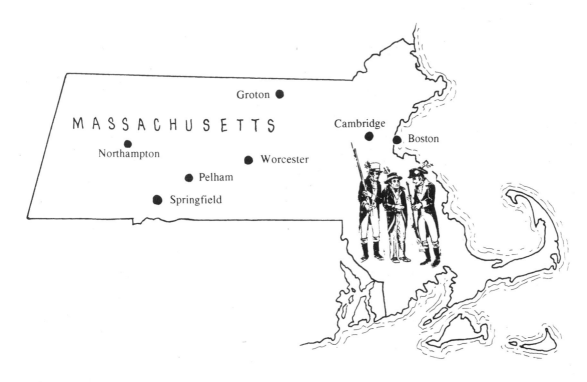

▲ **Shays' Rebellion sites**

ture and imprison criminals without a speedy trial. Adams and Theodore Sedgwick authored a Riot Act, which made sure that those acting in rebellion would be treated as criminals. These laws were proposed to the General Court in autumn 1787. They were passed in late October and early November.

Matters grew more tense when a group of the rebels gathered in Berkshire with the intent of capturing a government cannon that was mounted at Dorchester Neck. Although the mission failed, its leader, George Brock, was added to the list of wanted criminals. Yet overall, after the incident at Springfield, matters seemed to fall into a brief calm.

The next call to rebellion bore Shays' name, though he denied being its leader and later denied writing a letter that was circulated around the state between October 13 and October 20:

> Gentlemen: By information from the General Court they are determined to call all those who appeared to stop the court to condign

punishment. Therefore I request you to assemble your men together, to see that they are all armed and equipped with 60 rounds, each man to be ready to turn out at a minute's warning. Likewise be properly organized with officers. (Starkey, p. 91)

The letter drove the General Court to action. The Riot Act and the elimination of habeas corpus were quickly passed into law. The court, however, was not clear in its intentions, for in November it also passed an Indemnity Act, offering pardon to any rebels who agreed to surrender to the officials and swear an oath of allegiance before January 1, 1788. That offer had little effect; strong leaders such as Wheeler and Shattuck persisted in their mission to close the Court of Common Pleas. On November 28 they and their followers planned to close the court at Cambridge.

The state government was quick to act in this case; 160 men armed with warrants were sent to arrest Wheeler, the Gales, and Shattuck. Meanwhile, troops gathered in Cambridge to stop the rebels. Realizing the superiority of the state militia, the rebel leaders spread out to seek reinforcements. In the process, Shattuck was caught and arrested. Resisting arrest, he was struck on the back of the knee by a sword that severed a tendon. Thus crippled, he was carried off to a Boston prison. The rebels could not get information about his condition, and concern for his treatment aroused others, among them Shays.

Shays resists. Shattuck was the second rebel to meet harm. In response, another letter circulated, this time acknowledged by Shays to be his creation. It began: "The seeds of war are now sown; two of our men are now bleeding" (Starkey, p. 101). The letter called for all men to support the rebellion, for the cause of the rebels was everyone's cause; it should not be left to die and its leaders with it.

Shays continued to lead forces to close the Court of Common Pleas wherever it was scheduled to meet. In Dorchester, the opposing forces promised a bloody battle, but a driving snowstorm closed the court and saved the day. In Springfield, Shays, without using force, convinced the judges not to convene court.

A second showdown. Early in 1788 Shays briefly returned home to Abigail. On the way he is reported to have encountered an old commanding officer, General Rufus Putnam, and to have declared that he would gladly abandon the cause and his troops if offered a pardon. Hearing this from Putnam, the General Court saw an opportunity to rid itself of one of the strongest leaders of the rebellion. It granted a pardon to Shays to be delivered to him by the general. The rapid change of events, however, ensured that Shays would never see the pardon offer. He joined forces with Luke Day, Adam Wheeler, and Eli Parsons. They united in a plan to capture the Springfield Arsenal: While the others prepared to attack the arsenal, Day would bring reinforcements to support them. Day, however, had a change of heart and was slow to do his part. It was a standoff, as it had been at the Springfield Courthouse earlier. Shepard stood guard with a well-armed militia and artillery pieces to confront the men led by Shays. Again brother faced brother and neighbor faced neighbor as the lines closed. Shepard himself had no desire to have his men firing on their old friends. As the lines grew closer, however, he had to take action and ordered one artillery squad to open fire. Two shots from the cannon were fired over the heads of the rebels, but still they approached. Finally, a third shot was fired into their ranks and the rebels broke and fled. Three men were killed: Ezekila Root, Ariel Webster, and Jubez Spicer. John Hunter was so severely wounded that he later died. No one from either side had fired a musket.

Now the rebels were scattered and on the run. Shays and some of his men retreated toward home (on the way, they were ambushed by troops hiding in an outhouse). In Pelham, Shays was handed a demand for his surrender. He evaded it by fleeing to Petersham.

Punishment or pardon? In early February, with the rebel leaders on the run from forces led by the stern General Benjamin Lincoln, the General Court began to bring the rebellion to an end. In a closed session on February 3, the court appropriated 40,000 pounds from the general fund to repay loans that had been made to pay the state militia and called for a stronger state government lest anyone with a protest should lead another rebellion. As a first step, Samuel Adams prepared a measure that declared the acts of Shays and others to be rebellious and gave the governor broader powers to deal with rebellions. The court also denied a request, made by the same General Lincoln who had been scouring the country for rebels, to grant amnesty to, or pardon, some of those involved.

On February 9, the court set rewards for the capture of the leaders of the rebellion: 150 pounds for Shays and 100 pounds for each of three others, Day, Wheeler, and Parsons. Officers of the court remained divided, however, on how severely to punish the rebels. On February 16 the court again passed an amnesty bill granting pardons to all but officers in the rebellion on condition that each man serve three years probation. By this time, Shays, Day, and Parsons had fled to Vermont. Abigail joined Shays in exile there.

Back in Massachusetts, few people cared to pursue punishment for those captured. The government, however, felt that some penalty should be paid. The General Court debated what to do and finally decided to hang two representatives each from the most involved counties: Berkshire, Hampshire, Worchester, and Middlesex. Somehow the date of these hangings was delayed. Meanwhile, a new election replaced the anti-rebel governor of Massachusetts, James Bowdoin, with John Hancock.

Hancock was intent on fairness and justice. Although he faced considerable opposition from the old rebel Samuel Adams, he pushed for pardons for all involved. Shays was pardoned in a separate action on June 23, 1788, and those who had been confined to prison were pardoned on September 12. The affair that Shays denied ever leading, but which history gave his name, had reached its end.

Aftermath

Effect on American history. Two famous figures in American history were interested in the rebellion in Massachusetts. From Paris, France, Thomas Jefferson, who a few years earlier had helped write the Declaration of Independence, said that he thought a little revolution now and then was a good thing for a democracy and that such affairs were rarely entirely without excuse. George Washington, who had led the colonial army to victory and then retired to his farm with little interest in continuing in politics, was greatly disturbed when he heard of the affairs in Massachusetts. He demanded to know the cause so that it could either be remedied or the crisis put down through strong government action.

Shays' Rebellion may have been the stimulus that brought Washington back into public life and convinced the very independent colonies that they needed a stronger central government. Indirectly, then, Shays' Rebellion probably had a strong influence on the formation of the United States government.

Shays' final days. Shays remained in Vermont with his wife, Abigail, farming there until his pardon in June 1788. He then moved to Sparta in upstate New York. For some unknown reason, Abigail did not accompany him. He moved to Sparta alone.

After establishing himself, Shays met and married a local tavern owner, Darling Havens. By 1790 he began to receive a pension from the national government for his service in the Revolutionary War. He and Darling lived together on a farm outside Sparta until Shays died in 1825 at the old age of eighty-four.

> ## Thomas Jefferson on Rebellion
>
> "I hold it, that a little rebellion now and then, is a good thing, and as necessary in the political world as storms in the physical. It is a medicine necessary for the sound health of govenment." (Baker, p. 192)

For More Information

Baker, Daniel, ed. *Political Quotations.* Detroit: Gale Research Inc., 1990.

Ferdel, Frank, and Ernest May. *Shays' Rebellion.* New York: Garland Publishers, 1989.

Starkey, Marion L. *A Little Rebellion.* New York: Alfred A. Knopf, 1955.

Alexander Hamilton

c. 1755-1804

Personal Background

The Hamilton family. That he came into the world under less than perfect conditions did not, from an early age, slow Alexander Hamilton in his quest for power and influence. His mother, Rachel Faucett, of French-English heritage had moved to the Danish colony of St. Croix in the West Indies when she was about fifteen. There, at her mother's insistence, she married a Danish merchant. The couple divorced after three years, however, and Rachel later met and fell in love with James Hamilton, a poor merchant. Though Danish law forbade Rachel from marrying again, James and Rachel lived together as husband and wife and had two children, James and Alexander.

Young Alexander. Rachel gave birth to Alexander on the small West Indies island of Nevis. His date of birth is in dispute. While January 11, 1755, is an accepted date, he maintained that the year was 1757. About the time he was eleven or twelve, Alexander's mother died and his father left the care of the two boys to their mother's relatives. They soon put Alexander to work as a bookkeeping clerk at the trading company of David Beekman and Nicholas Cruger on the island of St. Croix. Alexander disliked the job. He wrote to a friend that working as a clerk was far from his own ambition to be prosperous and influential. At age thirteen he had already decided that the path to his goal was through the military; in fact, he

▲ Alexander Hamilton

Event: Creation of a national bank, the two-party system, and design of United States government.

Role: Alexander Hamilton's experiences in the War for Independence left him believing that the new country needed a strong central government. Convinced that the Articles of Confederation failed to provide that strength, Hamilton became instrumental in persuading the people of New York to ratify the Constitution. He also succeeded in interpreting the Constitution in a way that shaped the new central government's powers.

wished there were a war. Still, he disciplined himself to overcome his disdain for the job and perform his clerical duties well.

Businessman. Although Hamilton had little or no formal education, he began early to educate himself, reading such great literature as was available to him. His favorite author was the Greek writer Plutarch, who was noted for his biographies of famous Greeks and Romans. Hamilton also wrote a great deal, and discovered that he had a strong talent for it. When he was almost sixteen a violent storm struck the island and Hamilton reported on the event in a published letter that earned him a reputation as a writer. In addition, his work at the counting house had been so excellent that Cruger left him in charge of the business when he was called out of town on an extended trip. Young Hamilton wrote company letters, made decisions about shipments and the care of the company stores, and handled sales so efficiently that he earned a reputation as a fine businessman.

In the colonies. By age sixteen, Hamilton had positioned himself to attain a higher standing in society. He had nearly stopped any contact with his ne'er-do-well father and older brother, and had taken on the erect and sophisticated bearing that he would carry throughout his life. He made friends readily, and, it would turn out later, made enemies with equal ease because he was opinionated and headstrong. The boy grew to be five-feet seven-inches tall, slender, and handsome. His ambition, industry, and personality worked to win him support for more education. Friends raised money to send him to school in the colonies. In 1773 the sixteen-year-old sailed for Boston, Massachusetts, then New Jersey, where he enrolled in a grammar school at Elizabethtown. Alexander applied the same discipline to schooling as he had to his clerical job, rising early to study in the quiet of a nearby cemetery and reading and writing until midnight.

In a year, he was ready to enter King's College (now Columbia University) in New York. His study habits included long walks, during which he would talk to himself as if trying to convince an audience of his ideas. Now eighteen years old, he began to gain recognition as a writer when two of his articles, "A Full Vindication of the Measures of Congress...," and "The Farmer Refuted...," were published. The articles argued that the colonies were responsible only to the king and not to the British parliament. Therefore, Hamilton concluded, the colonies had every right to protect themselves from the tyranny of that assembly.

Military service. In 1776 the war that Hamilton had wished for so ardently as a young boy arrived. He quickly sided with the colonists, joining the New York infantry on March 14 as a captain in charge of an artillery unit. In less than a year he was promoted to serve as General George Washington's aide-de-camp. Colonel Hamilton handled Washington's letters and his appointments, and often issued orders in Washington's name. He was involved in almost all of Washington's actions, but the job of handling a general's communications was not what Hamilton wanted to do. Although his writing ability had carried him to this height, he was firmly convinced that his field of great ability lay on the battlefield. Hamilton pressed Washington for a position in command of troops.

In February 1781 Hamilton, in a fit of anger, resigned his post as aide-de-camp after being reprimanded by Washington for being slow in carrying out his orders. The bond was strong between the two men, however, and six months later Washington gave Hamilton command of a battalion of light infantry. Hamilton distinguished himself in the famous battle at Yorktown against Lord Cornwallis, driving his soldiers into the fray with what some thought was overly reckless abandon. Afterward, he returned to New York.

Marriage. In the midst of his military duty, Hamilton married Elizabeth Schuyler, the twenty-three-year-old daughter of a wealthy family. Hamilton described her to a friend as "a good hearted girl … though not a genius she has good sense enough to be agreeable, and though not a beauty, she has fine black eyes—is rather handsome and has every other requisite of the exterior to make a lover happy. And believe me, I am a lover in earnest" (Hecht, p. 60). The couple married on December 14, 1780, and over the years had eight children. Elizabeth, or Betsy as she was more fondly called, remained a loyal wife, supporting Alexander throughout his life. Though he had a reputation for straying, there was a steady affection between them for each other and their children.

Receiver of taxes. The month of July 1782 was a busy one for Hamilton. He was appointed Continental Receiver of Taxes for the state of New York on July 2, and soon after was admitted to the New York State Bar. On July 22 Hamilton was appointed by the New York State Legislature to be a delegate to the national legislature, the Continental Congress. He served as a member from November 1782 to July 30, 1783, and with James Madison campaigned unsuccessfully for a strong central government against those who wanted to preserve the rights of the individual states.

From 1783 to 1789 Hamilton attended to his law firm while continuing to press for a stronger federal government. He felt that the old Articles of Confederation, in effect since 1777, were not holding the states together. Incidents such as Shays' Rebellion (see **Daniel Shays**) further convinced him of the need for a stronger central government. Hamilton and others who favored reform of the Articles called for a Constitutional Convention. When this idea seemed to lag, he pressured friends in the New York government to encourage the convention. Partly because of his insistence, a Constitutional Convention to revise the Articles was finally scheduled for 1787. Hamilton became a New York delegate.

The Constitution. Hamilton attended the convention armed with his own proposal for the ideal government. He had little respect for public opinion, and he was opposed to a government by the people. In his view, only property owners should have been allowed to vote, since they would have the most to lose if the government failed and therefore would be less likely to behave corruptly. Hamilton's plan called for a president chosen for life by landholders. The president would have power over a popularly elected assembly that would actually have little voice in government. A second legislature would consist of propertied men elected for life by electors chosen by the people. The federal government would appoint a governor for each state, also for life, who would preside over a legislature and have an absolute veto over this body. Hamilton's proposal was not for a democracy. In fact, he had already found a model for the ideal national government:

Alexander Hamilton's Attire

- Hair—powdered and tied in back
- Blue coat with bright buttons and long skirts
- White waistcoat
- Black silk trousers
- White silk stockings
- Fine lace ruffles

The nearest approach to it is the popular conception of the empire of Japan—a mass of intelligent humanity, reckless of their lives, yet filled with the joy of life, eager for distinction, hungry for success, alert, practical and merry, but at the same time subordinate, humbly and proudly subordinate to a pure abstraction [a divine emperor]. (Cooke, p. 231)

As the convention worked its way through the many proposals, Hamilton came more and more to feel that America was not the right place for him. When the Constitution was completed, he felt it a "frail and worthless fabric," which would fail to provide the country the direction it needed. Still, in the end he said that he saw nothing wrong with experimenting with a republic. He approved the Constitution, even though "no man's ideas were more remote from the plan, than his own were known to be" (Cooke, p. 52) and set out to be one of its principal supporters and interpreters. Drawn with broad brush strokes, the Constitution had left much to be determined. But first, it was necessary to secure its approval by the states.

The *Federalist Papers* and Federalists. Returning to New York and to his law business, Hamilton began to campaign for New York to ratify the Constitution. Hamilton, along with James Madison and John Jay, became chief spokesman for this cause. The three men published a series of eighty-five articles defending the new Constitution and urging its acceptance. Hamilton is said to have written the first article, which was published in the *Independent Journal,* a New York newspaper, on October 27, 1787, exactly one month after the first publication of the proposed Constitution. Called the *Federalist Papers,* these articles spread throughout the states and were of major help in gaining support for the new Constitution.

> ## *Federalist Papers*
>
> As the debate over whether to ratify the Constitution got under way, Alexander Hamilton had the idea of publishing a number of articles to win support for the document. Enlisting the aid of James Madison and John Jay, he found a sympathetic newspaper willing to publish the pieces. The resulting essays, called the *Federalist Papers*, are regarded as the clearest, most complete explanation of the Constitution. They remain available today in book form.

Hamilton had remained in a country in which he was ill at ease and had supported a Constitution in the hope that it would somehow strengthen the faltering government. There remained the task of interpreting the Constitution in order to create that stronger federal government.

Participation:
The Debate Over the Shape of Government

Secretary of the Treasury. In 1789, with the Constitution in place, Washington was elected the first president of the country. Tremendous problems faced him. The new government was still in debt from the Revolutionary War, and the dangers of involvement in the continuing troubles in Europe threatened the new United States. The president immediately set about to appoint a cabinet of advisers. Jefferson became Washington's secretary of state and six months after the election Hamilton became the first secretary of the newly created Department of the Treasury. His first task in office was to prepare for Congress three reports: one on the public credit, one on the idea of a national bank, and one on "manufactures."

Restoring public credit. The first report dealt with the problem of restoring public credit, or faith in the nation's economic well-being. Hamilton proposed that the federal government establish its credit rating by stating its intention to pay off at full value all foreign debts incurred, or acquired, in the war. Hamilton further proposed that, as a means of uniting the states, the federal government also agree to pay all debts incurred by each state individually. Finally, the report proposed setting up a "sinking fund," an emergency fund to ensure the continued function of government. Hamilton's proposals were accepted, and the federal government was placed on solid financial ground with an emergency fund of 150,000 dollars. It was the beginning of consolidation of power in the central government.

A national bank and implied powers. In his second report, Hamilton urged the formation of a national bank that would be funded by the government at 10 million dollars and be managed by twenty-five governors, five of whom would be government employees. Such a bank would develop a system of notes to serve as money and make the payment of taxes easier. It would also be able to loan money to help build American businesses. As a control, the Department of Treasury would keep a tight check on the bank's books. Along with the bank, Hamilton proposed establishing a mint in order to make currency, which would be minted in small as well as large denominations to be of use to both poor and rich. Even before the proposal for the bank was officially made, however, there were mutterings against its formation. Some states already had their own banks and their own currency, and the new banks might help businessmen, but not the larger number of farmers.

The proposal was of great concern to Washington. He wondered about a national bank's effectiveness and listened to opponents of the plan. Instead of sending Hamilton's proposal to the legislature, Washington sent it to two members of his cabinet. Edmund Randolph, the attorney general, and Thomas Jefferson, secretary of state, opposed a strong central government. Hamilton's proposal had the potential to provide solid financing for such a government. Not surprisingly, the two cabinet members opposed the idea. Randolph immediately declared the formation of a bank unconstitutional and Jefferson wrote to the president condemning the plan. Not only was it a bad idea, he said, it had already been tried with little success. In fact, Jefferson noted, a bank set up to fund the confederation was already in existence and only needed to be renamed. Washington sent these two reports to Hamilton.

Accomplishments of Alexander Hamilton

- Captain of New York Artillery
- Aide-de-camp of George Washington
- Continental Receiver of Taxes
- Member of New York Legislature
- Representative to Continental Congress
- Founder of Bank of New York
- Founder of New York Society for the Manumission of Slaves
- Delegate to the Annapolis Convention (to bolster the Federation)
- Member of New York Assembly
- Delegate to the Constitutional Convention
- Secretary of the Treasury
- Inspector General of the Armed Forces
- Author of: The *Federalist Papers*
  Report on Public Credit
  Report on a National Bank
  Report on Manufactures

Hamilton and Jefferson had little in common, except for the fact that they were both ambitious. Each wanted to be the chief adviser to the president and had argued over issues before. Now, with two cabinet members opposing the idea, perhaps the president felt that the issue was dead and that once Hamilton saw the other reports he would not pursue the idea. Instead, in a week Hamilton responded with a letter to Washington in which he addressed each of Jefferson's issues and destroyed the basis for them point by point. After all, Hamilton contended, the Constitution demanded that the government regulate trade, collect taxes, provide for a common defense, and promote the "general welfare."

Some other powers must be implied, or suggested, by these sweeping demands, and one of these powers must be the ability to raise funds to accomplish these goals. Establishing a national bank would provide a means for the ready collection of taxes, which would support a strong military and help provide other services for the people. The Bank of the United States was chartered in February 1791 and was funded as Hamilton had proposed. More important, he had succeeded in giving a broad interpretation of the Constitution. The idea that the federal government has powers that are implied by that document, even though they are not specifically stated in it, persists even today.

Report on Manufactures. Hamilton remained as secretary of the treasury for two-and-a-half years. Before he left, he made a final report to Congress, a *Report on Manufactures*. This was an outline for building the economy of the new nation. It called for protective duties on imported goods to curb foreign competition with United States industries but for no duties on raw materials that could be used in American manufacturing. It also called for a business bonus for those who would import machinery for the new American industry. This proposal strengthened the federal involvement in the business of the nation. It was a continuation of Hamilton's fight for a strong central government. He had already said that the existing states ought to be abolished. Still, he returned to New York to practice law and to influence the state government and its role in national politics.

Disagreement with Adams. John Adams was vice president under Washington and before that had been one of the leaders of the Revolution and shapers of the government. His idea of national government was very different from Hamilton's, though both were counted among the Federalists who first directed the government. Adams planned for a government in which the individual states would have much authority. His view of the government follows:

> Kings we never had among us. Nobles we never had. Nothing hereditary existed in the country: Nor will the country require or admit of any such thing; but governors, and councils we have always had as well as representatives. A legislature in three branches ought to be preserved, and independent judges. (Morris, p. 105)

The two men disagreed from the beginning. By the time Washington stepped down from office in 1796 and Adams became president, Hamilton had already resigned from his Treasury post and retired to law and politics in New York. This, however, did not stop him from attempting to influence the shape of the national government. He began to correspond with Adams's cabinet members and so influenced them that the president, in annoyance, referred to Hamilton as "that bastard brat of a Scotch pedlar" (Cooke, p. 2).

Inspector general. Under John Adams, Hamilton became inspector general of the army. He served from 1798-1800, acting as the real day-to-day commander. Though he secured the right to build up the strength of the army, Hamilton's weakness as a leader of people was revealed in his slowness in recruiting and organizing the troops. He felt his real place was as a sort of Napoleonic leader of a militia (his all-time hero was Julius Caesar); in reality Hamilton's strength as a writer and an organizer of ideas proved much greater.

The political party system. The antagonism between Hamilton and Adams grew throughout Adams's presidency. The arrogant and outspoken Hamilton did little to make peace. In fact when Adams's term ended and he sought reelection, Hamilton campaigned for another Federalist candidate. This split the group into two parts, allowing those who advocated a weak federal government and strong states to establish themselves. Led by Thomas Jefferson, the Democratic-Republicans were carried into office in 1801 over the weakened and divided Federalists. Hamilton's bullheadedness and arrogance had been largely responsible for the creation of a system of two political parties. It also brought in a president whose intent was to weaken the national government.

Aftermath

Philip Hamilton. In 1801 an event took place that was to foreshadow Hamilton's own fate. His son Philip had just graduated from Columbia and was attending a New York theater when he met a lawyer, George Eacker, who had backed Jefferson and had earlier made speeches criticizing the Federalists. The two began to taunt each other and the argument ended with Eacker challenging both Philip and a friend to a duel. The duel took place November 23 and left Eacker unharmed and Philip mortally wounded. Hamilton was present at Philip's death and the event left him grief stricken. He now appeared gloomier than ever.

Aaron Burr. Jefferson's running mate in his bid for the presidency had been Aaron Burr. When it became obvious that the election would go to the Democratic-Republicans over the Federalists, Hamilton decided to try to influence the election. At that time the person with the highest vote count became president and the next highest, the vice president. Jefferson and Burr had tied in the election, so the outcome needed to be settled by Congress. Hamilton pushed his friends in Congress to elect Jefferson over Burr, and Jefferson was elected by a single vote.

A few years later, Hamilton again opposed Burr in his candidacy for governor of New York. The rift between the two men grew until Burr demanded an explanation of Hamilton's behavior or settlement by duel. That duel took place in Weehocken, New Jersey. Perhaps because of his long-standing hatred of duels, perhaps because of his son's experience, or perhaps because he no longer felt useful in the politics he loved, Hamilton fired in the air, obviously intending to miss his mark, and was mortally wounded by Burr. Apparently he had chosen "to reserve and throw away my first fire, and I have thoughts even of reserving my second fire" (Cooke, p. 241). Henry Adams described the event: Hamilton "allowed himself to be drawn into a duel but instead of killing Burr, he invited Burr to kill him" (Cooke, p. 241).

The duel erased many people's objections to Hamilton brought on by his superior attitude, fancy dress, and bitter tongue, and he became more of a national hero. Meanwhile Burr, then vice president of the United States, fell into oblivion save for a questionable escapade along the Ohio and Mississippi rivers. He was accused—but cleared—of trying to take over the American Southwest.

Elizabeth Schuyler Hamilton. Hamilton's wife, ever supportive even through reports of his unfaithfulness to her, lived to the age of ninety-four. In the fifty years after Hamilton's death, Elizabeth devoted much of her energy to collecting and preserving her husband's notes and correspondence. In this way, she preserved for history a vivid account of a man who was a brilliant planner and organizer, adored by some but hated by others for his lack of consideration and concern for the feelings or ideas of others.

Alexander Hamilton. Hamilton left an undying legacy to the United States. He was a man of military dreams whose pen proved mightier than his sword, whose speeches were noted for their clarity of thought and logic, and whose dress rivaled in silk and lace the finest dresses of the women of his day. From him came an interpretation of the Constitution that broadened the powers of the federal government and allowed it to operate. He put the nation on sound financial footing and created a plan for its development into a manufacturing giant. And, perhaps not by design, Hamilton was largely responsible for the mainly two-party political system that has operated in the United States since his lifetime.

For More Information

Cooke, Jacob E. *Alexander Hamilton.* New York: Charles Scribner's Sons, 1982.

Cooke, Jacob E. *Alexander Hamilton: A Profile.* New York: Hill and Wang, 1967.

Hecht, Marie B. *Odd Destiny: The Life of Alexander Hamilton.* New York: Macmillan, 1982.

Morris, Richard B. *Seven Who Shaped our Destiny.* New York: Harper and Row, 1973.

John Marshall

1755-1835

Personal Background

Early life. John Marshall's father, Thomas, was a frontiersman who grew up near Germantown, Pennsylvania, and became a planter there. As a young man, he married Mary Isham Keith and moved west to a valley at the base of the Blue Ridge Mountains in what is now Farquier County, Virginia. The place would become known in history as "The Hollow." John was the oldest of fifteen children, and was called upon to help with the raising and tending of his younger brothers and sisters. Historians later imagined that this gave him the attitude of affectionate helpfulness he carried throughout his life. All the children helped on the farm, which was a far cry from the large plantations east of them because John's father was a "planter of narrow fortunes" (Corwin, p. 25). John later recalled that, in his childhood, his mother and sisters used thorns for buttons on the family clothing, and that one of his favorite meals was hot mush flavored with a balm leaf. Although they were not wealthy, John's parents took a strong interest in educating their children.

Education. John's father saw to it that the life of his children was not all farmwork. He tutored the children himself because there were no schools on the frontier. He also encouraged them to read from his small library of classical writers, which included the works of William Shakespeare, John Milton, Alexander Pope, and John Dryden. John's favorite was Pope; by the age of twelve, he had

▲ John Marshall

Event: *Marbury v. Madison,* which defined the role of the Supreme Court.
Role: John Marshall, along with Alexander Hamilton and John Jay, was a founder of the Federalist political party, which stood for a strong federal government for the new United States. Marshall became chief justice of the Supreme Court and his decisions in his more than thirty-five years on the Court greatly defined the roles of legislative and judicial bodies in the government.

copied Pope's "Essay on Man," which taught the importance of justice. John's father took time to hunt and fish and take occasional trips with his boys. As an adult, John Marshall would give much credit to his father: "My father was a far abler man than any of his sons. To him I owe the solid foundations of all my success in life" (Corwin, p. 27). The Marshall children also learned from the people who visited the Hollow. One of his father's acquaintances whom young John came to admire was another planter, George Washington.

At age fourteen, John Marshall was given a brief taste of formal education. For a short time he was tutored by the Reverend Campbell, studying Latin and becoming acquainted with ancient writers such as Cicero, Livy, and Horace. He also briefly attended a nearby academy. Meanwhile, by 1770 cries for freedom from British taxes and government were resounding throughout the colonies. The rights of the colonists were being debated everywhere. Marshall, caught up in the excitement, began to read Blackstone, author of the law books of his day. By age twenty, he was beginning to study law with the intention of making his lifetime career.

Revolutionary War. The War for Independence changed his direction for a time. Marshall immediately enlisted in the army that was being raised by the newly appointed general George Washington. The new recruit participated in several major battles—Norfolk, Brandywine, Germantown, Monmouth, and Stony Point—and was with Washington at Valley Forge. Marshall had a strong and persuasive personality, and for his leadership ability was promoted to the rank of lieutenant early in the war. By war's end he had become a captain and a deputy judge advocate in the army. In this capacity he busily maintained order among soldiers and officers. One of these officers was Alexander Hamilton (see **Alexander Hamilton**), Washington's secretary at the time, and later the first secretary of the treasury of the United States. In 1780 Marshall was temporarily without a command and took advantage of this break in his wartime activities to attend lectures on law presented by the famous authority George Wythe at William and Mary College. At the same time, he met and began to court Mary Willis Ambler, the daughter of the treasurer of Virginia.

After the war Marshall resigned his commission and moved to Richmond. It had just become the capital of the state of Virginia and building was going on all around the city; the state capitol was not much more than a big barn then. Richmond had a single church, Farmicola's Tavern, and a collection of small, wooden houses. The city also had a strong group of experienced lawyers, which did not scare Marshall. He opened his practice there, even though he had had very limited training for the work.

The untrained lawyer soon demonstrated the qualities that would make him one of the country's most respected leaders. His ability to gather bits of evidence into a logical and convincing argument, which he built by searching for broad, underlying principles, soon earned him a place among the great lawyers of the day and a position in the Virginia Legislature. Though his abilities were widely praised, his appearance was perhaps less remarkable. He was described as a tall, painfully thin, unpolished speaker who had a small head and laughing eyes.

Marshall and Mary Willis Ambler were married in 1783. The marriage would hold strong for forty-five years, during which the couple had ten children. Six survived infancy and began a family line that included such prominent descendants as Thomas Marshall, vice president of the United States under President Woodrow Wilson. Early in their marriage, Mary developed a nervous disorder that sometimes made her weak. Marshall's concern for her revealed qualities that would later contribute to his excellence as a judge. He was generally thoughtful and considerate. Marshall loved his home and family and made them a priority in his busy life. Later, as a Supreme Court judge, he would rush from his three-month court service to Raleigh, South Carolina, where he served as circuit judge, and then directly to his home in Richmond. A Supreme Court colleague, William Story, described the marriage as Marshall's greatest achievement. According to Story, the purity of his affection for Mary and devotion to domestic life was Marshall's highest glory.

Political views. The Revolutionary War had clearly demonstrated the strength of the collective colonies, and afterward they had banded into a confederation. Yet such actions as Shays' Rebellion, in which farmers revolted against high taxes, demonstrated a weakness that disturbed Marshall and other leaders (see **Daniel Shays**). They feared that such uprisings would lead to the downfall of the new country. Marshall, among others, wanted to strengthen the federal government, giving it some of the rights claimed by states under the Articles of Confederation.

Hamilton was involved in the preparation of a written Constitution to govern the new country. By 1787 Marshall had joined Hamilton in pushing for the adoption of the Constitution, because he saw it both as a protection of human rights and as a base for a strong federal government. Marshall explained his position to the Virginia Convention as it was deciding whether or not to give its approval to the Constitution:

> We prefer this system because we think it a well-regulated democracy.... What are the favorite maxims of democracy?... A strict observance of justice and public faith.... Would to Heaven that these principles had been observed under the present government. Had this been the case the friends of liberty would not be willing now to part with it. (Corwin, p. 36)

In the minds of its preparers and champions, the new Constitution left much to be interpreted. What should be governed by the new national government and what by the individual states? How were the new divisions of government to function? (Marshall felt they should be as independent of each other as possible.) What powers would go to the president? To Congress? To the Supreme Court? Almost immediately after its ratification, Marshall became active in helping to define the roles of the various government officers. In 1796 and again in 1799 he supported the president's right to negotiate with foreign countries. He had been sent as an emissary to France in 1797 and had seen firsthand the turmoils of a government with a weak presidency. In defending President Adams's action in turning Jonathan Robins, a fugitive, over to the British, Marshall made it clear that he felt the president was the sole organ of the nation in its external relations, and its sole representative in foreign affairs.

Marshall had served for many years as a member of the Virginia Legislature. His popularity as a lawyer and his position for strong national government and for the Constitution had earned him consideration for a post in the new American government. George Washington had offered Marshall the position of attorney general, but he declined. He had also turned down the offer of John Adams to become either secretary of war or minister to France in his administration. Though he supported Adams, Marshall demonstrated his independence from the president by opposing the Alien and Sedition Acts, which made it a crime to criticize the government. Marshall did briefly serve as Adams's secretary of state. During this time, the Federalists faced opposition from a new group advocating more strength for the various states, the Democratic-Republicans.

Federalists and Republicans. Leading the Federalists were Adams, Jay, Hamilton, and Marshall. Those organizing the Democratic-Republicans were Thomas Jefferson and James Madison. By the end of the 1700s the Federalists were losing political ground. When Adams ran for a second term in 1800 against Jefferson, he was soundly defeated. The Democratic-Republicans threatened to control Congress as well as the presidency after this election. Hoping to salvage some power for the dying Federalist party, Adams stacked the courts with members of that party. The number of associate justices on the Supreme Court was reduced so that Jefferson would have no appointees and twelve high-ranking district judges were appointed from among the Federalists. In one of his last acts as president and without asking him if he would accept, Adams nominated Marshall for chief justice of the Supreme Court. The soon-to-be replaced Federalist-controlled Senate confirmed the nomination.

Participation: *Marbury v. Madison*

The Marshall Court. The Supreme Court of the United States in 1801 consisted of a chief justice and four associate justices. A pair of judicial acts (the first in 1789) had attempted to define the role of the federal courts, but in the turmoil of determining presidential authority and preserving rights for the states, just what the Supreme Court was to do had been a neglected question. The first chief justice, John Jay, had resigned after five years to become governor of New York. John Rutledge had filled the vacancy for a year, and then Oliver Ellsworth served as chief justice of a nonfunctioning Supreme Court from 1796 to 1799. Marshall became the fourth chief justice of the United States, serving under the administration of President Thomas Jefferson, who distrusted Marshall, and for whom Marshall had great disrespect.

Marshall had already won the respect of lawyers and judges with his ability to form a clear argument and present it thoroughly.

He had argued before the Supreme Court in *Ware v. Hilton* over Virginia's Sequestration (seizure of property) Act. He had further enhanced his reputation as a member of the ill-fated delegation to France in what became known as the XYZ Affair (in which a French official demanded a bribe from the Americans). His conduct in this matter was judged superior.

Thomas Jefferson on John Marshall

- "John Marshall is an unprincipled and impudent Federalist bulldog."
- "The germ of dissolution of our federal government is the federal judiciary; an irresponsible body." (Konefsky, p. 107)

As chief justice of the Supreme Court, Marshall quickly won the respect of the other justices so that almost immediately he was able to direct the decisions of the court. For many years, Marshall would write and deliver important court decisions that defined the role of the court and, at the same time, demonstrated his wisdom, selflessness, and commitment to the Constitution. The first of these cases was *Marbury v. Madison*.

Marbury v. Madison **(1803).** Just before he left office, Adams had nominated William Marbury to be justice of the peace of Washington, D.C. His appointment had been confirmed by the Senate and the necessary papers drawn up and signed, but Adams had left office before the papers could be delivered to Marbury. The new president, Jefferson, ordered Secretary of State James Madison not to deliver the appointment. Refusing to accept such treatment, Marbury petitioned the Supreme Court for a writ of mandamus to be delivered to Madison. A writ of mandamus was a command placed on an official to perform his duty—in this case to appoint Marbury as justice of the peace. Marbury based his petition on part of an act passed in 1789 (Judiciary Act of 1789).

Jefferson, a supporter of states' rights, believed that the states were the ruling bodies and that the federal government should be no stronger than was necessary to protect the states. As part of this belief, he favored a weak Supreme Court. Although he had been narrowly elected to the presidency, he was a powerful politician, and his party dominated Congress. Marshall, on the other hand, favored a strong central government, and he too was a powerful person. Marbury, like Marshall, was a Federalist. If the judgment were based on politics, Marshall would have ruled in favor of Marbury.

Marshall, however, was committed to making the Constitution serve as a guide for the United States. With this in mind, he wrote an unexpected decision for the Court. Congress, he said, had no authority to pass the part of the 1789 act upon which Marbury based his claim to his appointment as justice of the peace. Marshall further declared the act unconstitutional because it gave the Supreme Court powers that the Constitution had not intended. The Constitution had expressly defined the areas in which the Court could work, but had nowhere mentioned the right to issue a writ of mandamus. Therefore, Marshall said, the Supreme Court had no authority to decide the case in question. The Court refused to hear *Marbury v. Madison*. It was a brilliant decision for the Supreme Court and for the defense of the Constitution.

Marshall had established an important pattern. Laws had to be in keeping with the Constitution, and the Court would determine those that were. The 1789 act had already been passed by Congress and signed into law by the president. In *Marbury v. Madison*, the Court established its

> ### John Marshall on Thomas Jefferson
> • He insulted one man by calling him "as great a scoundrel as Tom Jefferson."

right to weigh the actions of Congress and the president against the directions of the Constitution. At the same time, Marshall had taken a position favored by Jefferson, who did not want Marbury appointed as justice of the peace. The decision thus avoided a conflict that would have otherwise erupted between the judicial and the executive and legislative branches of government. Marshall's commitment to the Constitution had established the power of the Supreme Court in this landmark case of 1803.

Aaron Burr. Three years later, Marshall would again behave ably and honorably in the trial of Aaron Burr. Burr became an instant villain when he killed Secretary of the Treasury Alexander Hamilton in a duel. Thereafter Burr embarked on a mysterious trip down the Ohio and Mississippi rivers gathering followers and arming them for some unknown, perhaps even "sinister," purpose. His activities upset the citizens of New Orleans. Pursued by the military, Burr was arrested for treason.

Marshall had no liking for Burr. After all, Hamilton had been Marshall's friend. The chief justice, like most Americans, was emotionally opposed to the defendant. Brought to trial, Burr drew a courtroom full of people who wanted to see him convicted of treason. Amid a clamoring, tense atmosphere, Marshall calmly listened to the opening arguments with his usual quiet assurance.

Burr was accused of attempting to establish a new country in the Louisiana Territory and Mexico. Hearing this about his one-time vice president, an angry Jefferson called for Burr's arrest. Marshall's handling of the case did little to soothe the president's anger. In the trial, Marshall established the principle of innocent until proven guilty, insisting that talking about rebellion and actually rebelling were two different issues and that it was necessary to prove an act of treason by the testimony of at least two witnesses to the act.

The world seemed ready to convict Burr, but, said Marshall, the Constitution defined treason in two ways: a treasonable act was an act of war designed to overthrow the government and it must be witnessed by at least two people who viewed the situation in the same way. Neither situation held in Burr's case. So Marshall refused to try him on the charge of treason. Instead, Burr was tried on a lesser charge, and even then found "not guilty."

Marshall had again defined the role of the Supreme Court, identifying it as interpreter of the Constitution and as limited in its powers by that document. He had, this time, made a decision that was opposed by the president and by many of the people. But in his written and spoken verdict, Marshall explained his position so clearly and logically that the president and the press realized that he had made the correct decision. The regard for and faith in the chief justice was strengthened.

Aftermath

For the next eleven years, Marshall would speak for the Supreme Court and seemingly make the Court's decisions. As chief justice, he wrote forty-four decisions, many of them laying the groundwork for the form of government still in operation in the United States. Three other cases often have been singled out as landmark decisions, defining the role of the Supreme Court and executive branch of government. In *McCulloch v. Maryland* (1819), the Supreme Court declared its right to review a state court decision, and in *Cohens v. Maryland* (1821), the Court reinforced its claim. In *Gibbons v. Ogden* (1824), the Supreme Court declared its right to regulate interstate trade, and in so doing established the precedent that the Constitution should be interpreted broadly. These cases, along with *Marbury v. Madison,* set patterns for understanding and interpreting the Constitution and for defining the power of the Supreme Court that have carried through to today.

The goal of building a strong federal government was behind many of the Supreme Court decisions during Marshall's leadership. Three years after the case of *Gibbons v. Ogden,* another case, *Brown v. Maryland,* reinforced the power of the federal government. This case canceled a Maryland state tax on imports, calling it illegal, and gave the right to regulate trade between the United States and other nations to the U.S. government.

John Marshall and Thomas Jefferson. Those presidents who favored more rights for the states and a weaker national government did not like Marshall or his court. Even before he became a member of the Supreme Court, Marshall had championed a strong union. In encouraging the Virginia Assembly to ratify the Constitution, he had opposed Patrick Henry, who argued that the ocean that separated the United States from Europe made it unnecessary to form a strong union for defense purposes. Marshall argued that, on the contrary, the ocean made the country's coast easy to reach by foreign intruders; unified protection was essential.

Since Jefferson believed in states' rights and a weak central government, he tried as president to weaken the federal armed forces. Marshall disagreed with this position, and the two men developed a near-hatred for each other. After Burr's case, relations between Marshall and the president worsened. The two were at odds throughout Jefferson's terms in office.

Andrew Jackson and the Cherokee. Jackson became president in 1828, succeeding John Quincy Adams. Adams's presidency had been filled with problems, including accusations of corruption, and Jackson felt it his duty to reform it. At the same time, he had to deal with continued unrest among the Indian tribes and white settlers while supporting his own position as a plantation and slave owner. Giving states more rights would better serve his purposes.

Jackson had already resolved one issue by abolishing the national bank, which Marshall had earlier defended.

One group of Indians, the Cherokee, lived mostly in Georgia. As white settlers pushed for more land, the state claimed much of the Indians' territory. In 1832 the Cherokee, who had developed their own written alphabet and were publishing their own newspaper, sued in the Supreme Court to keep their land. Marshall ruled that the state of Georgia had no right to claim Cherokee land. The state, however, chose to ignore this ruling and continued to demand the removal of the Indians.

Once more Marshall was in disagreement with a president of the United States. Jackson sided with the state, refusing to use the federal government to stop the state's action. It was reported that Jackson said that Marshall had made a decision, now let him enforce it. The Cherokee continued to resist the taking of their land. Six years later, General Winfield Scott rounded up 15,000 of them and marched them out of Georgia to Oklahoma (then called Indian Territory). On the sad march west, called the Trail of Tears, 1,500 Cherokee lost their lives.

Marshall's court. Throughout his term as chief justice, Marshall had struggled to build a strong union and to define the roles of the various branches of government under the Constitution. He had, for the most part, argued his decisions so convincingly that even his enemies came to believe he was right in his judgments. Yet Marshall's court met continued resistance from those who preferred strong individual states to a strong federal government. Maryland, Kentucky, and Georgia all ignored the Court's rulings, and their officials even spent some time in jail for their actions. In nearly every year during the 1820s Congress proposed some measure to curb the court. In 1821 Senator Johnson of Kentucky tried to undermine the power of the court by giving the right to try constitutional cases to the Senate. Another proposal was that any verdict of the court must be agreed to by five of the seven justices. When that failed to break Marshall's hold, Congress increased the total number of justices to ten and the number that must agree to seven.

The impact of Marshall's decisions is still felt today. Felix Frankfurter, a Supreme Court justice from 1939 to 1962, described Marshall's influence on the United States:

When Marshall came to the Supreme Court, the Constitution was still essentially a virgin document. By a few opinions—a mere handful—he gave institutional direction to the inert ideas of a paper scheme of government. Such an achievement demanded an undimmed vision of the union of the States as a Nation and the determination of an uncompromising devotion to such insight. (Konefsky, p. 267)

The Marshall family. The Marshalls built a home in Richmond in 1793 and lived there for the rest of their lives. During his lifetime, Marshall did allow his emotions to influence his decisions at least once—when he wrote an overly glowing biography of his longtime idol, George Washington. In later years, with his wife ill and so nervous that she became an invalid, Marshall spent hours at her bedside, confiding in her about his Supreme Court cases. She was ever his strong supporter and adviser. Mary died on Christmas day, 1831. Her death was a harsh blow to Marshall; almost immediately his health began to fade. Yet he remained active as chief justice of the Supreme Court until his death on July 6, 1835.

Perhaps more than any other American of his day, Marshall defined the roles of government and established the Constitution as the basic law of the land. His focus on justice and the union was constant and his decisions helped structure the country's government.

For More Information

Corwin, Edward S. *John Marshall and the Constitution.* New Haven: Yale University Press, 1919.

Fairlance, Robert K. *The Jurisprudence of John Marshall.* New York: Greenwood, 1980.

Hawkins, John. *The Foundation of Power: John Marshall, 1801.* New York: Macmillan, 1981.

Konefsky, Samuel J. *John Marshall and Alexander Hamilton: Architects of the American Constitution.* New York: Macmillan, 1964.

Rufko, Frances H. *John Marshall and International Law: Statesman and Chief Justice.* Richmond: University Press of Virginia, 1991.

Abigail Adams

1744-1818

Personal Background

Abigail Adams was born Abigail Smith on November 22, 1774, in Weymouth, Massachusetts, a farm community about fifteen miles southeast of Boston. Her family on both sides had lived in the colonies for several generations and were well-established in the more influential circles of society. Her father, William Smith, the son of a well-to-do Boston merchant, was a Harvard graduate who served as a minister in Weymouth. Her mother, Elizabeth Quincy Smith, descended from a long line of prosperous, educated, and well-reputed New Englanders.

Abigail, with her two sisters, Mary and Betsy, and one brother, Billy, enjoyed a happy childhood growing up in the Weymouth parsonage. The family was financially comfortable and had servants, a houseful of fine furniture, and a lush, productive farm. Their large, sprawling house sat on a hill overlooking farmland that spread across the surrounding area. The Smith home was busy and active—visitors came often and relatives lived nearby.

As a child Abigail was shy and quiet, but also determined and stubborn. Throughout her youth she suffered from one minor sickness after another. She later recalled being "always sick" (Akers, p. 5). Her parents, especially her mother, worried about their daugh-

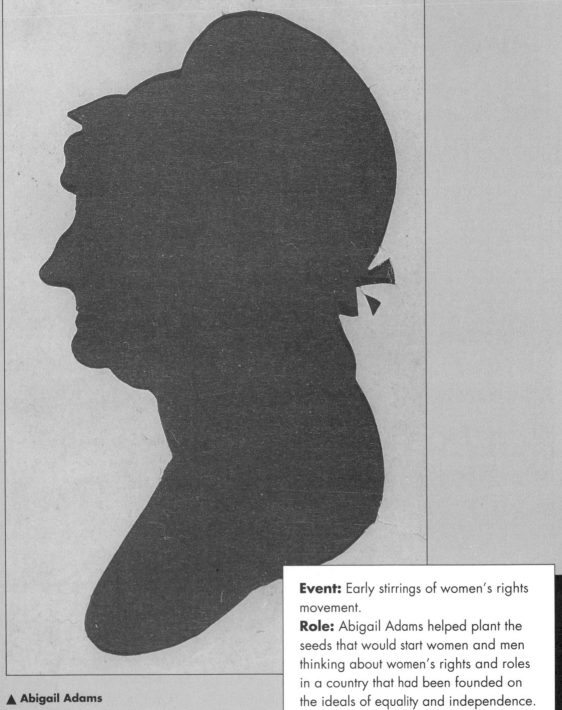

▲ Abigail Adams

Event: Early stirrings of women's rights movement.

Role: Abigail Adams helped plant the seeds that would start women and men thinking about women's rights and roles in a country that had been founded on the ideals of equality and independence.

ter's weak constitution, fearing that some disease or infection would cut her life short, as so often happened to children of this time.

Abigail often complained to her sisters about their mother's constant worrying and overprotectiveness. She sometimes felt smothered by Elizabeth's hovering presence. With her somewhat austere nature and strict approach to child rearing, Elizabeth insisted on obedient and excellent conduct from her children. However, life at the Smith home was not overly harsh or severe, for the father balanced out the parenting with his more easygoing and relaxed approach.

Overall, Abigail's early years were happy ones. At the Weymouth parsonage, amidst the security and guidance of a loving family, she developed the strict sense of values and strong moral fiber that would serve as a foundation for her later life.

Education. Like most girls of her time, Abigail received no formal education. Girls were taught reading and writing primarily so that they could read their Bible and write letters. They also learned basic arithmetic to help prepare them for their role as housewives, when they would be required to balance budgets and settle accounts. Although some Massachusetts towns did have primary schools for girls, called "dame schools," most families took responsibility for the education of their daughters at home.

The Smith girls were fortunate to have a father who loved learning and reading and who encouraged his children to share in this passion. To help with their education, William Smith gave his daughters and son full access to his extensive library of excellent books. Abigail shared her father's love of books and read widely in poetry, drama, history, theology, and political theory. As she grew older, Abigail became increasingly determined to educate herself, and by the time she was an adult, she had become one of the best-read women of her time.

In spite of this, the gaps in Abigail's education bothered her and were apparent in her letters. Her spelling was inconsistent and poor, and her inability to use punctuation properly and her poor penmanship embarrassed her. However, this did not prevent her from continuing in her quest to educate herself and further develop her mind.

For Abigail to have taken such a strong interest in her education was a brave stance for a woman of her time. The primary aim of eighteenth-century women was marriage and family. Education was often viewed as an obstacle that stood in the way of this goal. Women feared becoming too educated, believing that suitors would pass by girls who were "too" clever in favor of those who were more lighthearted and flirtatious.

Courtship. The first time John Adams met Abigail Smith, he might have been influenced by this cultural bias against intelligent women. The couple met at her sister Mary's wedding. Abigail was fifteen, and John, a twenty-seven-year old lawyer. In his diary, John wrote that the Smith girls were "wits" but that they were "not fond, not frank, or candid" (Levin, p. 7). The young man, who at the time had his eye on a franker, more straightforward girl, was put off by the Smith sisters' reserved, somewhat aloof manner, which made it difficult for them to show or express emotions or passion.

Two years later, John and Abigail met again, and this time he began to appreciate the special qualities in Abigail that before had escaped his notice. Now he described her as "Prudent, modest, delicate, soft, sensible, obliging, active" and addressed his letters to "Miss Adorable" (Akers, p. 14).

From this second meeting and throughout their fifty-four-year marriage, a strong love, mixed with flirtatious sensuality and intellectual companionship, grew and provided a sturdy bond for their relationship. Abigail thought of John as her best friend, and as an old woman, she still remembered the thrill she felt the first time he held her hand. To John, the relationship was equally satisfying and important; as he carved out his successful career, he relied heavily on Abigail's advice, support, and companionship.

In spite of their exceptional personal compatibility, in terms of looks, the couple were opposites. Whereas John was short and pudgy with a round, almost bland face, Abigail was tall and slender with sharp and striking features. Bernard Bailyn, an artist who painted the couple early in their marriage, left a vivid description of the twenty-two-year-old woman who sat for her portrait:

▲ John Adams

Abigail's face is extraordinary, not so much for its beauty, which, in a masculine way, is clearly enough there, as for the maturity and the power of personality it expresses. The face is oval in shape, ending in a sharp, almost fleshless, chin; a rather long arched nose; brilliant, piercing, wide-spaced eyes. It is about as confident, controlled, and commanding a face as a woman can have and still remain feminine. (Butterfield, p. 4)

Marriage and family. After their marriage on October 25, 1764, the newlyweds set up a home in Braintree (now Quincy), Massachusetts. Abigail soon became pregnant and found herself stuck in what would become a familiar pattern in their marriage. While she stayed at home, managing the vast responsibilities of an eighteenth-century household—overseeing servants, handling accounts, and stocking and preparing food—John traveled to Boston and other nearby communities pursuing his career as a lawyer. With cases in Maine, Boston, and other parts of New England, he spent weeks and months away from home; as his career prospered, his absences grew longer and more frequent.

Abigail hated these absences and sorely missed the companionship of her best friend. However, her growing brood helped lessen the loneliness. Within eight years Abigail had five children: Abigail, nicknamed Nabby, born 1765; John Quincy, born 1767; Susanna, born 1768 (died at age thirteen months); Charles, born 1770; and Thomas, born 1772. A sixth child, in 1778, was stillborn.

In 1768, early in their marriage, Abigail and John moved from the rural life in Braintree to the city life in Boston. Abigail delighted in the "Noisy, Busy town" (Akers, p. 25), where she could read four different newspapers a week and socialize with Boston's most influential families, including the Hancocks and the Bowdoins. Although stimulating, life in Boston was difficult. In just a few years, the family moved their large household several times. Also, the first movements of the revolution were stirring in Boston and war was daily becoming more and more likely.

The Adamses, of course, supported the colonists' cause. John, whose solid reputation and tireless ambition had thrown him increasingly into the public eye, was elected to serve as a delegate to America's first Continental Congress. Unfortunately, this commission would take John farther away from his family and for a longer time than ever before. Abigail, though she hated the prospect of facing her daily life without her partner, made no complaint about his acceptance. She felt it was a wife's duty to support her husband in all he aspired to and not prevent him from reaching his highest potential. But with John so far away, she had to take on even more responsibility for the household. John realized the weight of the burden he was leaving her with. Before he left, he wrote Abigail:

> I must entreat you, my dear Partner in all the Joys and Sorrows, Prosperity and Adversity of my Life, to take a Part with me in the Struggle. I ... intreat you to rouse your whole attention to the Family, the stock, the Farm, the Dairy. (Levin, p. 36)

With John in Philadelphia, Pennsylvania, Abigail entered a new period in her married and personal life. The increased responsibility of managing a large household gave her a growing sense of confidence and assurance in her abilities. With an adept and economical hand, she made sure the operations of the house and farm ran smoothly and efficiently. She even took it upon herself to make some investment decisions. After several years of this, she began to refer to the house and property as "my own affairs", rather than "ours." Long gone were the days when Abigail referred to these affairs in her letters to John as "your affairs" (Akers, p. 69).

Letter writing. During their long periods of separation, Abigail and John kept in close contact with a steady flow of intimate, frank letters. Beginning in her teens and throughout most of her life, Abigail devoted a significant amount of time and energy to correspondence with friends and family. Letter writing gave her a forum for expressing her ideas, sharpening her opinions, and sharing intellectual, domestic, and political concerns with others of like mind. She would, over time, share her opinion with shapers of the country, such as Thomas Jefferson and John Lovell, a delegate to the Continental Congress. Rarely dull, Abigail's letters cover a range of styles; in varying degrees, they are newsy, perceptive, flirtatious, warm, and intellectually challenging. In her writing, Abigail emerges as a self-confident, insightful, and sharp woman deeply involved in the activities of her day. At times, however, her letters reveal a judgmental and critical nature: she seemed unwilling to tolerate people who did not live up to her high standards of character or, in some cases, who did not share her views.

Though sometimes months passed between letters, Abigail and John's correspondence built and strengthened their relationship. Perhaps they grew even closer through their letters because writing allowed them to express thoughts and feelings that they might not normally have shared in person. Abigail told John that she felt freer to express her emotions in letters to him: "My pen is always freer than my tongue. I have wrote many things to you that I suppose I never could have talk'd" (Akers, p. 24).

Abigail addressed her letters to John "My Dearest Friend" and signed them "Portia." The letter below, dated May 18, 1778, written after months of not hearing from John or knowing of his safety and well-being, illustrates her close relationship with her husband, the pain she suffered from being apart from him, and her sense of patriotism:

> I have waited with great patience, restraining as much as posible every anxious Idea for 3 Months. But now every Vessel which arrives sits my expectation upon the wing, and I pray my Gaurdian Genious to waft me the happy tidings of your Safety and Welfare.... Difficult as the Day is, cruel as this War has been, seperated as I am on acount of it from the dearest connextion in life, I would not exchange my country for the Wealth of the Indies, or be any other than an American. (Butterfield, p. 211)

Participation:
Stirrings of the Women's Movement

Women in the late 1800s. A woman born in Adams's time had few choices in deciding the direction her life would take. At birth, a female child's life path was very nearly mapped out from childhood to old age. She received little formal education—just enough to manage her duties as a housewife—but was encouraged to pursue what were considered more feminine pastimes, such as sewing, music, letter writing, and hostessing. If she found a husband, she was expected to serve as his helpmate, creating a harmonious and peaceful home that he could happily return to after his dealings with the harsh, busy, and important outside world. By law, a married woman was subject to the will of her husband. A woman not lucky enough to find a husband had to depend on immediate family and relatives for her support. With such limitations, most women quietly submitted to the role that society demanded of them. Only the strongest few rose above the restrictions and established themselves as individuals in their own right, with opinions, ideas, and a contribution to make.

Adams was such a woman. With her strong character, sharp mind, and forceful opinions, she managed to fulfill much of her potential as a woman and an individual. Her example, along with her views promoting the rights of women, helped plant the first seeds of what would eventually grow into a successful women's rights movement in this country.

A woman's role. During her life, Adams thought a great deal about the role of women in society. She read widely on the subject, including the works of authors Reverend James Fordyce, who wrote, Adams claimed, with an "unfeigned regard for the female sex" (Levin, p. 28), and English political writer John Shebbeare, whose *Letters on the English Nation* addressed the unfairness of not educating women. Adams held accomplished, educated women in high esteem and was curious about women who had actually achieved a place for themselves in the world of men, such as the English historian Catherine Sawbridge Macaulay.

Adams considered women equals of men and believed women should be granted rights that acknowledged that equality. She did not view them as absolute equals, however, but as equal and complementary components functioning in separate spheres. Each sex had its own strengths and weaknesses, she felt, and clear distinctions existed between women's and men's roles. Adams advocated that women should be granted rights that made them equal to men in their own sphere, which centered around home and family.

> I will never consent to have our Sex considered in an inferiour point of light. Let each planet shine in their own orbit, God and nature designed it so. If man is Lord, woman is *Lordess*—that is what I contend for, and if a woman does not hold the Reigns of Government, I see no reason for her not judging how they are conducted. (Akers, p. 143)

Adams recognized the limited role women were allowed to play in the world, and for the most part accepted it. However, she insisted that a woman's role carried an equal amount of importance and responsibility to a man's. She believed that women deserved the opportunities and rights—including education and legal and political rights—that would enable them to live to their fullest capacity within the domestic sphere.

Education of women. One of Adams's greatest frustrations was that she had not been allowed to receive the classic education accorded to the males of her time. She adamantly believed that education was as important for women as for men. Adams felt that an educated woman could more capably perform the duties required in her domestic sphere, including child rearing, household management, and "retaining the affections of a man of understanding" (Akers, p. 189). She agreed with her friend Mercy Otis Warren who said that, since women were responsible for the early education of their children, they must themselves be educated so that they could adequately meet this responsibility.

In much of Adams's correspondence, to women and to men, she wrote passionately of her conviction about women's need for education. In a letter to her husband, she wrote: "You need not be told how much female education is neglected, nor how fashionable it has been to ridicule Female learning" (Akers, p. 66). Her commitment to promoting education for women was so strong that she pressed her husband to incorporate the issue into the body of laws that he and other founding fathers were drafting in 1776. She expressed the hope "that our new constitution may be distinguished for learning and Virtue.... If we mean to have Heroes, Statesmen, and philosophers, we should have learned women" (Gelles, p. 48). Surprisingly, John wrote back that he was in exact agreement with Abigail's views on this subject.

Adams's insistence on education for women stemmed from her own experience. Primarily self-taught, she had always placed enormous value on developing her mind, challenging her thinking, and continuing to learn. When living in England during the late 1780s, Adams had the opportunity to educate herself in science, an area which few woman dared, or were permitted, to tread. She signed up for a series of twelve lectures and attended five, whose subjects were electricity, magnetism, hydrostatics, optics, and pneumatics. The experience inspired her and gave her a heightened appreciation for the vast world of ideas that women had no access to. "It was like going into a Beautiful country, which I never saw before," she wrote. "A Country which our American Females are not permitted to visit or inspect" (Levin, p. 237).

"Remember the Ladies." Adams made her strongest appeal for women's rights in 1776, when John was in Philadelphia serving in Congress. As members of Congress drafted laws to guarantee the independence for which the colonies were fighting, Abigail wrote to John begging him to remember that women also needed to be given the right to independence. Her letter reveals a prophetic sense of the struggles to come, as well as an insightful understanding of the danger of making one group subject to the will of another:

> I long to hear that you have declared an independency—and by the way in the new Code of Laws which I suppose it will be necessary for you to make I desire you would Remember the Ladies, and be more generous and favourable to them than your ancestors. Do not put such unlimited power into the hands of the Husbands. Remember all Men would be tyrants if they could. If perticular care and attention is not paid to the Ladies we are determined to foment a Rebelion, and will not hold ourselves bound by any Laws in which we have no voice, or Representation. (Levin, p. 83)

Apparently, John did not take Abigail's heartfelt and forceful appeal seriously at first, for he wrote back in a laughing tone:

> As to your extraordinary Code of Laws, I cannot but laugh. We have been told that our Struggle has loosened the bands of Government every where. That Children and Apprentices were disobedient—that schools and Colledges were grown turbulent—that Indians slighted their Guardians and Negroes grew insolent to their Masters. But your Letter was the first Intimation that another Tribe [women] more numerous and powerful than all the rest were grown discontented. This is rather too coarse a Compliment but you are so saucy, I won't blot it out. (Levin, p. 83)

Undaunted, Adams shared her radical views with Mercy Otis Warren, and even spoke of petitioning Congress to consider her views. Although she did not do this, her proposal did have some effect. John seemed to have taken her ideas to heart and to have given the matter considerable thought as he struggled with the issue of voters' rights. He understood that a government built on the principles of freedom and equality and carried out with the consent of the people must by reason include women in that equation. With foresight, he wrote to Brigadier General Joseph Palmer on the issue of qualifying voters, "Depend on it, Sir, it is dangerous to open so fruitfull a source of Controversy and altercation, as would be opened by attempting to alter the Qualifications of Voters. There will be no end to it—New claims will arise—Women will demand a vote" (Levin, p. 87).

Ultimately, Adams probably brought about no immediate changes in the way women were treated or perceived. However, she was among the first women in the new country to begin to question a woman's rights and role in a free society. It would not be long before other women of like mind followed her lead and began working to bring about real and lasting change.

Aftermath

First lady. Adams supported her husband through every phase of his rise to power and fame. She never tried to hold him back when duty demanded his service, though often this meant being separated from him for long periods. The years of loneliness and struggle to raise a family and manage a home finally paid off when John became vice president to George Washington and later the second president of the United States. Adams saw herself as fully contributing to that success, and wrote him more than once that she had struggled and sacrificed more than most other women in the country.

Soon after she joined the new president in Philadelphia, Adams was caught in a whirlwind of responsibility and social activity. Rising at 5:00 a.m., she spent the morning tending to household and family matters. At 11:00 a.m. she dressed for the day and then spent the next two or three hours receiving visitors, often sixty a day. In the afternoon she traveled through the city visiting her own friends. She frequently planned and hosted large dinners, including one of the first Fourth of July celebrations.

At the same time, Abigail worked closely with John as he struggled with the many issues and problems that confronted him during his presidency. His dependency and reliance on her as his partner was apparent; he thought of her as his "fellow labourer." During his first months as president, as he waited for her to join him in Philadelphia, he pleaded with her to hurry to him: "I never wanted your Advice and assistance more in my life"; and later, "The Times are critical and dangerous, and I must have you here to assist me" (Akers, pp. 143-44).

As first lady, Adams maintained a mostly conservative stance. For example, she vigorously supported the Alien and Sedition Acts. These four acts, passed by Congress and signed by President Adams, placed restrictions on aliens who wanted to become citizens, treated aliens as enemies in times of war, and censured the press. These acts proved to be extremely unpopular with the public and were used against John in his bid for reelection.

Final years. After John's term ended, the couple returned to Quincy where they spent their remaining years. For the first time in thirty-six years of marriage, they lived peacefully together without the pressures and demands of political life or the necessity of any more long separations. Adams's last years, however, were not without hardship. Although she was near her family, her own chronic illness and the deaths of close relatives and friends, including her daughter, Nabby, to cancer, made life difficult. She died on October 28, 1818, after a brief illness. When she died, her son John Quincy Adams, who would go on to become the sixth president of the United States, wrote in his journal a private tribute to his mother:

> There is not a virtue that can abide in the female heart but it was the ornament of hers. She had been fifty-four years the delight of my father's heart, the sweetener of all his toils, the comforter of all his sorrows, the sharer and heightener of all his joys. It was but the last time when I saw my father that he told me ... [that] through all the good report and evil report of the world, in all his struggles and in all his sorrows, the affectionate participation and cheering encouragement of his wife had been his never-failing support, without which he was sure he should never have lived through them. (Mitchell, p. xxxiii)

For More Information

Akers, Charles W. *Abigail Adams: An American Woman.* Boston: Little, Brown & Company, 1980.

Butterfield, L. H., Marc Friedlaender, and Mary-Jo Kline, eds. *The Book of Abigail and John: Selected Letters of the Adams Family, 1762-1784.* Cambridge: Harvard University Press, 1975.

Gelles, Edith B. *Portia: The World of Abigail Adams.* Bloomington: Indiana University Press, 1992.

Levin, Phyllis Lee. *Abigail Adams: A Biography.* New York: St. Martin's Press, 1987.

Mitchell, Stewart, ed. *New Letters of Abigail Adams, 1788-1801.* Boston: Houghton Mifflin Co., 1947.

Lewis and Clark Expedition

1783
British fail to leave forts and fur-trading posts in Old Northwest, as agreed at end of Revolutionary War.

1791
Robert Gray sails to the Pacific Northwest, becomes the first non-native to "discover" the Columbia River.

1803
President Thomas Jefferson purchases the Louisiana Territory.

1802
Use of Mississippi River is closed to Americans.

1800
Spain cedes Louisiana to France.

1796
Congress sets up a string of government fur-trading posts.

1804
Meriwether Lewis and William Clark begin their journey across United States.

1805
Sacagawea joins the Lewis and Clark expedition.

1806
Lewis and Clark complete the journey back to St. Louis.

1815
Interest in exploring West resumes.

1812
Advance of whites onto frontier erupts in war.

1807
John Jacob Astor forms the American Fur Company. Interest in exploring West dwindles. War anticipated.

LEWIS AND CLARK EXPEDITION

The Lewis and Clark Expedition was a direct result of the Louisiana Purchase, which in 1803 doubled the size of the nation. The remarkable purchase occurred under President Thomas Jefferson. Like other Americans of his day, Jefferson had assumed that the nation would expand westward over time. It was believed that this expansion would happen gradually, with the United States gaining small areas piece by piece.

In 1803, however, French emperor Napoleon Bonaparte made a startling decision. In need of cash, he decided to sell not just New Orleans, which the Americans had asked to purchase, but the entire Louisiana Territory, all the land between the Mississippi River and the Rocky Mountains. America's diplomats, Robert Livingston and James Monroe, would pay 15 million dollars for 830,000 square miles of territory. They ended up giving France four cents an acre for the property.

Even before the purchase, Jefferson had laid plans for expeditions into the vast territory beyond the Mississippi River. The most famous of these expeditions, led by **Meriwether Lewis** and William Clark, was finally undertaken in 1804. Beginning in St. Louis (in present-day Missouri), the two-year expedition took the explorers across the continent and back again. They contacted native American peoples for the first time, collected scientific information about the region, and managed to discover an overland route to the Pacific Ocean.

▲ The Louisiana Purchase and Lewis and Clark expeditions

The expedition began with forty to fifty soldiers, hunters, and interpreters. Roughly twenty of these participants left the expedition before the journey's end. A few meanwhile joined the team. Among these later additions was the Shoshone Indian interpreter **Sacagawea.** Her help proved critical to the success of the journey, as did that of York, an African American servant whose presence eased relations between the explorers and native Americans.

The Louisiana Territory was a vast area occupied by native Americans and full of rugged terrain. Members of the expedition crossed thousands of unmapped miles through mountains and along rivers, including the Columbia River, "discovered" a generation earlier by **Robert Gray**. (Gray had approached the river by sea rather than over land.) Lewis and Clark continued to the Pacific Ocean and back again.

The expedition aroused the interest of Easterners, who began venturing westward to improve their fortunes. In the president's view, this type of movement preserved democracy. Jefferson, who was a farmer himself, felt that the availability of land was the solution to keeping society equal in the new democracy. Land, he reasoned, provided opportunities for all citizens to make a decent living.

The westward movement had disastrous consequences for native Americans. Easterners expected Indian peoples living between the Ohio and Mississippi rivers to give up their lands and become farmers themselves or move farther west. Eastern political leaders signed treaty after treaty with Indian chiefs in an effort to acquire tribal lands. There was some resistance, especially from Creek and Shawnee chiefs, but other Indians proved willing to exchange a portion of their territory for trade goods, yearly payments, and the promise that no more demands would be made on their lands. Fifty-three treaties were made with native Americans during Jefferson's and James Madison's terms as president. Lewis and Clark's descriptions of tribes they had encountered proved useful to the federal government in this treatymaking.

Another effect of the Lewis and Clark expedition was the spread of the American fur trade. The fur trade had flourished in the country for 200 years, centering in different regions as generations passed and resources dwindled. Lewis and Clark's journey made clear that an enterprising American could set up a chain of trading posts along the Missouri and Columbia rivers to compete with the powerful Canadian fur companies. **John Jacob Astor** won permission from Jefferson to form such a company.

The Great Lakes region had, until then, furnished rich supplies of furs, and American fur traders would continue to operate in this region afterward. They now had a new territory for their activities, though. By 1811 American fur tradeing had expanded to Oregon and from there moved into the Rocky Mountains, the richest fur trading region of all. Astor won control of this region, too, at the expense of the native Americans and a few independent mountain men who had occupied, hunted, and traded in this region before him.

Robert Gray

1755-1806

Personal Background

Early years. On May 10, 1755, Robert Gray was born in Tiverton, Rhode Island. Like many New Englanders, Robert grew up with a love of the sea. He joined the Continental Navy when he turned twenty and fought in the Revolutionary War. Following victory in 1776, Gray joined the merchant service and relocated to Boston, Massachusetts. For the next eleven years, he sailed in commercial vessels along the Eastern Seaboard and across the Atlantic Ocean, working his way up to ship's captain. He became commander of cargo vessels for Samuel Brown and Crowell Hatch, prominent Boston merchants, sailing out of Boston Harbor to ports in England, as well as up and down the eastern coast of the United States. Gray earned a good living as a merchant seaman and made his home in Boston with his wife and four daughters.

Captain Cook's influence. In his early thirties, Gray was coming into his own during an era of great change and excitement for the young United States. America had just won its independence and was beginning to expand westward. Untamed land west of the Mississippi River was being explored by land and sea, by not only American but also British and Spanish explorers. All were seeking to stake claim to the area and reap its rewards. The Pacific Northwest in particular offered both an abundance of animals whose valuable hides could be sold as fur and the promise of a Northwest Pas-

▲ Robert Gray

Event: First United States ship commander to sail around the world, as well as find and name the fabled "River of the West," the Columbia.

Role: In 1790 Robert Gray sailed around the world flying the flag of the United States, the first American shipman to do so. The following year, while on a second voyage to the Pacific Northwest, Gray became the first non-native to sail up the Columbia River, "discovering" the legendary great "River of the West" that so many explorers had imagined existed and had searched to find.

sage. If found, this fabled waterway through the United States would provide a shortcut for merchant ships sailing from China to the eastern United States and beyond. Explorer James Cook, who was sailing throughout the Pacific Northwest in search of a Northwest Passage, publicized his discoveries and raised considerable interest in the area, especially among the merchant marine. Merchants and traders, reading about the large numbers of sea otters (their skins were profitable) and the wide open, lush land in the Pacific Northwest, began to realize the potential for wealth there. Cook's articles excited them:

> This animal [the sea otter] abounds here: the fur is finer than that of any other we know of; and therefore the discovery of this part of the continent, where so valuable an article of commerce may be met with, cannot be a matter of indifference. (Bulfinch, p. 2)

Reading also that Russians were trading furs to the Chinese for up to 100 dollars per pelt, U.S. merchants were eager to enter into a Northwest-China fur trade. In addition, politicians such as President George Washington and Secretary of State Thomas Jefferson were encouraging exploration of the area, seeing it as a way to stake claim to the land for the United States before Spain or Britain acquired it.

Gray's employers outfit a ship. Gray's employers, attracted to the opportunities in the Northwest, began to discuss the possibility of outfitting a ship to send west with other area merchants. Together with James Barrell, Charles Bulfinch, John Derby, and J. M. Pintard, Brown and Hatch formed the Boston Marine Association. They raised enough money to outfit a ship, the *Columbia Rediviva,* and a sloop, the *Lady Washington*. Supplied with tobacco, guns, ammunition, and hardware (such as nails, hatchets, copper sheeting, and spikes), the ships were to voyage full circle around the world. They would sail to the Northwest, trade supplies with the native Americans for sea otter pelts, sail to Canton, China, to sell the furs and purchase tea and silk, and return to Boston.

With Barrell warning that "there is a rich harvest to those who shall first go in" (Bulfinch, p. 2), the partners chose commanders for the two ships. John Kendrick commanded the 220-ton *Columbia*

▲ **Lewis and Clark arrive at the mouth of the Columbia River, which Gray "discovered"**

Rediviva and Robert Gray headed the 12-man, 90-ton *Lady Washington*. The two vessels set sail for the Pacific Northwest on September 30, 1787, with consent from Congress and letters of introduction (to foreign leaders such as the Spanish governor of Nootka, a port on present-day Vancouver Island) from Washington, Jefferson, and John Hancock (governor of Massachusetts). At the age of thirty-two, Gray set his ship's course south out of Boston Harbor, little knowing as he headed toward the Northwest that he was sailing into history.

Participation: Exploring the Columbia River

The voyage. Heading down the East Coast of the United States, the ships plotted a course around the southernmost tip of South America at Cape Horn, stopping for fresh water and supplies at the Cape Verde and Faukland Islands along the way. From there the ships were to round the cape and head north up the West Coast of South America toward the West Coast of North America and finally to the Pacific Northwest (near latitude 50).

The *Columbia* and the *Lady Washington* traveled together until reaching Cape Horn in April 1788, but were separated in a violent storm as the ships crossed from the Atlantic to the Pacific Ocean. An experienced sailor, Gray had little trouble navigating the ocean on his own. He piloted his ship through the rough and unfamiliar waters and headed for the island of Masafuera off the coast of Chile to renew his crew's fresh-water supply and hopefully rejoin the *Columbia.* Though he had only a rough description of the island's location from previous explorers, he easily found it. But the rocky coastline and pounding waves made it impossible to land.

Without hesitation, Gray continued on toward the Juan Fernández Islands. Controlled by Spain and Chile and housing a penal colony, one of the three Juan Fernández islands was sure to have the fresh water Gray sought and would perhaps have a more approachable coastline. He set out for the islands but then decided to steer clear of them, fearing that the inhabitants might be too unfriendly. Refusing to endanger his men, Gray sailed north past the Juan Fernández, in search of St. Felix and the Ambrose Isles. He had latitude and longitude estimates for these unmapped islands and hoped to find them and fresh water.

Gray directed the *Lady Washington* toward its destination, imposing rations of two quarts of water per day per man as the ship's water supply began to dwindle. After sailing for nearly a month in the company of dolphins, flying fish, seals, whales, and porpoises, Gray's men finally spotted Ambrose Island. On shore the following day they "killed a vast number of seals and sea lions which were incredibly numerous" and caught many fish (Lyman, p. 26). The crew also gathered supplies and what fresh water they could find.

▲ The *Columbia Rediviva* and *Lady Washington*

As soon as they were finished, Gray ordered the ship back on course for the Northwest. It was noted by some of his crew that St. Felix was "but a few hours sail out of our way" and might prove to have more fresh water than Ambrose Island, but Gray "thought it not worth his attention" (Lyman, p. 26). A prudent and matter-of-fact man, Gray preferred to stay on course toward the Northwest, ration supplies, and even collect rainwater if necessary, rather than sail too far astray.

Gray reaches the West Coast. By August 1788 the *Lady Washington* landed on the West Coast of North America, which was then called New Albion. The *Washington* anchored off the coast of present-day Oregon near the border of Washington around August 10. Gray's sloop was greeted by a canoe carrying twelve native Americans of the Quinalt Indian tribe. Gray welcomed the chief aboard and the two exchanged gifts and discussed exchanging furs for some of the supplies that Gray had brought from Boston. The Quinalt struck a deal with Gray and, in addition to trading pelts, provided Gray's crew with crabs and smoked salmon to eat, which they exchanged for buttons and other merchandise. Relations appeared friendly, but one of Gray's crew noted a hint of underlying tension:

> The natives while we were at work on shore behaved with great propriety, frequently bringing us fruit but they always kept themselves armed and never ventured near us but with their knives in their hands. (Howay, p. 36)

Death halts Columbia exploration. Gray and his crew traded with the natives and explored the coastline for the next several days, slowly working their way north toward their final destination of the Nootka/Clayoquot area (Clayoquot was an American-controlled port next to Nootka). On August 15 Gray came to what he thought was the mouth of a great river, which was in fact the mouth of the Columbia. However, rough weather and sandbars prevented him from seeing into the channel or exploring it by ship at the time. Instead, he was forced to anchor in the bay.

Later that day, Gray sent several of his crew to shore by longboat to gather supplies for the last leg of the journey to Nootka sound. Although hundreds of Quinalt lined the shore, Gray assumed that the situation was perfectly safe. Relations with the natives up to this point had been fine. Marcus Lopius, a new crew member who had come aboard at the Cape Verde Islands, went ashore with the others. He began to dig for clams and, as he collected the shellfish, laid down his knife, whereupon one of the natives took it. Though the crew had been instructed not to fight with the natives, Lopius ran after the man. The two struggled, but Lopius was finally overpowered by a shower of arrows and killed on the spot.

Seeing Lopius dead, the other crew members on land immediately retreated to the ship. Gray's men already on board provided fire-cover as their shipmates quickly paddled back, and only a few suffered injury. But Gray, under orders not to attack the natives, decided to cut his losses and forge ahead rather than engage in a bloody confrontation. Once his whole crew was on board, he pushed out to sea. Later, one of his crew commented, "I must confess I should not have let them [the natives] enjoy their festival [war dance] so peaceably as Captain Gray but his humanity was commendable" (Howay, p. 39). Gray was forced to abandon his exploration of the mouth of the river (named "Murderer's Bay" after this event), but he did not forget the site. He was convinced there was a great river beyond the sandbars and would one day return to find it.

Second split with Kendrick. The *Lady Washington* traveled on from Tillamook Bay and arrived in Nootka Sound on September 16, 1788, nearly one year after setting sail from Boston Harbor. Five days later, the *Columbia* also arrived. Gray noted in his journal, "All well on board, except a small touch of the [disease] Scurvy" (Howay, p. 122). Having acquired a large number of furs during his weeks on the coast, Gray was ready to set sail for China immediately after Kendrick arrived. Gray wanted to leave before the seas turned rough with the onset of winter. But Kendrick, who had authority over Gray, preferred to rest through the winter and not set sail for China until the following spring. The crews set up camp in Clayoquot and prepared to stay the winter.

During these months the differences between Gray and Kendrick became very apparent. As Gray sailed around Vancouver Island and through the Straits of Juan de Fuca trading, trapping, and exploring, Kendrick stayed in camp, using supplies rather than collecting them. Gray warned his employer, Barrell, that "the voyage will not turn out to the owners expectation, all for the want of a nimble leader," (Howay, p. 123), suggesting that Kendrick's laziness was going to make the trip financially unsuccessful.

Fortunately for Gray, he and Kendrick were not partners for long. In July 1789, after continually delaying their voyage to China, Kendrick told Gray he wanted to go into business for himself and swapped the *Columbia* for the *Lady Washington.* Kendrick was to pay for the *Lady Washington* and embark on his own trade mission between the Northwest and China, leaving Gray in sole command of the Boston Marine Association's trade venture. Gray informed his employers of the split, saying, "Captain Kendrick thought it best to change vessels.... Kendrick never informed me whether he intended to come to Canton [China] or not … in case he does not arrive this month I shall conclude he means to stay another season or has met with some accident" (Howay, pp. 128-29). Oddly enough, Kendrick never arrived and did, in fact, meet with some accident.

En route to China, the *Lady Washington* passed a Spanish ship. When the Spanish fired the customary salute, Kendrick was accidentally shot in the chest as he stood on deck. He died instantly and the *Lady Washington* suffered a hole in her hull, which prevented her from ever returning to Boston.

Gray returns to Boston. As planned, Gray voyaged to China, traded his pelts, bought as large a cargo of bohea tea as he could afford, and returned to Boston. His ship arrived to fanfare from Governor Hancock, who threw a parade in honor of the first U.S.-flagged vessel to have sailed around the world. According to newspaper reports, when the *Columbia* arrived in Boston Harbor on August 10, 1790, "she saluted the flag of the United States (at the state capitol) with 13 guns ... and fired a federal salute—which a great concourse of citizens assembled on the several wharfs, returned with three huzzas, and a hearty welcome" (Howay, p. 145).

Unfortunately, as Gray had predicted, the mission was not a financial success because of the high import taxes imposed by the Chinese on the otter pelts and because of the steep costs of the three-year expedition. Nevertheless, there appeared to be so much potential for wealth in the Northwest that Gray's employers scheduled a return trip as soon as possible. Gray barely had time to see his family before he was off again, heading out just six weeks after he arrived.

Second voyage. Now thirty-seven and in full command of the *Columbia* and her trade mission, Gray retraced his path to Nootka Sound, arriving without incident in Clayoquot Sound on June 5, 1791. Once again, his crew set up camp and spent the summer and following winter hunting sea otters and collecting their pelts. During these months Gray and his crew also built a small sloop, the *Adventure,* which Gray put under the command of his second officer, Robert Haswell. On April 2, 1792, the *Columbia* and the *Adventure* left Clayoquot, with Haswell sailing north to acquire more furs and Gray sailing south to investigate the river at Murderer's Bay that he had been forced to abandon on his first voyage to the Northwest.

Gray meets Vancouver. On his journey to the site, Gray encountered his British counterpart, the explorer Captain George

Vancouver, off what is now the Washington coast. Vancouver was sailing north and asked Gray for help in finding the Strait of Juan de Fuca. Besides giving Vancouver directions, Gray described his own destination, the mouth of the river he had tried to enter on his first voyage. Vancouver remarked that he had just sailed by that location but "doubted very much the existence of any large river" beyond the bay (Skinner, p. 22). This did not discourage Gray, who continued south while Vancouver headed north.

The *Columbia* sailed into what is now called Gray's Harbor on May 7, 1792. According to the ship's log, the crew steered the vessel to an entrance that appeared to be a harbor. For the next several days the *Columbia* wound its way through treacherous sandbars and channels. Its crew received aid from Quinalt, Chinook, and Clatsop Indians who refilled fresh water caskets for the voyagers. Gray meanwhile proceeded up the river, searching for its main strait and forcing his way through the sandbars that had stopped so many previous explorers. After several attempts, Gray finally rammed his vessel through the rough entrance and sailed into the river. For days he explored the area and finally realized he had found the fabled "River of the West." He named the river "Columbia's," after the ship and for the United States (later, the possessive was dropped and the river was called simply the Columbia).

Typical of Gray's matter-of-fact and humble nature, he devoted just a single paragraph in his log to the discovery of "a body of water that had existed in men's imaginations for two centuries" (Holbrook, p. 27). An excerpt of his now-famous entry reads:

> At half past seven, we were clear of the bars [of Gray's Harbor], and directed our course to the southward, along shore. At eight p.m., the entrance of Bulfinch's Harbor bore north.... At four a.m., saw the entrance of our desired port.... When we were over the bar, we found this to be a large river of fresh water, up which we steered.... Vast numbers of natives came alongside; people employed in pumping the salt water out of our water-casks, in order to fill with fresh, while the ship floated in. So ends [the quest for this famous river]. (Morgan, p. 34)

Gray's discovery was hardly the end but rather just the beginning. The Columbia not only became one of the most important rivers to

American commerce but its naming by Gray helped the United States lay claim to the Oregon Territory, since an American was clearly the first non-native to sail into it.

After exploring the river, Gray returned to Clayoquot to meet with Haswell. Once there, Gray again met with Vancouver. As one historian wrote, "It must have given the Yankee merchant great pleasure to inform the British explorer that there had been a river behind the white-fanged bar" (Morgan, p. 40). Vancouver doubted the existence of the Columbia, which allowed the discovery of the great "River of the West" to be made by Gray and the claim to the Oregon Territory to be established by the United States.

Gray continues his voyage. Despite his momentous discovery, Gray immediately got "back to the business that had brought him to the Pacific, trading" (Holbrook, p. 28). Exchanging goods was his greater concern.

> ## Bulfinch's Sound Becomes Gray's Harbor
>
> The mouth of the Columbia River was first named by Gray for one of his employers, Charles Bulfinch. The name Bulfinch's Sound did not last long, however. After Gray's historic river trip the harbor was renamed "Gray's" by Captain George Vancouver, who recorded the explorer's findings in his journals.

It seems probable that Captain Gray was more pleased with his success at trading with the natives than with the fact that he had discovered and named a river. After all, he had crossed the bar simply to prove to himself that a river did empty into the Pacific and doubtless considered it of little importance except for his own satisfaction. (Holbrook, p. 30)

Aftermath

Second voyage to the Northwest. Gray completed his trade mission to China and returned to Boston on July 25, 1793, accomplishing a second full voyage around the world. The Boston Marine Association again lost money on the venture, however, and made Gray's second voyage to the Northwest its last. Gray's employers, having lost money twice, ceased sending ships west and concentrated instead on the Atlantic trade they knew best. Gray resumed captaincy of cargo ships sailing along the East Coast of the United States.

Final days. In 1799, during the undeclared war with France (1798-1800), Gray commanded a heavily armed privateer *Lucy*. A year later he again returned to the merchant service and died of yellow fever in 1806 while sailing off the coast of South Carolina. He left his wife and daughters very little property, forcing Mrs. Gray to petition Congress for financial assistance.

Because Gray was not interested in publicity and did not publish his own journals, his discovery of the Columbia River was not widely known until after his death. It was not until Vancouver published his journals, which included an account of Gray's discovery, and President Madison ordered a reprint of the *Columbia's* logs in 1816 to help settle the dispute over the Oregon Territory, that the world learned of the great feat Gray had accomplished.

Tragically, Gray died relatively unknown and in poverty. But his accomplishments helped secure the West Coast of the United States and laid the groundwork for future explorers such as Lewis and Clark (see **Meriwether Lewis**).

> ## Columbia and Washington Coins
>
> Gray's merchant backers thought the voyage to the Northwest Territory so important that they minted special coins. Several copies were made in bronze and silver and passed out to government officials and New Englanders. On one side, the coins showed the ship and sloop; on the other side, the names of the merchants.

For More Information

Bulfinch, Thomas. *Oregon and Eldorado: Romance of the Rivers.* Boston: J. E. Tilton and Co., 1866.

Holbrook, Stewart H. *The Columbia.* New York: Rinehart and Co., 1956.

Howay, Frederick W., ed. *Voyages of the Columbia to the Northwest Coast, 1787-1790 and 1790-1793.* Portland: Oregon Historical Society Press, 1990.

Meriwether Lewis

1774-1809

Personal Background

Early years. Mcriwether Lewis was born on August 18, 1774, on his family's plantation at Locust Hill in Albemarle County, Virginia. His father, an army officer who had fought in the American Revolution, died when Lewis was five. As a child, Lewis enjoyed the outdoors, hunting opossum and raccoon in the wooded hills near his home. When his mother remarried years later, he moved to Georgia into the home of her new husband, John Marks.

By age eighteen, Lewis began to show a great thirst for adventure. Hearing of then Secretary of State Thomas Jefferson's plan to fund a western journey to find a "river road" to the Pacific Ocean across North America, Lewis volunteered to go along. But Jefferson chose to have the older, more experienced Andre Michaux, a French botanist, make the journey alone. (Michaux found nothing but trouble and never made it past Kentucky. Jefferson recalled him for being a spy.) Disappointed by Jefferson's choice but not defeated, Lewis continued looking for adventure; by 1794 he found it.

At the age of twenty, Lewis enlisted as a private to help quell, or put down, the so-called "Whiskey Rebellion." Whiskey producers in western Pennsylvania were refusing to pay a whiskey tax, so President George Washington sent out 12,000 soldiers to collect it by force. Lewis probably saw little action in this short-lived con-

▲ Meriwether Lewis

Event: Lewis and Clark Expedition, 1804-1806.

Role: Meriwether Lewis was the official head of the first land-based journey by American explorers across North America. Following the Missouri River to the Continental Divide, on to the Columbia River and Pacific Ocean, Lewis and Clark charted the first direct continental route to the Pacific Northwest. The explorers encountered Indian tribes and flora and fauna, or plants and animals, previously unknown to white Americans. They also mapped the area and kept journals, which proved invaluable for establishing trade routes and moving into the territory.

frontation, since the "Whiskey Boys" surrendered at the sight of federal troops. However, the event opened a new and exciting chapter in his life. Lewis stayed on after the rebellion to become a soldier in the American army. Once enlisted, he was sent down the Ohio River to serve under General "Mad Anthony" Wayne and then reassigned to a rifle company commanded by Captain William Clark.

Lewis meets Clark. Like Lewis, William Clark came from Virginia. He had grown up in Caroline County, just miles from Lewis's childhood home. He shared the same love of the outdoors and had many of the same boyhood experiences as Lewis, such as hunting in the surrounding woods and rolling hills. Clark joined the armed services as soon as he turned nineteen.

In 1790, just a year after he had enlisted, Clark fought against the Creek and Cherokee Indians. This encounter sparked his great interest in and admiration for native Americans, which would later prompt him to jump at the chance at an expedition to further study their lands and culture. When Clark turned twenty-one, he was promoted to captain and put in charge of an elite infantry unit, to which Lewis was assigned in 1795. Lewis and Clark quickly became good friends. They did not serve long together, however. In July 1796 Clark had to resign from the army in order to help his family out of financial trouble brought on by his brother.

Lewis's wilderness training in the army. While Clark returned to his family farm in Kentucky, Lewis remained in the army and began rising through its ranks. He was promoted first to lieutenant and then to captain. From 1796 to 1801, Lewis led troops on expeditions up and down the Ohio River, making several journeys into "Indian country" and visiting frontier posts to deliver pay to remote army regiments. In 1801 newly elected President Thomas Jefferson wrote to Lewis at his barracks in Pittsburgh, Pennsylvania, requesting his presence in Washington.

The appointment to the Presidency of the United States has rendered it necessary for me to have a private secretary.... Your knowledge of the Western country, of the army and of all its interests and relations has rendered it desirable for public as well as private purposes that you should be engaged in that office. (Snyder, p. 9)

Lewis serves the president. Jefferson clearly wanted more than a secretary. He wanted someone who could help him realize his dream of exploring the West. Lewis, he knew, was just the man for the job.

For the next two years Lewis was treated like a member of Jefferson's family. He found himself in the company of the most notable scientists, poets, diplomats, and politicians of the day. He often traveled with Jefferson to Albemarle County, Virginia, a place that both had loved since boyhood. Together they discussed plans for a land-based expedition to the Pacific Ocean across what is now the northern United States.

In 1801 French emperor Napoleon Bonaparte, who controlled the Louisiana Territory, made a deal with the U.S. government that enabled such an expedition to take place. In a startling decision, Napoleon agreed to sell not just Louisiana, which the United States had asked to purchase, but the entire Louisiana Territory, which included present-day Louisiana, Arkansas, Oklahoma, Missouri, Kansas, Iowa, Nebraska, South Dakota, and parts of Minnesota, North Dakota, Montana, Colorado, and Texas. It doubled the size of the United States.

Jefferson saw this as just the beginning to claiming the entire West for the United States. He quickly petitioned Congress for money to back an expedition to explore the territory beyond the Rocky Mountains, the western boundary of the Louisiana Territory. In January 1803 Congress agreed to the president's request and issued 2,500 dollars to get the expedition under way. As he and Jefferson had discussed, Lewis was chosen to head the discovery mission. Its purpose, according to Congress, was to extend "the external commerce of the U.S." (Snyder, p. 13). Jefferson and the explorers, however, intended to accomplish more than just furthering U.S. business interests. The money Congress gave for the expedition fell far short of what it would cost, but Jefferson considered the gesture a major victory. He was at last on the verge of realizing his dream of westward exploration and would come up with additional funds for the trip as they were needed.

Participation: Lewis and Clark Expedition

Preparation. With Jefferson's complete trust and official backing from Congress, Lewis began preparing for the long and difficult expedition. He recruited men, gathered supplies, and acquired transportation for a trip that would last two years and cover 8,000 miles of virtual wilderness. One of Lewis's first and most important tasks was to choose a co-captain for the mission, someone capable of leading the expedition should anything happen to him. Without hesitation he nominated his old friend, William Clark, and Jefferson agreed to his choice. Lewis wrote to Clark in June 1803, saying:

> If there is anything ... in this enterprise, which would induce you to participate with me in its fatigues, its dangers and its honors, believe me there is no other man on earth with whom I should feel equal pleasure in sharing them as with yourself. (Snyder, p. 15)

Though the mail was slow and Lewis did not receive Clark's reply for more than a month, Clark eagerly accepted the invitation. Jefferson and the War Department refused to officially recognize Clark as Lewis's co-captain, however. They insisted Lewis remain above his friend in command. Angry over the decision, Lewis wrote to Clark:

> It will be best to let none of our party ... know anything about the grade [rank difference]. You will observe that the grade has no effect upon your compensation, which by God, shall be equal to my own. (Snyder, p. 15)

Thus, as Lewis insisted, the crew considered Lewis and Clark equal leaders.

Before setting off, Lewis traveled to the East Coast to pick up information and supplies that he needed for the expedition. In Lancaster, Pennsylvania, he purchased a telescope and took a crash course in astronomy from astronomer Andrew Ellicott. In Philadelphia, he obtained medical advice from three of the most knowledgeable doctors in the United States: Benjamin Barton Smith, Casper Wistar, and Benjamin Rush. Since there would be no doctor along on the trip, it was essential that he, as well as Clark, know something of medical treatment and available herbal remedies.

Laden with dried food and cured meat, weapons, whiskey, scientific instruments, blank journals, and presents for native Americans (blankets, trinkets, mirrors, tomahawks, beads, etc.), Lewis and his party of ten men departed from Pittsburgh on August 31, 1803. Traveling by keelboat down the Ohio River to Louisville, Kentucky, Lewis's party met up with Clark, his slave, York, and nineteen other volunteers. From there they sailed north of St. Louis and set up camp at Wood River, where the Mississippi and Missouri rivers meet. The party wintered in camp and the following May finally began their excursion into uncharted territory.

The journey begins. On May 14, 1804, the fifty-five-foot keelboat *Discovery* started up the Missouri. Each one of the twenty-nine members of the permanent expedition had his own talent necessary for the group's survival. There were carpenters, hunters, cooks, blacksmiths, boatwrights, gunsmiths—even a pair of fiddlers for entertainment. As co-captains, Lewis's and Clark's talents worked perfectly together. Lewis was well educated—skilled in writing, botany and biology. Clark was a fine cartographer (mapmaker), geographer, and navigator and had a high regard for native American peoples. In personal traits, Lewis was more of a loner, often taking walks by himself to enjoy the peacefulness of the empty land. Clark, on the other hand, liked being with people; he was "hearty and good-natured, preferring the company of men" (Snyder, 37). Clark was loved by the crew; Lewis, respected.

The well-rounded group traveled first to St. Charles, with Clark leading the keelboat and two canoes called "pirogues" up the river and Lewis riding over land with his dog, Scannon, to meet them. Within a few days the entire group set sail from St. Charles, the last taste of civilization they would get for two years.

Lewis, who had had a reputation for moodiness and worrying about his health prior to the trip, apparently underwent a change as he explored the uncharted territory. Joy took over, and he grew excited to discover what might be around the next bend. He assembled something of a traveling museum as he went, gathering jackrabbit skins and live animals—a shiny black-and-white magpie bird, a weasel, a coyote, a red fox—and sending them by keelboat back East for inspection. (The magpie was for President Jefferson, who studied birds.) Lewis roasted a prairie dog to see how it tasted and found that he liked it. Later he discovered a forty-five-foot-long skeleton, probably the remains of a dinosaur. It was too difficult to send, so he shipped some of its bones back home.

Along the way some native Americans had their first meeting with immigrant Americans when Lewis and Clark arrived. The explorers met a host of Indian peoples; among them the Omaha, Missouri, Teton Sioux, and Mandan. Many of the Indians were fascinated to meet a black man, Clark's slave, York, and Lewis amazed them with his knowledge of medicine. He would treat the Mandan people and his own men for frostbite during the winter, sometimes having to amputate a patient's frozen toe.

Averaging fifteen miles a day, Lewis and Clark guided their expedition into Mandan and Minnetaree country, toward the Knife River, where they built a log fort, Fort Mandan, for shelter during the winter of 1804. The journey to the site had been long but far from dull. The hunters had added meat to the daily diet by advancing ahead of the boats to kill game. They hung their kill from tree branches over the river for the main expedition to pick up. The muddy Missouri had made navigation difficult for the whole crew; the mosquitoes made the men miserable. Black gnats pestered the men's eyes, while great flies (greenheads) bothered the horses. Dripping with blood, the horses would bolt from camp in fits of pain. The men set fires at night to drive off these pests.

By bestowing gifts and making clear their peaceful intentions, Lewis and Clark were able to obtain from native Americans valuable information on the flow of the Missouri and the outlay of the land to the Continental Divide. Especially helpful were the Minnetaree Indians. By the time the expedition reached its winter campsite, it had lost one man, Sergeant Charles Floyd. The only man to die on the entire trip, Floyd probably suffered from a ruptured appendix and could not have been saved even had he been in a hospital.

Sacagawea. When the party resumed its journey West in April 1805, three more had joined the venture: a French-Canadian fur trapper, Toussaint Charbonneau, who would serve as an interpreter; his Shoshone wife, Sacagawea; and their newly born son, Jean Baptiste, whom Lewis helped deliver at Fort Mandan during the winter. Sacagawea became the first and only female member of the expedition and soon proved to be more valuable to the team than her husband (see **Sacagawea**).

By August 1805 the expedition reached the end of the Missouri River and entered Shoshone territory. Sacagawea helped arrange for Lewis and Clark to buy horses from her tribe in order to cross the Continental Divide. Storing their boats for the return trip, the explorers began their trek by horseback through the Rocky Mountains, a trip that would have been nearly impossible by foot.

Lewis's journal. Throughout the entire journey, as the expedition forged its way through the rugged country toward the Columbia River, Lewis eagerly explored the countryside. He jotted down notes in his journal and drew sketches of birds, flowers, and landscapes he had never seen before. Lewis vividly described his first glimpse of the Rocky Mountains, saying, "Every object here wears a dark and gloomy aspect. From the singular appearance of this place I called it the *gates of the rocky mountains*" (Snyder, p. 134). Days later, when the party reached Nez Perce Indian country, Lewis described the unfamiliar people as "stout likely men and handsome women" (Snyder, p. 140).

Lewis's journals not only paint a vivid portrait of the landscape, but reveal much about his feelings. On the explorer's thirty-first birthday (at the Continental Divide), he wrote that he had "done but very little, very little, indeed, to further the happiness of the human race, or to advance the information of the succeeding generation" (Snyder, p. 138). In the midst of one of the greatest journeys ever undertaken, which certainly furthered the understanding of the next generation, Lewis's words seem strangely out of place and show a self-doubt that continually haunted him.

> ### Lewis's Dog, Scannon, Saves Men from Being Trampled
>
> In May of 1805, while Lewis and his men slept in their tents, a buffalo stumbled through the darkness and found its way into the campsite. The great animal charged toward Lewis's and Clark's tent but just as it was about to trample their heads, Lewis's dog, Scannon, jumped out and barked, causing the buffalo to change its course. One crew member said, "If the buffalo had trod on a man it would have killed him dead." The dog had saved both Lewis and Clark from a tragic fate that could have stopped the expedition. (Snyder, p. 118)

Pacific reached—return home. Most grueling was the journey across the Rockies and through the present states of Montana and Idaho. At times the party was forced to kill and eat several of the horses and to melt snow for water. The expedition finally reached the Clearwater River in the Pacific Northwest and resumed their travel by boat. Making canoes from hollowed-out pine trees and riding rapids from the Clearwater to the Snake and onto the Columbia rivers, Lewis and Clark finally sighted the Pacific Ocean from a high peak on November 18, 1805. In Lewis's words:

> We could not ascertain the direction of the deepest channel, for the waves break with tremendous force … but the Indians point nearer to the opposite side as the best passage. After remaining for some time on this elevation, we descended across the low isthmus, and reached the ocean at the foot of a high hill. (Lewis II, p. 269)

They set up camp at Fort Clatsop on the Columbia River, near present-day Astoria, Oregon, and remained there exploring and trading through the rainy winter before returning east in March 1806. Sacagawea again proved valuable in this part of the country. Serving as an interpreter between the explorers and the Columbia River tribes (including her own Shoshone and the Clatsop, Flathead, Chinook, Clackapoo, Wappatoo, Mutnomah, Cushook, Eloot Nation, and Wapatoo Island tribes), she helped persuade the natives to accept and assist the expedition. Lewis encountered a new food here, anchovies, and before winter was over, preferred them as his favorite snack: "I find them best when cooked in Indian style, which is by roasting a number of them on a wooden spit … I think them superior to any fish I ever tasted" (Lawrence, p. 224).

On their return trip, the explorers retraced their path to the Missouri River. Lewis and Clark split at Lolo Creek (near the Missouri Falls) to investigate and map separate territory. Lewis and his group explored the Marias, the land north of the Missouri controlled by Hidatsa and Blackfoot Indians. He had hoped to avoid an encounter with the Blackfoot, who were rumored to be hostile, but on July 26 he and his men crossed their path. Seeing eight Blackfoot Indians traveling on horseback, Lewis boldly chose to meet the band head-on. All appeared friendly at first as the Indians and explorers smoked a peace pipe and set up camp together. During the night, however, Lewis was awakened by a cry from his watchman alerting him that the Indians were trying to drive off their horses and steal their guns. A confrontation ensued and one of Lewis's men stabbed an Indian through the heart. Lewis himself shot and killed another. Fearful that the violence would spread, Lewis quickly ordered his men to pack up and leave the area. These were the only native Americans killed on the entire journey.

Lewis and his men were able to rejoin Clark's group with no further hostile encounters. However, when Clark reunited with his co-captain in early August, he learned that Lewis had been shot in the leg. It seems that one of Lewis's men, who was blind in one eye, had accidentally shot him, mistaking him for a elk. Clark treated the wound and Lewis was able to continue on to Fort Mandan, where both explorers sought to convince Mandan and Minnetaree chiefs to accompany them to Washington to meet President Jefferson. Reluctantly, the Mandan chief Big White agreed to accompany the explorers, bringing along his family, and the party headed toward St. Louis, back into "civilization." But before the explorers left the wilderness, they said goodbye to their friends Sacagawea and Charbonneau, and paid them 500 dollars. Sacagawea would later place her son in the care of Clark, who oversaw the boy's education, including a tour of Europe.

> ## Lewis and the Wild Animals
> Lewis thrilled at the sight of an endless stretch of buffalo, elk, deer, and antelope all feeding off the same plain. He also had several harrowing experiences with grizzly bears; one of them chased him for seventy-five yards.

On September 23, 1806, Lewis and Clark arrived back in St. Louis. Dashing off a letter to Jefferson, Lewis informed him of the mission's success: "We have penetrated the Continent … to the Pacific Ocean, and have discovered the most practical route which does exist across the continent" (Snyder, p. 195). Jefferson, who had received no word from his secretary in nearly two years, was overjoyed and planned a huge reception in his honor. Lewis and Chief Great White attended, while Clark, anxious to get back to a young woman he would soon marry, headed straight for his home in Virginia.

Aftermath

Reward and sorrow. For their efforts, Lewis and Clark each received money and land from the president, along with governorships of Louisiana and Missouri, respectively. But Lewis's new post proved to be not a blessing but a curse. Not cut out to sit behind a desk, Lewis was miserable in his job and quickly made many enemies among other state officials. Additionally, he began to drink and quarrel with the federal government over reimbursement for expenses.

During much of 1807 and 1808, Lewis sought to escape his troubles. He traveled to Philadelphia and met with artists and publishers, with the intention of having his journals of the expedition professionally illustrated and published. He worked on the project for more than a year and finally returned to the Louisiana Territory in 1808. By this time his friendship with Jefferson was very strained and his political troubles as governor continued to plague him. In the summer of 1809, after the federal government had refused to repay him 500 dollars (the cost of returning Chief Big White to Mandan country), Lewis became enraged and decided to travel to Washington to confront the situation, as was his habit.

Along the way, however, it appears that Lewis's growing depression got the best of him. On September 15, 1809, he arrived at Fort Pickering in Tennessee. The fort's commanding officer, Captain Gilbert Russell, noted that Lewis arrived at the fort "in a state of mental derangement. He had made [en route] two attempts to kill himself, in one of which he had nearly succeeded" (Cutright, p. 51). Russell took personal charge of Lewis and, when the captain appeared to be fully recovered two weeks later, sent him on toward the nation's capital. On October 10, with his traveling companion, Major James McNeelly, Lewis stopped at a roadhouse called Grinder's Inn in to rest. McNeelly noted that earlier in the day Lewis had "appeared at times deranged in mind" (Cutright, p. 51). That night he was awakened by gunshots coming from Lewis's room. Hearing the shots, McNeelly rushed in to find Lewis dead, shot twice in the head and chest, apparently by his own hand.

Though hotly debated, Lewis's premature death at the age of thirty-five most certainly was suicide. A letter from Jefferson indicates the extent of Lewis's depression after the expedition, saying:

> He was much afflicted and habitually so by hypochondria. This was probably increased by the habit into which he had fallen

[drinking] and the painful reflections that would necessarily produce in a mind like his. (Cutright, p. 50)

Whatever the cause of his death, whether murder or suicide, Lewis's tragic end saddened all of his friends, most especially Clark. On hearing the news, Clark lamented, "I fear O! I fear the weight of his mind has overcome him" (Snyder, p. 198). Lewis was buried in the Tennessee hills where his life ended.

For future generations. After his death, Lewis's journals were finally published, complete with the illustrations he had commissioned. Clark died in St. Louis in 1838 at the age of 68, leaving behind his second wife and six sons.

The Lewis and Clark expedition has been called "the most perfect journey of its kind" (Lamar, p. 665). It forever altered the course of American history. At a cost of less than 40,000 dollars and three deaths (two native Americans and one crew member), Lewis and Clark charted some 8,000 miles of unknown territory and opened the gateway to the West. In addition, the explorers introduced countless native varieties of plants and animals to the immigrant Americans, and provided some of the first and fullest descriptions of native Americans ever written.

For More Information

Cutright, Paul Russell. *A History of the Lewis and Clark Journals.* Norman: University of Oklahoma Press, 1976.

Lamar, Howard R. *The Reader's Encyclopedia of the American West.* New York: Thomas Y. Crowell & Co., 1977.

Lawrence, Bill. *The Early American Wilderness As the Explorers Saw It.* New York: Paragon House, 1991.

Lewis, Meriwether. *History of the Expedition. 3 vols.* New York: Williams Barker Co., 1906.

Snyder, Gerald S. *In the Footsteps of Lewis and Clark.* Washington, D.C.: National Geographic Society, 1970.

Sacagawea

1788-c. 1812/1884

Personal Background

The Shoshone way of life. Sacagawea was born in 1788 in a small Shoshone Indian village in what is now Lemhi Valley, Idaho. The Shoshone tribe originated in Mexico, then traveled north and settled in the basin between the Rocky Mountains and the Sierra Nevadas. Through many generations, the Shoshone relied on the basin environment for their food, mostly gathering plants and hunting small rodents and birds. Eventually the climate changed, and their home evolved into an arid desert, making it impossible to survive on what little food and water still existed in the intense heat of the land. This change forced the Shoshone people to become nomads, moving from place to place in search of sustenance.

They began living in small groups, scattering themselves about and finding just enough food to survive. Their diet included deer, buffalo, jackrabbits, and badgers as well as fish, birds, seeds, roots, and medicinal herbs. The Shoshone made use of all parts of an animal, eating the meat, carving the bones into tools, shaping teeth into jewelry, and sewing hides into clothing, using animal tendons as thread.

Grass Maiden of the Shoshone. Sacagawea was given the name Boinaiv at birth, meaning "Grass Maiden." Her father was a respected chief, No Retreat, and her mother, Fragrant Herbs,

▲ Sacagawea

Event: The Lewis and Clark expedition.
Role: Sacagawea traveled with Lewis and Clark from the newly acquired Louisiana Territory to the Pacific Ocean, proving valuable as an interpreter between the explorers and Indians. She did not, however, guide Lewis and Clark across the continent. In fact, she was familiar with only one area of value to the explorers, an area near today's Montana-Idaho boundary, east of the Rocky Mountains, where they could get horses for the crossing.

worked hard to provide for Sacagawea and her brothers, Cameah-wait (Never Walks) and Spotted Bear, and her sister, Rain Girl.

Sacagawea, like every other young Shoshone girl, was trained to recognize and gather more than 100 different types of edible bulbs, roots, and berries, as well as several kinds of medicinal herbs. Because the Shoshone tribe she belonged to was nomadic, Sacagawea was used to moving about and became extremely skilled at finding things to eat wherever the tribe was settled.

Moving from place to place also helped Sacagawea learn about traveling through different kinds of terrain. She expertly climbed rocky mountains, crossed rivers, hiked through grassy plains, and walked over miles of hot desert land.

The capture. When Sacagawea was about ten, she camped with her band between present-day Butte and Bozeman, Montana, in Three Forks Valley, where three rivers join to form the Missouri River. The Shoshone men had ridden off to hunt buffalo, and Sacagawea was busy picking berries near her mother when, suddenly, a shot rang out in the distance. An enemy tribe, the Minnetaree (or Hidatsa), were attacking Sacagawea's people. Some Shoshone braves managed to flee on horseback, but others were not so lucky. Powerless against the guns of the Minnetaree, many Shoshone men were shot and killed. All around Sacagawea lay the bodies of men. The women and children ran in every direction to escape. Panicked, Sacagawea jumped into one of the three rivers, only to be grabbed from behind by a mounted Minnetaree warrior and thrown on the back of his horse. In a matter of moments, Sacagawea was violently separated from everything and almost everyone she knew. In the attack a few other Shoshone girls were taken captive as well.

Sacagawea was able to recognize the territory she passed through for a few miles, but then she lost her bearings. She was taken much too far away to ever find her way back. Finally she and her captors arrived at a Minnetaree camp, located close to what is now Mandan, North Dakota. She was told that she had been brought to the camp to work in the fields with the other captives. She was probably given the name Sacagawea, interpreted as "Bird Woman," upon arriving at the Minnetaree camp. Sacagawea worked for several years, learning the language and customs of the Minnetaree and, in turn, teaching them some Shoshone words.

Sacagawea becomes a wife. When she reached her early teens, Sacagawea was considered old enough for marriage, so she was sold as a second bride to a French Canadian fur trader by the name of Toussaint Charbonneau, who lived among the Minnetaree as an interpreter for the Indians and the traders. (He was said to have won Sacagawea while gambling.) Charbonneau was regarded by the rest of the tribe as a bumbling, slow-witted white man. His first wife, also a Shoshone woman, had already born a child. Sacagawea was forced to live in a hut with her as well as Charbonneau and the baby. Although her husband was "not known for unkindness" (Skold, p. 20), Sacagawea was undoubtedly displeased with her position as a second wife to this dull man, yet she had no choice in the matter. Several years passed, and she became pregnant by Charbonneau in the summer of 1804.

Meeting the white explorers. While Sacagawea was preparing for motherhood, two American explorers appointed by President Thomas Jefferson were blazing a land trail to the Pacific Ocean from the newly purchased Louisiana Territory. The explorers, Meriwether Lewis and William Clark, had traveled through several different Indian villages between the Louisiana Territory and the North Dakota area. As they traveled farther west, they began running into some difficulty because of the language barrier. They were unable to communicate with many of the tribes. As the winter months approached, the explorers began preparing to camp for the season in what is now Bismarck, North Dakota, very near where Sacagawea and the Minnetaree were settled. Used to trading with white men who passed through the area, the Minnetaree Indians were anxious to visit with the exploring party. The meetings that followed were peaceful; the explorers and Minnetaree spent long hours smoking peace pipes, talking to each other through an interpreter, and trading gifts.

> **Sacagawea the Interpreter**
> From Meriwether Lewis's journal, on speaking with the Tushepaw Indians: "I spoke to Labieche in English—he translated it to Charbonneau in French—he to his wife in Minnetaree—she in Shoshone to the boy—the boy in Tushepaw to that nation." (Jackson, p. 519)

Joining the party. Clark first wrote of Sacagawea in his journal in November 1804, when she and Toussaint's other Shoshone wife visited the explorers' camp. Sacagawea and her husband are said to have visited several more times and, days before going into labor, she actually stayed in the explorers' camp. Meanwhile, Charbonneau was making arrangements to continue on with the expedition as an interpreter for the Minnetaree and the white men. Sacagawca was asked to come too, since an interpreter was badly needed to help acquire horses from the Shoshone, the tribe nearest the Rocky Mountains. According to *Sacagawea of the Lewis & Clark Expedition,* "only Sacagawea could speak Shoshone. So, although it is obvious from their journals that the captains neither respected nor liked him, Lewis and Clark hired Charbonneau as an interpreter, specifying that he should bring Sacagawea along" (Clark and Edmonds, p. 15). Charbonneau had three wives at the time.

The birth of "Little Chief." On February 11, 1805, Sacagawea went into labor. The process was long and difficult until a Frenchman, Rene Jussome, suggested giving her part of a rattlesnake's rattle to help bring on the birth of the child. She swallowed the rattle and, coincidentally or otherwise, within minutes gave birth to a baby boy. She and Charbonneau named the child Jean Baptiste. Clark quickly grew attached to the child, nicknaming him "Pomp," which means "Little Chief." The following spring, mother and baby were ready to join the expedition.

Participation: Lewis and Clark Expedition

The explorers set out again on April 7, 1805, with Charbonneau, Sacagawea, and Jean Baptiste, who rode on his mother's back in a cradle board. Sacagawea was only about seventeen years old when she set out with the explorers. The party used the Missouri River as the main guide on their quest to reach the Pacific Ocean. Along the way, Sacagawea collected edible plants, such as prairie turnips, wild onions, gooseberries, and red currants. The explorers otherwise drew from their own supply of foods, which included salt pork, parched corn, and flour. Sometimes they caught rabbits or birds and enjoyed fresh meat, accompanied maybe by a side dish such as suet dumplings (flour and fat boiled in water).

On May 14, the party ran into some trouble when a boat, holding valuable supplies and attended by Sacagawea and Charbonneau, was tipped over by a strong gust of wind. Characteristically, Charbonneau panicked, and Sacagawea calmly salvaged the supplies that had fallen into the river. Several days later, the captains named part of this river "Birdwoman's River," in honor of Sacagawea.

The hardships begin. However strong and able, Sacagawea could not fight off a terrible sickness she caught in early June that left her near death for two weeks. The captains were very concerned with the well-being of their interpreter, for her pulse grew more weak and irregular with each passing day. Clark was working extremely hard to keep her well by bleeding her, as was a customary remedy at that time, feeding her tree bark and opium, and making her drink fresh mineral water from a nearby spring. She responded well to the water and quickly recovered, much to the satisfaction of the entire party.

> ### Lewis Describes Sacagawea
> Lewis write of Sacagawea in his diary: "If she had enough to eat and a few trinkets to wear I believe she would be content anywhere." (Clark and Edmonds, p. 21)

The exploring party started out again four days later. While following the Missouri River, an enormous flash flood accompanied by rain and hail overcame them. Sacagawea escaped near death again, clinging to the rocks on the side of the river with one arm, and holding her baby with the other. Charbonneau was of no help, but Clark assisted Sacagawea by staying underneath her, pushing her up toward safety whenever possible.

Three Forks recognized. Despite torrential rains and generally poor conditions, the explorers made it through the difficult river within a month. It was now August. Exhausted, they trudged on, unsure of what lay ahead until Sacagawea recognized the part of the river known as Three Forks, where she had been abducted by the Minnetaree as a child. This discovery was of great help to the party because the explorers knew that one of the forks would take them west to the Rocky Mountains. Further exploration eliminated two of the forks, so they started following the third, known now as the Jefferson River.

Reunited with her people. Not far up the Jefferson, Sacagawea again aided the party by recognizing Beaverhead Rock, in western Montana, as the place not far from where her people and their horses could probably be found. They continued hiking and, on

August 17 as Clark was walking behind Sacagawea, she joyfully noted that she recognized the band of Indians up ahead. They were her people, the Shoshone, and largely because of her presence, the Indians received the explorers well. There followed a conference between the Shoshone chief and the explorers, who intended to barter for horses to help them finish the journey across the Rocky Mountains. Then Sacagawea entered the circle, raised her eyes to the chief, and burst into tears of joy. Standing in front of her was her beloved brother, Chief Cameahwait. He apparently promised Sacagawea he would provide her party with fine horses and several Shoshone guides. When the council ended, Sacagawea learned of the deaths of most of her family, with the exception of Cameahwait, another brother, and her sister's son, a child she immediately adopted as her own but was forced to leave behind with her brothers.

Crossing the Rockies. The explorers crossed the Rockies on horseback in about a month's time with the help of their Shoshone guides. The arrival of September brought snow, making the journey especially treacherous. In early October, the party finally reached the plains west of the Rocky Mountains, where they met the Nez Perce ("Pierced Nose") tribe. The Nez Perce drew maps of the three rivers that had to be followed in order to reach the Pacific Coast: the Clearwater, Snake, and Columbia. The Indians seemed to trust the explorers, considering Sacagawea and Jean Baptiste "tokens of peace." Some of the Nez Perce even decided to join the fast-growing party as guides.

Reaching the coast. On November 7, 1805, after surviving the rush of the three great rivers, the explorers caught the first glimpse of the Pacific Ocean nearly twenty miles in the distance. They had reached the lower part of the Columbia River, yet they could go no farther because winter was upon them again. They decided, with Sacagawea's help, to set up camp near the Oregon coast. The party built a log cabin in which they spent the winter months, naming it Fort Clatsop, after a nearby tribe of Indians. This is where the explorers exchanged Christmas gifts, watched Pomp take his first steps, and shared what precious little meat and tobacco they had.

Soon after the start of the new year, Clark, Charbonneau, Sacagawea, Pomp, and eleven others traveled the remaining twenty miles to the sand to see a beached whale, the likes of which had never been seen by the explorers. Sacagawea was not invited at first, but she showed great disappointment and even confronted Clark on what she considered to be a very rude gesture: speaking of the final stretch of the trip in her presence and not including her after she had been such a devoted member of the exploration. Clark promptly agreed and invited her to accompany them. This was the only recorded instance in which Sacagawea showed anger on the long and difficult trip.

The journey home. When the seasonal rains finally let up on March 23, 1806, Sacagawea, now eighteen years old, and the exploring party were ready to head back toward the Louisiana Territory. Lewis and Clark split up into two parties, one led by Lewis, the other led by Clark. The idea was for Lewis's party to travel north of the Missouri River in order to find yet another route around it. The two parties were to reunite at a prearranged spot along the shores of the Missouri. The return trip went considerably smoother, now that the explorers were familiar with the terrain. Sacagawea and Charbonneau were assigned to Clark's party, traveling back to the Shoshone land and then on to the Yellowstone River to make canoes in which they would travel to Missouri to meet with Lewis's party.

Upon arriving at the land of the Minnetaree on August 14, 1806, Sacagawea and Charbonneau were no longer needed as interpreters. They ended their journey where they had begun, gaining newfound respect from the Minnetaree tribe. Sacagawea stood out as the heroine, mostly because she was regarded as a symbol of peace between the explorers and the Indians. In contrast to popular belief, though, she had not guided Lewis and Clark through the country. Rather, she had located foods to eat along the way, served as an able translator and symbol of peace in dealing with Indian peoples, and assisted in the explorers' effort to obtain Shoshone horses.

Aftermath

The explorers also recognized Sacagawea's importance to the expedition, as shown by Clark in a letter he wrote to Charbonneau:

Your woman who accompanied you that long dangerous and fatigueing rout to the Pacific Ocian and back diserved a greater reward for her attention and services on that rout than we had in our power to give her.... As to your little son (my boy Pomp) you well know my fondness for him and my anxiety to take and raise him as my own. (Jackson, pp. 315-16)

After the exploration, Sacagawea was given a medal by Lewis and Clark. It had Jefferson's face on one side and a tomahawk on the other, symbolizing peace between the Indians and the white explorers. Wearing the medal with pride, she retold her story to the Shoshone. It has become an important part of their history.

However dedicated she was to her original tribe, Sacagawea had also become a part of the Minnetaree. She decided to return to Minnetaree land with her husband, but the journey had changed her. She now had ideas of more explorations, perhaps without her family this time. The notion of exploring alone appealed to her, but she still had her husband and son to consider.

Throughout the journey, Clark had become very attached to Pomp, regarding him as a son. He asked Sacagawea if he could take the boy to St. Louis and enroll him in school. Sacagawea considered, then declined the offer, because Pomp was not weaned yet. She promised that after the infant lived with her for a year, he could be raised by Clark.

Sacagawea's mysterious fate. Sacagawea and Charbonneau remained with the Minnetaree for a little over a year. In 1808 Sacagawea took Pomp to Clark in St. Louis, as promised, and remained with them until 1812. She then left her son in the care of Clark. It was rumored that she afterward reunited with her husband at Fort Manuel, on the border of North and South Dakota. The only evidence that she engaged in more exploration is an account from the Shoshone people that she took an extended trip back from St. Louis to Fort Manuel. She was reported by a fort clerk to have died at Fort Manuel of fever on December 20, 1812, at the age of twenty-four. She also was reported dead by Clark in a journal entry written sometime between 1825 and 1828, yet he could have been misinformed. He mistakenly claimed in the same entry that another member of the party was dead, when he indeed lived to an old age.

The Shoshone's traditional spoken story differs greatly from these accounts. They claim that Sacagawea returned to the

Shoshone camp sometime after leaving her husband at Fort Manuel. Meanwhile, Sacagawea married again and had more children. She told her story of the exploration until her death in 1884. A distinguished native American researcher and writer, Dr. Charles Eastman, wrote this of Sacagawea's last years:

> I report that Sacagawea, after sixty years of wandering from her own tribe, returned to her people [the Shoshones] at Fort Bridger and lived the remainder of her life … in peace until she died April 9, 1884, at Fort Washakie, Wyoming. (Clark and Edmonds, p. 129)

It is impossible to know which account is correct, and both are argued equally by historians. Regardless, Sacagawea is remembered as an essential link in the chain of western exploration—in spoken stories by the Indian people and in landmarks by the explorers.

For More Information

Clark, Ella E., and Margot Edmonds. *Sacagawea of the Lewis and Clark Exploration.* Berkeley, Los Angeles, and London: University of California Press, 1979.

Jackson, Donald. *Letters of the Lewis and Clark Expedition, With Related Documents.* Urbana: University of Illinois Press, 1962.

Skold, Betty Westrom. *Sacagawea: The Story of an American Indian.* Minneapolis: Dillon Press, Inc., 1977.

John Jacob Astor

1763-1848

Personal Background

Astor Family. In 1750 John Astor, Sr., a butcher in the small town of Waldorf, Germany, married Marie Vorster. They bore two daughters and four sons; the youngest, John Jacob, was born July 17, 1763. John Jacob's mother died when he was three years old, and the infant's father remarried. He and his new wife bore six more children, so John Jacob's stepmother had little time to give to him. It was a large family to support and each of the boys, in turn, helped his father in the butcher business.

Life in Europe. Although busy with work and not wealthy, John Astor, Sr., provided for his sons' education, employing Valentine Jeune to tutor them. The Seven Years' War was coming to an end, and Hessian soldiers were returning home with tales of events throughout Europe. Excited by these stories, Jeune taught the Astor boys about the world beyond Germany, including happenings in far-off America.

While John Jacob was still a young boy, his brother George left the family to seek his fortune in London, England. He found work there with his uncle, who manufactured musical instruments. When war erupted in America in 1776, another brother, Henry, became a Hessian mercenary hired by the British and was sent to New York to fight against George Washington's Continental Army.

▲ John Jacob Astor

Event: The growth of the American fur trade.

Role: While the Hudson Bay Company concentrated its fur trading efforts in Canada, John Jacob Astor persuaded President Thomas Jefferson to encourage United States fur traders to compete with the French and British of Canada. Given the rights to that trade in the Ohio Valley, Astor grew to become the wealthiest man in America.

When his unit was moved out of the city, however, Henry gave up his fighting job and stayed in New York. There he fell back on the family profession, opening a butcher's business in the Fulton Market. Soon the third brother, Melchior, left home to become a tenant farmer in nearby Heidelberg. John Jacob was left alone, for a short time, as a helper in the family butcher shop.

In London. The youngest Astor also was eager to go out into the world. At the age of sixteen, he left home to join George in London. By this time George had set up his own small factory to build musical instruments. John Jacob worked in this factory for four years. A very serious young man, he spent his hours away from the factory reading the Bible and the Lutheran prayer book.

America. Meanwhile, Henry kept writing to his two brothers in London about the great opportunities he felt would open in America when the war between the colonies and Great Britain ended. John Jacob began planning for that day. He would become a representative of George's company, selling musical instruments in the United States. The opportunity to cross the ocean came in 1783. John Jacob packed his bag of musical instruments and set sail from London just as winter set in.

On the voyage Astor met a fellow traveler who was in the fur trade. The stories of the riches to be gained in this business stirred his interest. There were, however, obstacles. Most of the American fur trade was controlled by British traders. (In fact, all trade was required to pass through Great Britain from the North American centers at Montreal and Toronto.) Then, too, Astor had little capital to start any new venture and it had been largely invested already in his musical instrument business. The biggest obstacle of all was that he knew nothing about the fur business.

Bad luck, good luck. Life in America began with a new problem. The ship Astor had taken from London was caught in a sudden freeze of Chesapeake Bay. Ice formed around it and the ship could not dock. As the ice thickened and prospects of landing dimmed, some passengers began to pack their belongings and walk across the ice to the safety of land. Astor, however, refused to follow them. The ship was obligated to feed him and provide him a room until it docked; he had come to America with only five pounds in British money. While others left, he remained on board for free food and board. He stayed on the ship two weeks before joining the others in the trek across the icy bay.

Making his way to Baltimore, Maryland, he befriended a local merchant, Nicholas Tuchdy. As a young man, Astor inspired respect and affection from the people he met. Tuchdy took a liking to Astor and offered to take the musical instruments into his own shop to sell with no commission for himself. Astor accepted this offer and soon had pocketed the money from the sale and headed for New York to look up his brother Henry.

New York. Henry and his wife, Dorothy, arranged for Astor to stay with George Dietrich, a baker who needed a salesperson. In exchange for lodging, Astor agreed to walk the streets of New York peddling pastries.

> **J.J. Astor's Total Wealth**
> **Upon Arrival in America, 1783**
> 7 flutes
> 1 or 2 clarinets
> 5 pounds British money
>
> **In 1844**
> 30 million American dollars

Two important events occurred during the short time Astor worked as a pastry salesman. While walking the streets, he passed a boarding house run by the widow Todd and her daughter Sarah. He met Sarah as she was sweeping the front steps of the boarding house and stopped several times to talk with her. However, he could sell more pastries near the docks where many men worked at loading and unloading ships, so he spent most of his time there.

The ships and their cargoes excited young Astor. The idea of buying and selling had already been in his plans. He noticed that Indians of several neighboring tribes came to the docks to sell pelts at very low prices. One of the merchants who bought these pelts was Robert Browne. In 1785 Astor soon began working for Browne to learn the fur business. His first job in furs paid two dollars a week for beating the pelts to keep them free of moths. Soon he began to invest his earnings, buying pelts from the Indians to sell in London.

Browne taught Astor which pelts were the best to buy and how to prepare them for sale in England. The best pelts were those known as *castor gras,* those whose fur had been worn next to a human body for months, allowing the human body oil to soften the fur. For a little extra, many Indians were willing to do this work also. Astor began to understand that there were large profits to be gained from buying pelts at very low prices from the Indians and selling them for nine or ten times that amount in England.

Through his work with Browne, Astor became acquainted with William Backhouse, the greatest fur merchant in America. Backhouse was charmed by Astor. The young man became a frequent visitor to the Backhouse home, where family talk often drifted to the great possibilities in the fur trade.

Trade at Albany. In April 1785, still working for Browne, Astor traveled to Albany, then a trading post seven days up the Hudson River from New York. There he watched as trappers traded their furs to waiting merchants. Albany was at the edge of Indian country, however, and Astor believed that he could make better purchases if he left Albany to trade directly with the Iroquois Indians.

Adventure Among the Iroquois. Taking a pack of trading materials, a rifle, ammunition, and a flute with which to entertain himself in the evenings, Astor set out to explore Iroquois territory. Once more fortune smiled on him. He discovered that the Indians were fond of the flute music, which warmed relations and helped trade. Soon Astor returned to New York with two canoes full of pelts. He had arranged this trip as part of his work for Browne, who now offered him a raise in pay. Astor, however, had learned enough to strike out on his own.

Marriage. Astor reached another important turning point in 1785; he married Sarah Todd. Along with this marriage came a dowry of 300 dollars and two rent-free rooms in the Todd boarding house. He then pursued the risky fur business while Sarah carried on the more steady music business. She turned one of the two rooms in the boarding house into a store. While Astor traded in furs, Sarah became the American agent for George's London music house. Astor was very careful with the little money he had for his business. He proved to be so thrifty that the couple stayed in the two rooms of the boarding house even though one room was used for business and they soon had a child.

Astor and his wife remained together until her death in 1833. The couple had eight children, of which Magdalena was the oldest, and John Jacob Astor II, the oldest son. Astor and Sarah were so devoted to their children that John II, who was born feeble and mentally handicapped, lived a pleasant life to the age of seventy-eight.

Albany trade center. Astor was a city man. Although he was tall and muscular, he found no great joy in tramping through the woods looking for Indians and trappers from whom to buy furs. Still, each year he took the first ship to Albany to meet the trappers at Cornelius Persen's store. The pelts he bought from them were stored in a warehouse and prepared for market at the home of another friend, Peter Smith.

Sometime in 1786 or 1787, Astor was invited by a trapper named Alexander Henry to join other trappers and hunters gathered in Montreal to sell to the British North West Company. Astor quickly saw the advantages of Montreal. It was a stable settlement from which furs could and indeed were required to be sent to London for sale. In contrast, the beginning American states were still struggling over what form of government to create.

His time in Montreal allowed Astor to see how the North West Company had organized itself. Before 1780 fur hunters had operated quite independently and had encountered great dangers from the various Indian tribes. Sixteen Canadian fur traders had decided to band together for protection, and Alexander Henry was one of them. Together they formed the North West Company. By the time Astor arrived in Montreal, the company had established 117 trading posts around the Great Lakes to buy furs from Indian and European (mostly French) trappers. Every year the managers of these posts gathered at Fort Williams to exchange news and bring pelts to the company's warehouse. By the time Astor had arrived in Montreal in 1788, the company had located its largest trading post on Michilimackinac, an island in Lake Michigan. Henry arranged for Astor to visit and observe the gatherings at Fort Williams and Michilimackinac.

New York base. Astor established a New York base for his fur operations. While continuing to travel to Montreal to buy furs and ship them to market, he now sent some furs home to Sarah to sell in their musical instrument store. Still, he needed to find a reliable

London trader to deal with. By the end of 1790 he had made several trips to England and had established a business relationship with Thomas Backhouse, a London merchant. Ships carrying his casks of furs to Backhouse were returned with goods to sell in the United States. Casks marked with the Astor mark, J-JA, became familiar items aboard British ships.

Participation: The American Fur Companies

Sir Alexander MacKenzie. In 1793 a Canadian named Sir Alexander MacKenzie proposed that all the American fur business be brought together by building a series of trading posts from ocean to ocean. The trading posts were to be connected by wagon or river trails. Then in 1794 Chief Justice John Jay secured a treaty with the British. It lifted the requirement that American furs be sold in Great Britain. Now Astor was free to sell the furs he bought in Montreal and Quebec anywhere in the world.

The Value of Furs in the 1790s
Bought from Indians
10 beaver skins = 1 gun
8 beaver skins = 1 blanket
5 beaver skins = 1 petticoat
Price in London Market in American Money
1 beaver skin = $7.00

He began to bring his furs to New York and ship them from there to markets throughout Europe. To supply his needs, he contracted with fur traders to buy large numbers of furs—such large numbers that he was really buying the trader's catch for the entire next year. These contracts helped him control the cost of pelts from the traders, who became reliable business associates. Astor, however, had little respect for the traders, finding them too lazy and too independent to suit him. He preferred men who followed orders.

Trade with China. By 1800 Astor was ready to take control of his own shipping and explore new markets. He chartered the ship *Severn* and sent it to Canton with a shipment of furs. It returned eighteen months later with a cargo of silks and chinaware for sale in the United States. China was the world's largest potential market, but the travel time from the East Coast was too great. Astor began to dream of a port in the Northwest that could be used for the trade in beaver pelts with China. He also dreamed of trading the fur of the

The Cataract of NIAGARA, some make this Water-Fall to be half a League while others reckon it no more than a hundred Fathom.

▲ Trappers told tall tales about the industrous beavers

Pacific Ocean sea otter, whose smooth skin was in high demand. In less than five years, Astor would own the *Severn* and three other ships.

American patriotism. The travels of Lewis and Clark between 1804 and 1806 showed that a chain of trading posts suggested by MacKenzie eleven years earlier was, indeed, possible. Until that time, the fur trade in the Northwest Territory and as far west as the Rocky Mountains had been controlled by Canadian companies. The men who blazed the trails west had been, for the most part, French Canadians.

Although Jay's Treaty had made the time ripe for expansion of an American company, the American government stood in the way. Government trading posts competed with the private companies in the West and President Thomas Jefferson did nothing to discourage this unfair competition. In fact, he added a new problem for businessmen. In 1807, just as Astor was beginning to expand his trade with China, the president placed an embargo on trade with Britain and France. The embargo and British retaliation placed severe restrictions on American ships sailing anywhere.

Tricking a president. Astor was not to be drawn away from trade with China by a presidential edict. Instead he found a friend who knew the president, Senator Mitchell of New York, and persuaded him to carry a message to Jefferson that a Chinese merchant had come to America on business and now found it nearly impossible to return home. Since "Punqua Wingchong" was an important businessman, Astor asked the president if he could send one of his own ships, the *Beaver*, to take Wingchong home. The unsuspecting Jefferson approved. The *Beaver* sailed with the mysterious Punqua Wingchong and furs for the China trade valued at 45,000 dollars. The ship returned with 500,000 pounds of tea along with silk and china for sale in America. Punqua Wingchong was never heard from again.

Aiming for high profits, the businessman was committed only to himself. He seemed to take no interest in democracy or the welfare of America. Yet, strangely enough, he became the first American to corner a large share of the fur business as he continued to play on American patriotism.

He asked Jefferson to grant him exclusive rights for a company that would compete with the two Canadian fur giants: the North West Company and the Michilimackinac Company. Jefferson approved the idea and Astor made plans to build a series of trading post/forts along the Missouri and Columbia rivers. Never one to begin any adventure unprepared, Astor looked for experienced traders in the North West Company and made them partners in a new Pacific Fur Company. Each partner received small amounts of stock in the company, while Astor retained half of the total value of the venture.

Eventually, the Astor organization began to buy out the Canadian competitors until there were virtually only the Astor companies and the Hudson Bay Company in the far north. Astor was, however, primarily a merchant, not a fur trader. When the businesses he bought up began to wane, he found another use for his minor partners; he sold the worn-out businesses to them.

Astoria. An important part of the Astor plan was the Pacific Coast trade center that he had proposed to build: a fort and port called Astoria near the mouth of the Columbia River. This was to be the Pacific terminal of the string of trading posts along the Missouri and Columbia rivers. Astor's Pacific Fur Company began to explore sites for the base in the early 1800s, then sent a team to build Astoria. First to arrive was a sea party under Captain Jonathan Thorn. Unfortunately, Thorn knew little about Indians and fur trading. So a company partner aboard his ship the *Tonquin* selected a spot near Baker's Bay at the mouth of the Columbia River. The partner stayed to supervise the building of Astoria while Captain Thorn sailed north in search of furs.

When Thorn tried to trade with the coastal Indian tribes, however, he angered them. Offering to make peace, about 200 Indians boarded the *Tonquin* and pretended to trade furs for knives. They promptly used the knives to kill or wound nearly all the crew. The next day, the same Indians returned and were welcomed aboard by a survivor, Mr. Lewis. Lewis then blew up the ship's powder magazine, sinking both the ship and the Indians. The year was 1811. A famous author of the day, Washington Irving, wrote about the settlement and the incident in his book, *Astoria*:

> Arms, legs, and mutilated bodies were blown into the air and dreadful havoc was made in the surrounding canoes ... the bay presented an awful spectacle after the catastrophe. The ship had disappeared but the bay was covered with ... Indians swimming for their lives or struggling in the agonies of death. (Irving, p. 113)

Upon learning of the tragedy, Astor did not even interrupt his visit to the opera. His attitude seemed to be that the incident had already

▲ **Fort Astoria**

happened and he could do nothing about it. Perhaps his feelings were cooled by the misdeeds of Thorn, who had left three company partners at the southern tip of Chile and had so angered his crew that some abandoned ship in Hawaii. Besides that, Astor had already sent supplies to Astoria on another ship, the *Beaver.*

The land party. Seven months later a land party, which had followed the trail of Lewis and Clark, arrived at Astoria, and the post began its fur trading. Few people in the West seemed aware of the British-American problems that were about to erupt into the War of 1812. The war spread over the continent and in 1814 a contingent of members of the Canadian North West Company arrived in Astoria proposing that Astor sell everything to that company rather than have the town blown up by a nearby British frigate. The American Fur Company sold its holdings, which included more than 200,000 dollars worth of furs for 80,000 dollars. Astor vowed to get the money back and did within the year by investing 2 million dollars in government bonds issued to pay off the war debt. He also managed to get a shipment through the British blockade and continue his trade with Europe and China.

War of 1812. The war between the two countries was a bother for Astor. He continued to buy furs in Montreal and smuggle them to New York for shipment, but England was blockading American ships. To get around the British blockade, Astor persuaded a French general, Jean Victor Marie Moreau, to offer his services to the British. Astor then convinced the British to let him transport the general to Europe in one of his ships, the *Hannibal.* Naturally, Astor's ship transported more than 50,000 animal skins along with the general.

Astor and Sons. Astor stepped-up operations in Europe and the United States once the war ended in 1815. By then he was firmly established on three continents as a millionaire merchant. In an effort to strengthen his position in European trade, Astor invited former Secretary of the Treasury Albert Gallatin to become a partner in his organization. When Gallatin refused, Astor decided that he would make his son William a partner. William had been educated at Heidelberg University and Gottingen University. Father and son revived the old American Fur Company.

Now Astor began to build the string of trading posts from the plains to the Pacific. When the federal government's bureaucracies slowed his efforts in Michigan, he enlisted the governor of that state, Lewis Cass, to plead his case and win his way. It was later revealed that Astor had paid Cass 15,000 dollars for his efforts.

Across America. With ever-increasing power and wealth, Astor attacked yet another business opponent. George Washington had been the first to propose that the government establish trading posts or "factories" in frontier lands to conduct trade with the Indians. These government-supported factories had grown in number and were competition to Astor. He now had the money to destroy them. Astor instructed his agents to tempt the Indians away from the liquor-free government posts with whiskey. In 1822, while he was traveling in Europe, Astor and others who were opposed to these government posts finally succeeded. Congress voted to do away with them. The path was now clear for the American Fur Company to expand across the continent.

Company representatives, often ex-officers in the Continental Army, were assigned to develop posts in specific areas of the West. These officers recruited trappers and hunters, sending them in small units to areas likely to be rich in fur-bearing animals. One of Astor's posts was managed by Jim Beckwourth, a trapper who became a chief among the Crow Indians.

Astor's posts also traded with Indian tribes, paying them mostly in liquor. The posts would advance whiskey to Indian trappers against future deliveries of furs, thereby encouraging their dependency on alcohol. In widespread use at Astor's posts, this practice was already popular at the Canadian companies. Astor hired many of his more experienced crew from the rival North West and Michilimackinac Companies; the use of rum for trade continued to be important.

Astor's company developed a large-scale trade across not only America but the world. Furs from all sources were brought to the posts. They were carried next by riverboats to U. S. ports, then by ships to other ports throughout the world.

Sale of the American Fur Company. In the 1830s, the market began to change. Silk began to replace beaver as the material of choice for top hats. The thirst for pelts had thinned the animal population and made trapping more difficult. Trappers had to travel farther into the mountains and stay longer to get their catches. Furs were becoming more expensive to buy and more difficult to sell. In addition, the American Fur Company was beginning to receive complaints about its use of liquor in trade with the Indian tribes. At the same time, Astor's health began to fail. In 1832 he sailed to England for medical help and stayed there for a year and a half. He returned home to find that his wife, brother Henry, and daughter Magdalena had all died while he was away.

Astor had, from the beginning, used the fur trade only as a means to his own goal—to gather money and power. In 1834 he sold the American Fur Company to a group of his regional directors and turned his attention to his real estate.

Aftermath

New York. Astor was extremely thrifty and cautious. He and Sarah stayed in the two rooms at her mother's boarding house until their second child was near birth. Astor then bought a house in the city for 850 dollars. By the early 1800s he had become a millionaire. In 1803 he set out to invest in the growth of New York, buying a large portion of land on Manhattan Island for 184,000 dollars. Other purchases include the Eden Farm, located between present-day Broadway and the Hudson River at about 42nd Street. Each of the next two years, Astor invested additional sums of 80,000 dollars. Among those from whom he bought land were Aaron Burr and Governor George Clinton (from whom he acquired what is now Greenwich Village). He broke these plots into city lots and sold them at a profit.

Even before 1834, Astor began to take a more active interest in his real estate. While away in Europe, he had arranged for workers to begin to tear down a city block of old houses near where he lived. He planned to build a hotel there, the finest in New York. The Astor House had 6 stories, 300 rooms, and 17 bathrooms. Its walnut woodwork and elegant living commanded a daily room rate of two dollars. The rich and famous of the day—for example, Charles Dickens, the Prince of Wales, and Davy Crockett—stayed at the Astor House. When Crockett discovered what it cost to build the Astor House, he is said to have exclaimed, "Lord help the poor bears and beavers!" (Cowles, p. 540).

In 1834 Astor stopped selling land. He instead bought acres and rented lots. In fourteen years he bought over 800,000 dollars worth of property and took in over 1.25 million dollars in rent. His greed seemed to increase with his fortune. Over the years Astor's personality changed. Earlier, he had earned a reputation as a cunning but fair employer and an honest dealer. In later life, he became known as a harsh, selfish, and greedy man.

In his last dozen or so years, Astor, who had earlier traveled upstate and throughout Europe frequently, never left the city of New York. Instead he moved between his home on Broadway and his summer home a few miles away on the East River.

Astoria. In these same years, Astor took an interest in literature. He had met Washington Irving in Paris and hired him to write a book about his attempt to found Astoria. Irving lived in an Astor home while he and his staff created *Astoria*. In the book, Irving presented Astor as the hero of the fur trade.

161

▲ **Astor's New York home**

The New York Library. The scholar Joseph Cogswell also lived with Astor for a time. Cogswell presented him with the plans and the idea to build New York's first public library. However, when Astor learned that the new library would cost 65,000 dollars in the first year, he put off the decision to finance it. He did, however, order one book for the unbuilt library—Audubon's *Birds of America*—for which he paid the pre-publishing price of 1,000 dollars after protesting that he had no money in the bank.

Astor turned eighty years old in 1844. Knowing that his years were numbered, people from all over the world came to stand outside his house, hoping to catch a glimpse of the richest man in America. Astor played his role to the hilt, dressing in rich furs and wearing an ermine cap as he was carried into his ornate sleigh for his brief rides about town.

Meanwhile he continued to tend to his rental property. One story tells of him berating an employee for not collecting rent from a widow whom the employee felt should be given more time to pay. Astor disagreed and sent the employee to collect, but, as the story goes, son William intercepted the collector and paid the rent himself. Whatever the truth of the story, Astor's thrifty attitude earned him blasts from some New Yorkers upon his death. The *New York Herald* claimed that he should pay the city at least 10 million dollars because it grew and made his property valuable. Horace Mann criticized Astor because he had given less than half a million dollars for public projects in his lifetime.

In the end, most of the Astor money went to the Astor family; Astor did not forget any member. He also remembered his interest in Joseph Cogswell and left 400,000 dollars for the construction of New York's first public library. The one surprise item in his will was 50,000 dollars to the city of Waldorf, Germany, for a home for the poor.

Astor died March 29, 1844. When he died, William continued control of the family fortune and, through the careful management learned from his father, added considerably to the 30 million dollars at which his father's estate was valued. William became known as the "Landlord of New York."

For More Information

Cowles, Virginia. *The Astors.* New York: Alfred A. Knopf, 1979.

Haeger, John Denis. *John Jacob Astor: Business and Finance in the Early Republic.* Detroit: Wayne State University Press, 1991.

Thomas, Lately. *The Astor Orphans, A Pride of Lions.* New York: William Morrow, 1971.

Birth of American Literature

1630s

Tales passed on orally by North American Indian tribes are set down in writing by Jesuit missionaries.

1732

Benjamin Franklin prints *Poor Richard's Almanack*.

1789

First American novel written, by William Hill Brown.

1775–1776

Thomas Paine writes *Common Sense;* Thomas Jefferson writes most of the Declaration of Independence.

1775

Phillis Wheatley, a slave, writes poem on George Washington.

1772

Revolution inspires poetry. Philip Freneau and Hugh Henry Brackenridge write "On the Rising Glory of America."

1794

Susanna Rowson's *Charlotte Temple* is printed in America.

1819

Washington Irving publishes collection of short stories, including "Rip Van Winkle."

1823

James Fenimore Cooper writes *The Pioneers*, the first novel in his Leatherstocking series.

1852

William Wells Brown writes *Clotel, the President's Daughter*, first novel by an African American.

1841

James Fenimore Cooper writes *The Deerslayer*, last novel in the Leatherstocking series.

1828

Noah Webster prints *The American Dictionary of the English Language*.

BIRTH OF AMERICAN LITERATURE

The origin of American literature is generally traced back to the early 1800s. In fact, however, the earliest writings were of native American tales recorded by Jesuit missionaries in the 1630s. These native tales, stories of creation, tricksters, heroes, marriage, and journeys to other worlds, constituted the first body of written literature in North America. The European missionaries recorded them as part of their reports on experiences with native Americans of the continent. Most writing for the next two centuries would, like these Jesuit reports, serve some practical purpose.

Purely imaginative stories were frowned upon by most of the serious-minded immigrants of colonial days. They believed writing should be used to serve some useful purpose, not to entertain. Thomas Paine's *Common Sense,* for example, argued in favor of independence from England. The Declaration of Independence, written mainly by Thomas Jefferson, outlined the basic principles of the American democracy.

Yet the seeds of imaginative writing were planted during this period by Benjamin Franklin in *Poor Richard's Almanack,* first published in 1732. Along with the usual information on weather, tides, and eclipses for farmers, these almanacs featured a character called Poor Richard, whose sayings on life, death, doctors, lawyers, drinking, eating, and wealth aimed to instruct and also entertain readers. Some of the sayings were serious; others, comical. Franklin's almanacs became second only to the Bible in popularity throughout the colonies.

The Revolutionary War inspired some poetry but only much later were novels written about it. The first novels in the nation were imported into America from Europe. Then, in 1789, William Hill Brown, an American, wrote *The Power of Sympathy,* a novel about a young man who kills himself after learning that his sweetheart is really his half-sister. The English-American actress Susanna Rowson followed it up with *Charlotte Temple,* a tremendously popular novel first published in England and reprinted in America in 1794. It concerns an English girl tricked into coming to America, where she dies in childbirth after being abandoned by the man who had promised to marry her. Both novels, though set in America, contributed nothing new to fiction-writing.

This changed with the writers of the 1800s, who gave birth to a truly American fiction. In 1819 the publication of *The Sketch Book* by **Washington Irving** marked a milestone in American literature. No American author had yet received the worldwide acclaim accorded Irving. His short stories "Rip Van Winkle" and "The Legend of Sleepy Hollow" would later be considered the first masterpieces of American literature. The stories drew on old German folktales as well as Indian legends, and their setting is American: the Hudson River and the Catskill Mountains of New York. Considered a master of style, Irving used humor and rich descriptive language to create other stories uniquely American in content and tone.

Some Americans, however, continued to regard short stories and novels as inferior even after Irving's success. **Noah Webster,** for one, complained that fiction was harmful, especially to the minds of young readers. Yet Webster, like Irving, laid the groundwork for future American writers. At the time, many words were not spelled in any uniform way, so Webster took on the task of creating order out of disorder. He wrote books on spelling and grammar that were used by schoolchildren throughout the country. Webster is perhaps best known, though, for his *The American Dictionary of the English Language,* first printed in 1828, and still widely used today in a revised form.

While Webster and others continued to frown on reading fiction, its popularity grew in America. **James Fenimore Cooper,** writing at the same time that Webster assembled his dictionary, was the first to earn worldwide respect for the American novel. From the 1820s to the 1840s Cooper wrote a series of five novels known as *The Leatherstocking Tales.* Writing in the style of British authors of his day such as Jane Austen, who created stories about family life, and Walter Scott, who wrote tales that mixed history with fiction, Cooper forged a new path for American novelists by creating a distinctly American main character, Natty Bumppo. A hero of the American forest, Bumppo was neither completely savage nor completely civilized. Cooper gave Natty a self-reliant, pioneering spirit, traits Americans could call their own with pride. The author also wrote fine action-filled chase scenes; Cooper, in fact, excelled in the escape-chase adventure pattern, which runs through the five novels of the series.

Early fiction helped shape a separate American identity out of the mix of immigrants and natives that made up the nation. Native Americans figured prominently in some stories by Irving and Cooper. Irving based the plot in "Rip Van Winkle" in part on an Indian legend, and Cooper featured some of the first native American characters in his novels, though he was faulted for creating unrealistic ones. In 1852 William Wells Brown wrote *Clotel, the President's Daughter,* the first published novel by an African American. He, along with other writers, added to the foundation laid in the early 1800s. Others would later build on this base to more fully develop the American short story and novel in the nineteenth century.

Noah Webster

1758-1843

Personal Background

"I wish to enjoy life, but books and business will ever be my principal pleasure. I must write; it is a happiness I cannot sacrifice" (Rollins, *The Autobiographies,* p. 5). These words, which Noah Webster wrote to George Washington in 1785, capture Webster's devotion to words and writing. He wrote so much that a bibliography of his works would fill 600 pages. His *American Spelling Book* became, next to the Bible, the top-selling book in the country.

Early years and family. The fourth of five children, Noah Webster was born October 16, 1758, on a small farm in West Hartford, Connecticut. His ancestors had lived in New England almost since the days of the first pilgrims. In fact, his mother, Mercy Steele Webster, was the great-great-granddaughter of William Bradford, the second governor of Plymouth Colony in Massachusetts. His father, Noah Webster, Sr., descended from John Webster, one of the founders and a former governor of the Connecticut colony. Webster's father owned a ninety-acre farm that he struggled to make productive. The elder Webster also worked as a justice of the peace for the state legislature and as a deacon at his church. Apparently, Noah was not very close with his parents, for in all of his later writing he barely mentioned either his mother or father.

Noah's childhood was like that of most children raised under

▲ Noah Webster

Event: Shaping and defining an American cultural identity.

Role: Called America's schoolmaster, Noah Webster worked to shape the American educational system, thereby influencing the new country's culture. His crowning achievement was to single-handedly compile *The American Dictionary* of the English language, which became a literary standard.

similar circumstances in the mid-1700s. Most New England children grew up on farms, sharing in the daily chores and getting some schooling when their parents could spare them from the fields. Younger children went to school during the summer, while the older children attended during winter months and worked on the farm the rest of the year. Young Noah was not the most hard-working farm boy, for his father often found him reading under the shade of a tree when he should have been working on the farm.

Education. Noah's natural leaning toward books convinced his father to allow him to study with Reverend Nathan Perkins, a pastor at the West Hartford Church and a graduate of Princeton. The young pastor tutored Noah in a range of subjects to prepare him for college. Noah entered Yale in 1774, joining a growing number of young men who traveled from all over the colonies to attend college. These young men had more choices and, in some ways, fewer opportunities than their fathers. Earlier generations had grown up knowing they would inherit a parcel of their father's land. Now, with a limited amount of land and a growing population, young men were forced to decide what they would do for a living and to carve out their own futures. Noah was no different from his classmates; there was no future for him on his father's small farm. His father supported his decision to go to Yale, but had to mortgage his farm to pay Noah's way through school. Noah never repaid the loan, and, his father, unable to honor his debt, eventually lost the farm.

Revolution broke out while Noah was still in school, and the war had a strong effect on him and his classmates. In the winter of 1776, Yale had to send students home because the school was running out of money and food. However, the raging fight for independence affected the young men's minds and hearts more than their stomachs. As they watched their world transform, the young students saw for themselves a future filled with possibilities. The valedictorian address given by Timothy Dwight to the class of 1776 illustrates the mix of responsibility and excitement that the students felt about their role in forging a new nation:

> You should by no means consider yourselves as members of a small neighborhood, town or colony only, but as being concerned in laying the foundations of American greatness. Your wishes,

your designs, your labors, are not to be confined by the narrow bounds of the present age, but are to comprehend succeeding generations, and be pointed to immortality.... Remember that you are to act for the empire of America. (Morgan, p. 19)

At the same time, ideas from the Enlightenment influenced the educated people of the late 1700s. This movement, which originated in Europe and especially France, emphasized the power of human reason. Educated people looked to science as a way of understanding God and the universe. Enlightened thinkers believed that a person determined his or her own fate, and could improve it through education and reason. Many felt that America was the perfect place to put such theories to the test. These ideas, of course, influenced Noah Webster; he developed a strong and lasting interest in science and a deep nationalistic pride. His essays about America describe it as the "empire of reason" (Rollins, *The Long Journey,* p. 16).

During his years at Yale, Webster gained an education that would enable him to pursue a literary and scholarly career. Although he showed promise, rough edges had begun to surface in his personality. Throughout his life he was often described as self-promoting, vain, and self-involved. He may not have been very popular with his Yale classmates, for his tutor, Joseph Buckminster, suggested that he tone down his forceful nature and be less haughty because people "will be disposed to ridicule you and perhaps set you down among those who have too high an opinion of their importance" (Moss, p. 4).

Schoolteacher. After Yale, Webster struggled to find his life's work. With a war going on, it was a difficult time to start a career. He hoped to go into the legal profession, but did not have the finances to devote himself to study. His father, making it clear that he could offer his son no help or support, turned Webster away from the family farm.

Depressed and uncertain of what to do, Webster spent three days alone in his room considering his future. Having few options open to him, he decided to go into teaching. For the next couple of years he taught at several schools in Connecticut. Although he began taking an interest in the American educational system and suggesting reforms, Webster was not very happy with his chosen profession. This was understandable since teachers worked for low pay and were near the bottom of the social scale. Webster complained, "It's a poor business, the wages not equivalent to a support, and the knowledge gained by it not worth a farthing. I shall soon dismiss it" (Morgan, p. 31).

Meanwhile, he managed to study law and eventually passed the bar. Now he could sign his name Noah Webster, Junior, Esquire, Attorney at Law, which he seemed to enjoy doing even though he had few chances to apply his legal training. There were already too many lawyers in New England, and Webster had a hard time competing. By 1780 he had turned back to teaching and opened his own school in Sharon, Massachusetts.

Rejection and failure. In Sharon, Webster fell in love twice; both times he was rejected. The young schoolmaster had red hair and a proud, jutting chin; he was slim and of average height. He was also quite sociable, especially with women, and the ladies probably found him attractive. However, the first woman who captured Webster's heart, Juliana Smith, thought he was vain and snubbed him. Commenting on a fable he had written for a magazine, Smith wrote: "Mr. Webster has not the excuse of youth ... but his essays ... are as young as yours or brother Tommy's while his reflections are as prosy [commonplace] as those of our horse.... In conversation he is even duller than in his writing" (Morgan, p. 35). Although Webster probably never read these stinging words, he must have felt the blow of Smith's distaste for him.

Soon after, another woman, Rebecca Pardee, was more encouraging toward Webster but ultimately just as disappointing. Webster fell in love with her, spent several months courting her, and then proposed marriage. Sadly, Pardee had another boyfriend—an officer in the army—and when he returned from war, she chose him over Webster.

Emotionally wounded, Webster closed his school and left Sharon. In the three years since graduating from Yale, he had moved seven times, going from one job to another, switching from teaching to law and back again. He was always in debt, and in love he had been rejected twice. After wandering around New England, he ended up in Goshen, New York, with seventy-five cents in his pockets. There he spent the winter, suffering "extreme depression and gloomy forebodings" (Rollins, *The Long Journey,* p. 22). Years later he would remember this time with painful clarity. However, it was during this period that Webster began to focus on his future and find a purpose for his life. From this point on, Webster devoted himself to language and writing.

Participation:
Shaping and Defining American Culture

Early writings. As a schoolteacher, Webster had become interested in educational reform and had begun writing his ideas down. He criticized the crowded classrooms in American schools. Commonly, schools packed seventy to eighty students into one classroom with one teacher. Webster proposed twenty to twenty-five students per teacher, saying this would offer students more opportunity for individualized instruction. He also spoke out for a less commanding teaching style, believing that children should be encouraged to enjoy learning rather than being frightened or forced into it. Many of his ideas were very much ahead of their time; some were applied in his day and some were not.

Webster spoke out for more than educational reform. He wrote books, pamphlets, and essays in support of the principles for which he believed the revolution had been fought. Many of these principles had their roots in Enlightenment philosophy. Webster, a fierce nationalist, pushed for such values as social equality, abolition of slavery, separation of church and state, and religious tolerance. His goal was to help Americans to develop a cultural identity all their own, separate from England. What better place to accomplish this than in the schools?

The American Speller. While living in Goshen, Webster completed a book that would not only educate the children of America, but also introduce them to nationalist ideas and themes to build what Webster saw as an American cultural identity. Before this, American schoolchildren had been learning from books written in England by English people teaching English customs, loyalties, and geography. Webster planned a set of three books that would educate American children not only in the basics of reading, spelling, and writing, but also about customs and ideas unique to their country. Webster saw this as a final way of cutting ties with England. "America must be as independent in *literature* as she is in *politics*," he declared to a friend, "as famous for *arts* as for *arms*, and it is not impossible but a person of my youth may have some influence in exciting a spirit of literary industry" (Rollins, *The Long Journey*, p. 36).

Spelling Changes That Webster Introduced

British Spelling	American Spelling
honour, colour, valour	honor, color, valor
theatre, centre	theater, center
publick, musick	public, music
gaol	jail
plough	plow
axe	ax
draught	draft
mould	mold

The speller introduced students first to letters and their sounds, then to groups of letters, and finally to full words. It also presented complete sentences and included short fables that contained moral lessons. Webster's speller made several improvements on previous spellers. For example, he divided words into syllables in ways that made it easier for the student to learn: *ha-bit* became *hab-it, le-mon* became *lem-on,* and *va-lor* became *val-or.* He also made the endings *tion* and *sion* into one syllable, whereas before they had been two (e.g., *na-ti-on* became *na-tion.*)

Of the three books in the set, the spelling book was by far the most popular. In 1783 Webster paid for the paper, ink, and labor to have 5,000 copies of the speller published. Initially, he called the book *A Grammatical Institute of the English Language,* but renamed it *The American Speller* in 1787 and *The Elementary Spelling Book* in 1829. The little blue book, 119-pages long, became one of the best-selling books in American history. Estimates place the number of copies sold at about 100 million. By the mid-1800s, more than 150 editions of the book had been published and Webster had revised it four times. Proceeds from the book would help support Webster until his death.

The American Speller was the product of Webster's attempt to standardize the American language while providing a consistent and complete system of education. He sums up his goal for the book in his introduction:

It is the business of Americans to select the wisdom of all nations as the basis of her constitutions,—to avoid their errors,—to prevent the introduction of foreign vices and corruptions and check the career of her own,—to promote virtue and patriotism, to embellish and improve the sciences,—to diffuse an uniformity and purity of language,—to add superior dignity to this infant Empire and to human nature. (Morgan, p. 47)

The American Magazine. In the years immediately following the publication of *The American Speller,* Webster returned to Hartford for a time and then began to travel through the South and New England. He promoted his book and lectured on the need for a standardized American language. Around this time, he also began to lobby for a national copyright law, a cause to which he devoted much effort and which he eventually won.

In 1787 Webster moved to New York to start *The American Magazine.* In this short-lived venture, he sought to provide readers with a national voice on a wide range of subjects, including history, geography, science, satire, poetry, economics, and the Constitution. A primary focus of the magazine, however, was educational reform in America. Webster also used the magazine to deliver an antislavery message; he was a fervent abolitionist. As editor Webster wrote many of the articles under the pseudonym "Giles Hickory." He worked tirelessly to keep the magazine going, but public interest waned; when the magazine folded in 1788, it had only 200 subscribers.

Webster's personality made him few friends in New York. Although he had become a national figure by this time and knew such key personalities as George Washington, Benjamin Franklin, and James Madison, he apparently was not well liked. His vain, brusque, overbearing manner made him many enemies. He was often criticized in biting satires that made fun of his shortcomings. One story illustrated his excessive pride: In reply to a friend congratulating him upon his arrival in Philadelphia, Webster supposedly said, "Sir, you may congratulate Philadelphia on the occasion" (Morgan, p. 106). Further evidence of Webster's tiresome character is his writing of a sixty-four-page pamphlet in response to a critic who accused him of being a sciolist, a person having only a superficial show of learning.

Webster seems to have been more popular with women than with men, and after his initial rejections in love, was able to find a loving and well-suited mate. In 1789 he married Rebecca Greenleaf. After years of wandering and struggling to establish himself, marriage and family provided Webster with the security he needed to continue with his writing career. Interestingly, in sharp contrast to his public relationships, Webster was a warm, loving, and devoted husband and father; he treated his wife with caring respect and showed deep concern for the welfare of their eight children.

The American Dictionary of the English Language.
Early in his career, Webster had set out to develop and define a language uniquely American. Yet nearly a half-century later, when he published *The American Dictionary,* he described the work as being of the English language, not the American language. In the end, a separate American language became less important to Webster than what he saw as a need for a regular, dependable, uniform way of writing and speaking. In fact, his purpose for writing the dictionary was to preserve the similarities between the two languages. The huge shift in Webster's thinking in his later years is evident in a message he included with a copy of the dictionary that he sent to Queen Victoria in 1841: "Our common language is one of the ties that bind two nations together; I hope the works I have executed will manifest [show] to the British nation that the Americans are not willing to suffer it [the English language] to degenerate [decline] on this side of the Atlantic" (Rollins, *The Long Journey,* p. 127). Whereas sixty years before, he had struggled to separate America as far as possible from the mother country, now he sought to highlight their common ties.

Webster's dictionary filled a definite need. Although Samuel Johnson's English dictionary was widely circulated, even the most educated people still maintained a fairly casual attitude toward spelling. A look at writings from the eighteenth century and earlier shows different spellings for the same words. Many people in the developing country also saw the need for careful and clear definitions of words. Rufus King, one of Webster's strongest supporters, claimed that words such as *liberty, democracy,* and *honor* were "in the mouth of everyone and used without precision by anyone; the abuse of words is as pernicious [destructive] as the abuse of things" (Rollins, *The Long Journey,* p. 124).

At the same time, however, many critics ridiculed Webster for his efforts. Such criticism was not unknown to Webster, who, though respected by many, was often treated with scorn by others. When Webster first announced his plan for a dictionary, printers attacked him for the idea.

Sensitive to criticism, Webster altered many of his ideas in the years he spent writing the dictionary. As a young man, he had urged radical reform in spelling. Although some of his spellings were accepted, many others were seen as ridiculous and unnecessary. In his earlier writings, Webster wanted to change the spellings of the words in column one to the spellings listed in column two:

bread	bred
mean	meen
head	hed
grief	greef
health	helth
wrong	rong
tongue	tung
breath	breth
is	iz
determine	determin

He let go of this position in the face of criticism, but still managed to bring about some significant and lasting changes in spelling.

Webster spent twenty-five years completing the monumental work. At first he sought only to assemble a dictionary that would correct errors in earlier dictionaries and to add new words that had since entered the language. As he set about his task, however, he soon became immersed in the study of language and the roots of words. In his office at home in Amherst, Massachusetts, where he had moved for financial reasons, he wrote endlessly at his desk. Some of his research involved sitting at a semicircular table covered with dictionaries from twenty languages. Moving from one end of the table to the other on a chair set on wheels, he would trace a word through the different languages, making notes as he went. Eventually, the strain on his hands from writing continuously caused him constant pain and soreness.

The final result was an achievement worthy of Webster's untiring and devoted effort. The dictionary contained 70,000 words with definitions that were more complete and more modern than previous dictionaries. Webster had achieved more working entirely alone than the Englishman Samuel Johnson had with the help of several assistants. And, at 58,000 words, Johnson's dictionary was smaller. Surprisingly, Webster's dictionary at first sold better in England than in America. Not long after publication, *The American Dictionary* became the standard dictionary for the English-speaking world.

Aftermath

Later works. When he finished the dictionary, Webster felt satisfied that he had completed his life's work. Yet he also had accomplished many other achievements of note in his busy and active life. In 1799 he completed a study of the causes and treatment of epidemic diseases, entitled *A Brief History of Epidemics and Pestilential Diseases.* This well-researched work is still valued by medical historians. In 1814 Webster helped to found Amherst Academy, which later became Amherst College, serving as president in 1820.

In his long life, Webster underwent many changes in his thinking and positions on important issues. He acknowledged this by quoting Benjamin Franklin, who said, "I have been all my life changing my opinions." To this, Webster added, "Now at seventy-six years of age, I can say the same thing" (Rollins, *The Long Journey,* p. 139). In his youth, Webster was a liberal idealist who believed fiercely in the potential of the young nation. In his old age he became increasingly conservative, believing more in authority and less in the power or rights of the people. As a young man, religion had meant little to him, but when he was fifty, he underwent a conversion to Christianity that was to have a powerful effect on the remainder of his life.

After publishing the dictionary, Webster continued to keep busy into his eighties. In 1833 he published his own version of the King James Bible. A year later he published *Value of the Bible.* Meanwhile, he kept up steady correspondences and remained interested in politics and national affairs.

Last years. Around 1840, however, Webster began to slow down his pace and withdraw from public life. He spent his last years quietly and peacefully, focusing mostly on his private life with his family. Webster died at age eighty-four on May 28, 1843. Today in the United States, the dictionary that bears his name remains the standard for the spelling and definition of the English language.

For More Information

Morgan, John S. *Noah Webster.* New York: Mason/Charter, 1975.

Moss, Richard J. *Noah Webster.* Boston: Twayne Publishers, 1984.

Rollins, Richard M. *The Autobiographies of Noah Webster: From the Letters and Essays, Memoir, and Diary.* Columbia: University of South Carolina Press, 1989.

Rollins, Richard M. *The Long Journey of Noah Webster.* Philadelphia: University of Pennsylvania Press, 1980.

Washington Irving

1783-1859

Personal Background

Family and childhood. Washington Irving was born in New York City on April 3, 1783, just five days before the official end of the American Revolution. In honor of the occasion, his parents named him Washington, after the famous general who had helped lead American forces to victory.

Washington's father, William, had immigrated from Scotland to the colonies some twenty years earlier with his wife, an Englishwoman named Sarah Sanders. In America, he built a fairly profitable business trading wine, sugar, and hardware. Washington was the youngest of eight children, and he received the pampering and coddling that children in that position often do. Somewhat spoiled and very much loved, he grew into a sociable, easygoing, and likeable man, though he sometimes was prone to long periods of melancholy and depression.

Although the family was warm and loving—Irving maintained strong and affectionate bonds with his siblings throughout his life—William Irving, a Presbyterian deacon, insisted on a strict and serious household. The Irving children were not allowed to dance, to attend the theater, or to engage in light reading. Furthermore, all of them had to participate in long nightly prayers. Such severe rules went against the grain of young Washington's lighthearted, spirited,

Event: The birth of American literature.
Role: With his essays, short stories, and historical pieces, Washington Irving helped establish the international reputation of American literature.

▲ Washington Irving

and friendly personality. He came to view religion as being against everything he found pleasant. However, his spirit was too strong to be broken or even subdued. He rebelled against his father's rules by sneaking out at night to see plays in the nearby theater district. After catching the first act, he would return home in time for nightly prayers and pretend to go to bed. Then he would crawl out his bedroom window, climb down a tree, and run back to the theater just in time to catch the last act of the play.

> ## Washington Irving Meets His Namesake
>
> At age six, young Washington had the good fortune to meet his namesake. While out with his nurse, Lizzie, the boy saw George Washington ride past on his large white horse and dismount in front of a nearby store. Boldly, Lizzie pushed her way through the crowd that had gathered and introduced the young boy to the president of the new United States. President Washington looked down at the small boy, kindly shook his hand, and gave him his blessing.

In school Washington was a poor student. He did not excel in any subject and he never learned how to spell very well. Small for his age and sensitive, he was a playful and dreamy boy. At school, he often neglected his studies to read fairy tales or adventure books such as *Robinson Crusoe.*

Sometimes he played hooky to wander through the woods and fields that still covered much of Manhattan. Though a bustling and important center, New York had only 60,000 inhabitants and was a small town compared to the metropolis it is today. In the late 1700s horse-drawn wagons clattered down the city's cobblestone streets, while on the nearby Hudson, ships from all over the world brought and carried goods. In the midst of all this activity, the Irving family lived a fairly quiet life, keeping much to themselves and too poor to be a part of New York's high society.

Legal work. At sixteen, instead of following his brothers to college at Columbia, Irving made a decision that he would later regret. He decided to stop his education and enter the legal profession. Though he spent six years studying law and eventually passed the bar examination, he found the work uninspiring and tedious. To relieve his boredom, Irving secretly began to take dance lessons and learn the flute. He also began to write during this time. His first efforts were humorous essays on the theater and New York society. Irving's first published writing, *The Letters of Jonathon Oldstyle, Gent,* appeared in the *Morning Chronicle* on November 15, 1802, when he was just nineteen years old.

On the continent. After a few tedious years working in law, Irving's family sent him on a two-year journey to Europe in the winter of 1804. His health was poor and they thought the trip would give him renewed strength. In fact, this trip would be just the first of Irving's many adventurous travels to exotic parts of the world. In Europe he visited London, Paris, Rome, and Sicily, among other places, spending months at a time in each location.

Wherever he went, Irving's happy and pleasant manner, his good heart, and his desire to be liked won him many friends. He enjoyed a lively social life, regularly attending parties, balls, and the theater. A handsome man with blue eyes and dark brown hair, Irving was popular with women.

Throughout his travels in Europe, Irving kept a detailed journal, making careful observations about the people and places he saw. His intent was to take these rough notes and shape them first into letters and later into complete works. During this trip alone he compiled six volumes worth of notes.

Salmagundi. In spring 1806 Irving returned to New York a more mature and worldly young man. His health was improved and he was in high spirits, until he realized that he would have to return to working at law. Halfheartedly, Irving went back to legal work, though he still found time to pursue his growing interest in writing.

With his three brothers and several friends, Irving formed a literary club. They called themselves Salmagundi, which stands for a spicy salad of meat, anchovies, peppers, and onions. The purpose of their literary efforts was "to instruct the young, reform the old, correct the town, and castigate [criticize] the age" (Williams I, p. 82). The highly popular *Salmagundi Papers,* published in 1807, were satirical, humorous, and gossip-filled essays that spoke about current issues and goings-on around the city.

The literary club was also a social club, and Irving spent much of his time engaged in mindless fun—drinking, dancing at balls, going to parties, and flirting with ladies. However, his carefree, lighthearted approach to life soon changed when Irving fell deeply in love.

Matilda Hoffman. In his early career in law, Irving had worked as a clerk for an attorney named Josiah Hoffman. Though Irving was not the most praiseworthy worker, Mr. Hoffman liked the amiable young man and began inviting him on social outings with his family. A strong and lasting friendship developed between Irving and the Hoffman family, especially with the two teenaged girls, Ann and Matilda. At first, it seemed Irving's eye would settle on the older, more sophisticated, and vivacious Ann, but over the years, he slowly developed a deep and abiding love for Matilda, who was shy, serious, and soft-spoken. By the time he was in his early twenties, Irving was visiting the Hoffman's every day, but it was not until he was twenty-five, and she, seventeen, that he finally realized the depth of his feelings for Matilda.

The couple became engaged, and Irving, somewhat reluctantly, accepted Hoffman's offer to join him as a partner in his law firm. Although Irving still hated the law, he had no choice but to accept this generous offer. He wanted to marry Matilda and he had to prove to her father that he could take care of her. He demonstrated his devotion to Matilda by buckling down to work hard without complaint at the profession he hated.

In 1809, before they could marry, Matilda died unexpectedly of pneumonia. The loss crushed Irving; he sank into a depression for many months, a depression from which he finally emerged when he began to write again. In fact, this crisis was the starting point of Irving's serious literary career.

Participation: The Birth of American Literature

American literature in the early 1800s. An American writer in the early nineteenth century had several advantages over writers of earlier centuries. First, printing was becoming increasingly widespread, so the number of published books was growing at a rapid rate. Newspapers and magazines also were gaining popularity and being produced in large numbers; in 1801 approximately 200 newspapers were being published in the country. And writers were benefiting from new protections under a 1790 copyright law that prevented their work from being used without their permission. With all this, writers had many more opportunities to have their writing published. Meanwhile Americans were fast becoming avid readers and enjoyed reading works by writers from their own country.

Irving answered this need with a form of writing that was still not accepted in some literary circles: fiction. Literary and political figures such as Thomas Jefferson and Noah Webster (see **Noah Webster**) scorned fiction, believing that it would corrupt impressionable young minds with false ideas about the world. However, by the late 1700s fiction was growing in popularity and readers increasingly demanded more stories by and about Americans.

A History of New York. Irving wrote his first major work after Matilda's death. He spent several months at an old farmhouse outside the city recuperating from his grief and writing in solitude. Interestingly, during this time of sorrow and depression, he wrote a humorous history of New York, which he introduced to the public through a hoax in the daily newspaper.

On October 26, 1809, readers of the New York *Evening Post* puzzled over the following piece of news about an old Dutchman who apparently was missing:

> Left his lodging some time since, and has not been heard of, a small elderly gentleman, dressed in an old black coat and cocked hat, by the name of KNICKERBOCKER. As there are some reasons for believing he is not entirely in his right mind, and as great anxiety is entertained about him, any information concerning him ... will be greatly appreciated. (Williams I, p. 112)

Nearly two weeks later came a letter in response (written, as the first piece of news had been, by Irving) to this plea for help in finding the elderly Knickerbocker. The writer claimed to have spotted the old man. Now the city was abuzz with gossip about this curious mystery. When it was reported (again by Irving) that a manuscript was found in the old man's hotel room, the public eagerly waited to see the writing in print.

Irving's first large work, published under the name of his imaginary missing Dutchman, Diedrich Knickerbocker, was thus received with much excitement. Though it did well and he earned a good deal of money from it—3,000 dollars—he was still very depressed. He wrote that he "cared nothing for the money, it seemed to come too late to do me good. . . . I could not bring myself to write, I had grown indifferent to literary reputation. I felt a degree of apathy growing on me, which was dismal" (Seton, p. 49).

Irving put away his pen for a long while and joined his brothers as a silent partner in their hardware and cutlery business.

The Sketch Book. Just as Matilda's death had impelled him to write, Irving began his second serious literary work after more crises upset his life. In 1815, depressed and bored with his life in New York, he left for England, "determined to break off from idle habits, idle associates, and fashionable dissipation [wastefulness]" (Seton, p. 55).

In England Irving visited his brother Peter and his sister Sally Van Wart and her family. He was soon caught up in the social whirl of London, enjoying his time with his family and friends. This happiness was shaken, however, when he learned that the family business back home was failing and his brothers were nearly bankrupt. Adding to this misfortune, Irving's mother had died, and the loss left him deeply grieved.

For the first time in years, Irving turned to writing to help cope with his feelings of grief and sorrow. He also wanted to do everything he could to help his brothers, and a successful book could bring the family money to help the failing business.

The result of his efforts, *The Sketch Book,* is a collection of short fictional stories set in England and America. First published in 1819 and 1820, the book was printed in both countries. More of Irving's stories were added to the collection in later printings.

"Rip Van Winkle." The two most popular stories from *The Sketch Book* are "Rip Van Winkle" and "The Legend of Sleepy Hollow," both set in the Catskill Mountains of New York. "Rip Van Winkle" is about a henpecked husband who would rather fish or listen to town gossip than work. Rip wanders off high into the mountains with his dog, Wolf, where he witnesses a strange fairyland scene of goblins bowling at nine-pins.

> They were dressed in a quaint, outlandish fashion; some wore short doublets, others jerkins, with long knives in their belts, and most of them had enormous breeches, of similar style with that of the guide's.... One had a large beard, broad face, and small piggish eyes; the face of another seemed to consist entirely of a nose.... They all had beards, of various shapes and colors. (Wagenknecht, p. 37)

▲ Rip Van Winkle

Rip watches the event and drinks the brew that the goblins pass around and soon falls into a deep sleep. Upon waking, the sleepy man returns to town to find his wife and most of his friends dead and gone. After much confusion, he finally realizes that he's been asleep for twenty years. During his long nap, the American Revolution had been fought and won and the thirteen colonies had become the United States of America. Such historical touches, along with the setting of the story and the birthplace of its author, make "Rip Van Winkle" distinctly American. Irving weaves in some Dutch American history and, in a postscript after the story, credits native Americans for the inspiration he got from them: "In old times, say the Indian traditions, there was a kind of Manitou or Spirit, who kept about the wildest recesses of the Catskill Mountains" (Neider, p. 15).

"The Legend of Sleepy Hollow." Also set in New York, "The Legend of Sleepy Hollow," like "Rip Van Winkle," contains distinctly American details. The tale centers around Ichabod Crane, a schoolteacher with a strong interest in witchery and the supernatural. Among Ichabod's belongings is a history from Massachusetts Bay Colony on the subject of witchcraft.

Irving describes Sleepy Hollow as one of the "quietest places in the whole world," where "a drowsy, dreamy influence seems to hang over the land and to pervade the very atmosphere" (Wagenknecht, p. 52). In this otherworldly place, tales abound of ghosts, hauntings, music and voices heard out of nowhere, and other strange happenings. The most eerie and powerful tale in Sleepy Hollow is that of the Headless Horseman, the ghost of a headless soldier who rides through the sleeping land in the dark hours of night. The story recounts Ichabod's courtship of a rich local farm girl, Katrina Van Tassel; his rivalry with Brom Bones, a brawny farm boy also courting Katrina; and, finally, his mysterious end at the hands of the Headless Horseman, who, as it turns out, was probably more bones than spirit.

International literary fame. *The Sketch Book* drew many favorable reviews on both sides of the Atlantic and gave Irving instant and lasting fame. Americans especially appreciated the arrival of a national literary figure. He was respected in the highest literary circles; one friend described him as "the most fashionable fellow of the day" (Williams I, p. 193). The top literary figures of the

▲ **The Headless Horseman of Sleepy Hollow**

time, including the poet Lord Byron, welcomed the newcomer into their fold. The book also made Irving financially well-off; with the money he made from sales, he was able to help his family pull out of their business troubles.

Irving had achieved worldwide popularity and established himself as an important writer. He had also done something beyond this: with the publication of the *The Sketch Book,* Irving helped define the form of the short story. This new type of literature included rich detail, a leisurely pace, an emphasis on atmosphere, and a sharp climax. Many believe that American literature came of age with the short story. The works of American authors began to be taken seriously, as a part of world literature.

Tales by a traveler. Ever restless, Irving left London to spend a year in Paris with his brother Peter. He enjoyed an active social life while working to complete *Christmas at Bracebridge Hall,* a book of sentimental sketches of life in England, focusing especially on Christmas traditions and customs.

After the book's publication in 1822, Irving traveled to Germany, where he lived for more than a year, learning the language, observing the people and their customs, and trying to learn as much local folklore as he could. In Dresden he fell in love for a second time, with an eighteen-year-old girl named Emily Foster. He proposed marriage to her, but she refused him. Although she cared for Irving, who was twenty-two years older than she, Emily did not love him. Irving left Germany crushed, feeling that his time for love and marriage was now behind him.

After this second disappointment in love, Irving returned to Paris to write *Tales of a Traveller,* published in 1824. These stories of Italian thieves, haunted English inns, and other fanciful subjects, were written in haste. The book was not well-received by the critics, who described the work as trivial and shallow with dull, unrealistic plots. They even accused Irving of copying someone else's writing and of being a snob. One critic belittled the work in this way: "Nothing that can excite controversy, nothing that can occasion dissatisfaction; all, pensive, gentlemanly, and subdued; all, trivling and [as] acquiesent [agreeable] as a drawing-room conversation" (Williams I, p. 277).

Irving, who had a strong, lifelong need to be liked, was shocked by the hostile criticism. He thought the book contained some of his best work and was deeply hurt that the critics did not agree. The public, however, enjoyed the book, and in spite of the reviews, the work sold well.

Biography of Columbus. By 1826 Irving had spent eleven years in Europe. Now, at age forty-three, he ventured to Spain, a country whose language, customs, and literature had long fascinated him. With his brother Peter, he traveled by mule across the towering Pyrenees Mountains to what he described as that "stern, melancholy country" (Seton, p. 84). He had been invited to Spain to translate into English a biography of Christopher Columbus. With so many source books at his disposal, some dating back to the twelfth century, Irving became deeply interested in the explorer's life and decided instead to write his own biography of Columbus.

Still stinging from the critics' attacks on *Tales of a Traveller,* Irving wanted to show the literary world that he could produce more serious work than just stories and sketches. He aimed to make his biography "the most complete and authentic account of Columbus and his voyages extant" (Seton, p. 85). Irving labored over the project for two years, working from just after dawn until seven or eight o'clock in the evening. When *The Life and Voyages of Christopher Columbus* was published in 1827, the work was greeted with many positive and appreciative reviews. The critics described the book as detailed, reliable, and exciting.

Return to the States. After this, Irving stayed on in Spain for a while longer, traveling to visit the Alhambra, a Moorish palace in Granada. Later, he published a book of sketches called *The Alhambra,* another critical success, which presents legends of Spain in a style similar to *The Sketch Book.* He spent several more years in Europe, mostly in London.

Finally in 1832, after seventeen years on the continent, Irving returned home. With great excitement, Americans welcomed their beloved national hero, who had achieved worldwide literary fame since leaving the young country. Irving attended a banquet in his honor and, though publicity embarrassed him and he hated speaking before crowds, he gave a moving speech promising to stay in America for the rest of his life.

Aftermath

Diplomat. During his lifetime, Irving had a second career; he served twice as a diplomat for the United States. In 1829, while enjoying the peaceful beauty of the Alhambra, he was summoned by President Andrew Jackson to return to London and serve as a secretary of legation (chief diplomat). Though he was honored by the request and felt duty-bound to serve his country, Irving hated to leave the Alhambra, where he had spent many relaxing months and felt so peacefully at home. Reluctantly, he returned to the fog and bustle of London to work under Louis McLane, minister to England. As secretary of legation, Irving was involved in helping to resolve issues such as American trading rights in the West Indies and the mutual distrust between England and America. Although he accepted the post willingly, he found it demanding, saying that it was "a complete interruption to all his literary avocations [activities]" (Williams II, p. 5).

Two decades later Irving served his country a second time as minister to Spain from 1842 to 1846. This time the request came from President John Tyler, who was relying on Irving's knowledge of the country and the language to help with diplomatic relations between Spain and the United States. The post placed Irving directly at the forefront of a dramatic intrigue taking place in the Spanish Court. The reign of Ferdinand VII's twelve-year-old daughter, Queen Isabella, was being disputed by many people in the country, including Isabella's own uncle. An eighteenth-century Spanish law had ruled that a woman could not reign, but Ferdinand had revoked this law in his will. As a result, the country was torn and at the brink of revolution. Irving felt sympathetic toward the young girl at the center of this controversy and the two became friends. When he left his post to return to America, the young Queen was sad to see him go and commended him by saying that his "frank and loyal conduct has contributed to draw closer the amicable relations which exist between North America and Spain" (Seton, p. 162).

Out West. Irving's travels also included a trip to the American West. At the age of 50 he had a desire to see more of the country he loved, so he ventured on a rough-and-tumble journey by wagon and horseback beginning at the eastern end of the Santa Fe Trail. The man who had spent most of his life enjoying the soft luxuries of genteel society now slept nightly on the cold, bumpy ground, hunted buffalo, braved the threat of Indian attack, and ate whatever food could be caught in the wild, including, on one unhappy occasion, skunk.

From this expedition came two works: *The Western Journals of Washington Irving* and *A Tour on the Prairies*. Both offer readers a vision of the old West in the days before many Americans had traveled across this rough and wild land. Irving paints scenes of buffalo country, wild horses running freely across the open prairies, and encounters with Pawnee Indians. One excerpt describes a busy camp against a background of vivid beauty:

> Picturesque scene of camp—some roasting bear's meat and venison—others stretching and dressing skins … horses feeding…. Camp nearly surrounded by deep glens with clear pools at the bottom, in which the autumnal glory and mellow evening skies are beautifully reflected. (Seton, p. 137)

Sunnyside. Irving lived the last years of his life surrounded by family at a peaceful retreat in Tarrytown, New York. He spent years remodeling the tiny Dutch salt-box house that stood on ten acres of land. On the grounds he built stables, servants' quarters, bridges, and even ponds. The peaceful happiness of the last years of his life was troubled only by the exhausting effort Irving put forth to complete his final work, which he hoped would be his crowning achievement. The five-volume biography of his namesake, George Washington, was in fact somewhat tedious and is not remembered as one of Irving's great works.

In 1859, Irving died suddenly of a heart attack just as he was about to go to bed. The next day, flags were raised at half-mast as the nation grieved the loss of one of its first national literary heroes. Irving lies buried at a grave in Sleepy Hollow.

For More Information

Neider, Charles, ed. *The Complete Tales of Washington Irving.* Garden City: Doubleday & Co., 1975.

Seton, Anya. *Washington Irving.* Boston: North Star Books, Houghton Mifflin Co., 1960.

Wagenknecht, Edward, editor. *Washington Irving's Tales of the Supernatural.* Owings Mills, Maryland: Stemmer House, 1982.

Williams, Stanley T. *The Life of Washington Irving.* Vols. I and II. New York: Oxford University Press, 1935.

James Fenimore Cooper

1789-1851

Personal Background

On an autumn day in 1785, James Fenimore Cooper's father, William, rode alone on horseback across one of the vast tracts of unsettled wilderness that still covered much of the new country. He had a plan for the raw New York land: he wanted to establish a settlement and name it Cooperstown. The feeling he got from gazing at the endless stretches of uninhabited land deeply affected him. Years later, in a little pamphlet entitled *A Guide to the Wilderness,* William wrote about his first impression of the "rough and hilly" land that would soon become Cooperstown, New York:

> There existed not an inhabitant, nor any trace of a road. I was alone, three hundred miles from home, without bread, meat, or food of any kind; fire and fishing tackle were my only means of subsistence … I laid me down to sleep in my watch coat, nothing but the melancholy Wilderness around me … I explored the country, formed my plans for future settlement, and meditated upon the spot where a place of trade or a village should afterwards be established. (Franklin, p. 10)

William's reverie took place some four years before his son James was born; however, the elder Cooper's romance with unexplored wilderness had a powerful and lasting effect on his son. As a child James formed a deep attachment to the woods that surrounded his

▲ **James Fenimore Cooper**

Event: The birth of the American novel.
Role: James Fenimore Cooper was the first author to write novels with themes, characters, and settings that were distinctly American.

family's mansion and the nearby lake. This attachment would show through later in his most memorable writing.

Early years. Cooper was born on September 15, 1789, in Burlington, New Jersey, the twelfth of thirteen children. His father descended from English Quakers who had immigrated to the colonies in the late 1600s. His mother, Elizabeth Fenimore, also a Quaker, came from a wealthy Burlington family. Her inheritance and William's profits from buying and selling land made the Coopers very wealthy. When James was a little over a year old, his family moved to Cooperstown, where his father had purchased land and then sold lots to settlers.

As a boy in Cooperstown, James had the privilege of being a member of the most honored and well-off family in town. He benefited from the unusual combination of a cultured, educated, and civilized upbringing while living on the edge of a wild, unsettled countryside that stretched for miles all around. His parents were living examples of this contradiction between polished society and untamed wilderness. His mother enjoyed the more delicate, cultured activities that she learned as a girl in wealthy Burlington. She loved to read, listen to music, and mingle with other members of refined society. Even though her husband built her a fine mansion in Cooperstown, Elizabeth longed for the life she had left behind in Burlington.

William, on the other hand, thrived on the challenge of living in the raw wilderness. He was rough and vigorous. A physically powerful man, he promised his farm to anyone who could wrestle him down. People who knew William described him as "impulsive, outspoken, and combative," but also "sagacious [intelligent], tactful, and gentle" (Long, p. 14).

James, like his father, also adored the adventure of the wilderness. His sister Hannah described him and his brother as "very wild," showing "plainly that they have been bred in the woods" (Long, p. 14). At the same time, James received an excellent formal education at the local academy, where he delighted in playing sports and exhibited a love of reading.

When he was just thirteen, James enrolled at Yale College in New Haven, Connecticut. Although he was well-liked and a strong student, he was expelled before graduating. This was his own fault, for he had indulged in a few practical jokes. Apparently, James stuck some gunpowder in the keyhole of a classmate's door and blew it up; also, he is said to have led a donkey into a classroom and somehow made it sit in the professor's chair. Interestingly, James was not the first Cooper to tarnish the family name in this way; his brother William had been expelled from Princeton for a prank that could have led to the school's burning down.

After being expelled from Yale, James returned home, where he studied under Reverend William Neill for a short time. Neill described the young Cooper as a "rather wayward" student, who "cordially disliked hard study … and he was especially fond of reading novels and amusing tales" (Long, p. 15).

At sea. With his academic career cut short, Cooper entered the navy in 1806. During his three years as a midshipman, he spent a great deal of time on the open sea. He learned firsthand about the unique life aboard a ship and came to love the sense of freedom and adventure that he associated with the sea. He later drew on this experience when he wrote such novels as *The Pilot, Red Rover,* and a biography, *Ned Myers,* about a sailor during the War of 1812. The biography reveals how it felt for an American sailor to be impressed, or forced to sail for the British. Ned, at one point, becomes prisoner on a British ship, along with others, including three native Americans.

Marriage and family. When Cooper was just twenty years old, his father was killed in an unpleasant incident. William Cooper, who had become a judge in Cooperstown, was struck from behind and killed by a political opponent while leaving a meeting in Albany. His father's death made Cooper a very wealthy young man. He inherited 50,000 dollars as well as a share with his four brothers in an estate worth 750,000 dollars.

Soon after, Cooper met and fell in love with Susan Augusta De Lancey, a young woman from one of the finest families in Westchester, New York. The eighteen-year-old De Lancey was one of the most eligible ladies in the area; she had property, wealth, and good breeding. In addition to this, she was also bright, loving, and a good friend and partner to Cooper. In a letter to his brother, Cooper described her charms:

> Like all the rest of the sons of Adam, I have bowed to the influence
> of a fair damsel of eighteen. I loved her like a man and told her like
> a sailor.... Susan De Lancey is the daughter of a man of very
> respectable connections and a handsome fortune—amiable,
> sweet-tempered and happy ... but ... it is enough she please me in
> the qualities of her person and her mind. (Phillips, pp. 63-64)

De Lancey and Cooper married on New Year's Day, 1811. At his
new wife's request, Cooper resigned from the navy and settled into
married life. In the early years of their marriage, the young couple
lived in Westchester and Cooperstown, moving back and forth
between the two. For a time, Cooper lived the life of a country gentlemen, gardening, managing a small farm, participating in an agri-
cultural society and a Bible society, riding horses in the countryside, and playing the flute. He and his wife had five children who
survived infancy, four girls and a boy.

This fine manner of easy living probably would have continued
for a long time if Cooper's finances had not taken a serious down-
turn. Between 1813 and 1819 each of his four brothers died—all
were barely middle-aged—leaving Cooper in charge of the family
estate and of supporting their surviving children and wives. His
brothers had lost much of their inheritance by living beyond their
means, spending foolishly, and investing unwisely. Now Cooper,
who had never worried about money, had to figure out some way of
making a living. By a strange turn of events, he decided, almost by
accident, on a career as a writer.

Participation: The Birth of the American Novel

Writing career. Cooper's entry into the literary profession
came about partly from financial need and partly as a result of a
challenge from his wife. One night in 1820, when Susan was feeling
ill, Cooper read to her from a new novel just brought over from England. His daughter Susan tells the legendary story as follows:

> My Mother was not well; she was lying on the sofa, and he was
> reading this newly imported novel to her; it must have been very
> trashy; after a chapter or two he threw it aside, exclaiming: "I
> could write you a better book than that myself!" Our Mother
> laughed at the idea as the height of absurdity—he who disliked
> writing even a letter, that he should write a book!! He persisted in

his declaration, however, and almost immediately wrote the first pages of the tale. (Railton, p. 37)

Cooper's first novel, which he dashed off just to prove his boast, was a romantic book called *Precaution*. Set in England, the story centers around three daughters of a wealthy country gentleman, all seeking suitable marriages. One daughter marries sensibly, one throws herself away on a dishonest, unworthy man, and the last, Emily, falls in love with a man whom she later learns is the wealthiest young man in England. In its English country setting and its romantic yet moral tone, *Precaution* resembles the writing of English author Jane Austen and comes close in name to her novel *Persuasion*.

It is difficult to say whether Cooper achieved his aim of writing a better novel than the one he had read to his wife that fateful evening. *Precaution* received some negative criticism and only mild success. Cooper, however, seemed to enjoy his new status as a writer and immediately set about working on a second novel, *The Spy*. He later wrote, "having accidentally produced an English book, I determined to write one purely American, by way of atonement" (Railton, pp. 63-64). Set in Westchester County, New York, during the Revolutionary War, *The Spy* was published in 1821. The novel achieved tremendous success; it was read worldwide and translated into several European languages, including French, German, Spanish, and Italian. Almost overnight, Cooper had become a literary star.

Success. With his new fame, Cooper's life soon changed. He moved his family to New York City, where he formed an intellectual society with several friends. The Bread and Cheese Club—also known as the Cooper Club—included such famous figures as Samuel B. Morse, the painter who later invented the telegraph, and William Cullen Bryant, the poet and newspaper editor. Another famous writer, Washington Irving, who was abroad in Europe, was named an honorary member. The club met in the back room of a bookstore owned by Charles Wiley, who was Cooper's publisher.

While enjoying an active social life, Cooper continued to write at a steady and rapid pace. He does not seem to have edited his writing, but rather, sent first drafts directly to the printer. After the success of *The Spy,* Cooper published several other novels, including *The Pioneers* (1823), *The Pilot* (1824), *Lionel Lincoln* (1825), and *The Last of the Mohicans* (1826).

With these novels and his later writing, Cooper established himself as an important American author. In fact, he, along with Washington Irving, was helping to lay the foundation of American literature (see **Washington Irving**). Whereas Irving's writing helped to define the American short story, Cooper's fiction was the first to define the American novel. His themes, settings, and characters were distinctly American. Even his writing style—informal, sprawling, and energetic—reflected the raw, boundless American landscape.

What's in a Name?

Does the name James Cooper sound far less appealing than James Fenimore Cooper? Had it not been for a promise to his mother, the novelist would, in fact, have been simply James Cooper. Elizabeth Fenimore Cooper was the last in her line and asked her sons to try to carry on her family name. Cooper agreed, and in 1826 he legally changed his name to include his mother's maiden name.

The Leatherstocking Tales. Cooper is perhaps best remembered for his series of five novels that came to be called *The Leatherstocking Tales.* Published between 1823 and 1841, the novels are set in the American wilderness and revolve around a frontiersman named Natty Bumppo.

The first published book of this series, *The Pioneers,* is set in Cooperstown in 1793. The novel takes the reader through four seasons in the new frontier settlement. Against the backdrop of warm, homespun settings, Cooper examines the lives and struggles of people living together on the outskirts of civilization. Natty Bumppo, nicknamed Leatherstocking by the villagers, has lived like a hermit for many years by the lake and watches with growing resentment as the settlement takes form around him. He resents new laws that make deer hunting illegal during certain seasons, and he hates to see the settlers reducing the number of game in the woods.

Cooper's second novel in the series, *The Last of the Mohicans,* made him hugely popular during his time and is still widely read. The action-filled adventure tells a romantic, exciting story set during the French and Indian War. On a trek across the eastern countryside, a party of two sisters, Cora and Alice Munro, and an American Army major, Duncan Heyward, are escorted to Fort Henry by Hawkeye (the Natty Bumppo character) and his two Mohican Indian companions, Chief Chingachgook and his son Uncas. On the way, they face the constant danger of attack by an enemy Indian, Magua, and his warriors. Cora and Uncas fall in love, but die tragically in the end. An excerpt describing the colonists' fear of Indians gives a fine example of Cooper's writing style:

> The alarmed colonists believed that the yells of the savages mingled with every fitful gust of wind that issued from the interminable forests of the west…. Numberless recent massacres were still vivid in their recollections; nor was there any ear in the provinces so deaf as not to have drunk with avidity the narrative of some fearful tale of midnight murder, in which the natives of the forests were the principal and barbarous actors. (Cooper, p. 4)

The other three books in this series are *The Prairie* (1827), *The Pathfinder* (1840), and *The Deerslayer* (1841). Cooper, whose regard for his own talent seems to have been modest, correctly predicted that *The Leatherstocking Tales* would be the works that he would be remembered by:

> If any thing from the pen of the writer … is to at all outlive himself, it is, unquestionably, the series of the "The Leatherstocking Tales." To say this, is not to predict a very lasting reputation for the series itself, but simply to express the belief that it will outlast any, or all, of the works from the same hand. (Grossman, p. 3)

Aftermath

Souring success. Cooper's tremendous popularity in his country did not last. In 1826 he and his family left America for a seven-year stay in Europe, most of which they spent in Paris. While abroad, Cooper learned a great deal about politics through his friendship with an earlier hero of the American Revolution, the Marquis de Lafayette. Cooper's writing began to reflect his growing interest in political philosophy. Unfortunately, the American public did not welcome his views, some of which were quite critical of Americans and the democratic system. Not surprisingly, by the time he returned to native soil, he had grown considerably less popular.

In his later years, Cooper also suffered harsh attacks from critics. One viciously described him as a "slanderer who is in fact a traitor to national pride and national character" (Grossman, p. 131). Cooper brought many lawsuits against such critics and usually won.

One famous critical piece was a humorous attack against Cooper's writing, penned a half-century after his death by Mark Twain. In the essay "Fenimore Cooper's Literary Offenses" Twain writes some harsh criticism of Fenimore Cooper's book *The Deerslayer.* Claiming that Cooper had scored 114 offenses against literary art out of a possible 115, Twain goes on to write:

> He prized his broken twig trick above all the rest of his effects, and worked it the hardest. It is a restful chapter in any book of his when somebody doesn't step on a dry twig and alarm all the reds and whites for two hundred yards around. Every time a Cooper person is in peril, and absolute silence is worth four dollars a minute, he is sure to step on a dry twig. (Neider, pp. 463-464)

Twain does not stop there. He accuses Cooper of having no ear for the language, of being a poor observer, and of giving his characters shifting personalities that change during the course of a tale. According to Twain, Cooper's work:

> Has no invention; it has no order, system, sequence, or result; it has no lifelikeness, no thrill, no stir, no seeming of reality; its characters are confusedly drawn ... its English a crime against the language. (Neider, p. 472)

Influence on American Literature. Although much of Cooper's writing has not proved lasting and many have harshly criticized his work, he is considered the father of the American novel. Cooper was the first American novelist to achieve worldwide fame and the first to make a successful living at writing novels. He influenced later writers such as Nathaniel Hawthorne and Herman Melville. Hawthorne wrote historical novels, which Cooper had made popular; and Melville perfected the sea-going adventure that Cooper had first fictionalized in his sea tales. Certainly most of the other writers of the nineteenth century read Cooper and were, to some degree, influenced by him.

As the first popular American novelist, Cooper understood his responsibility as a leader in this new form of writing. He strove to make his works distinctly and purely American, and "in the settings and subjects of his books, helped to introduce the young country to itself—even though it did not always like what it saw there" (Railton, p. 4).

Cooper set a pattern for writers after him who included Indian characters in their works. He apparently had little contact with Indians himself but read about them in accounts of the Lewis and Clark expedition and other sources. In his own writing Cooper presented Indians as symbols of a less civilized people than the American immigrants had become. Historians criticized Cooper's Indian characters, saying they were not realistic. Nevertheless, his treatment of Indians as symbols was modeled by later writers.

Final praise. Cooper clearly succeeded as a writer in his lifetime and influenced others afterward. A measure of his importance as the first American novelist was the memorial tribute paid to Cooper after his death. He died of liver failure on September 14, 1851, one day short of his sixty-second birthday. Five months later, on February 24, 1852, America's leading literary figures gathered at the Metropolitan Hall in New York to commemorate him. Writers such as Washington Irving, Ralph Waldo Emerson, Nathaniel Hawthorne, and Herman Melville gave speeches praising the novelist's significant contribution to American literature.

For More Information

Cooper, James Fenimore. *The Last of the Mohicans*. New York: The Book-of-the-Month Club, 1993.

Cooper, James Fenimore. *Ned Myers; or, A Life Before the Mast*. Annapolis: Naval Institute Press, 1989.

Franklin, Wayne. *The New World of James Fenimore Cooper*. Chicago: University of Chicago Press, 1982.

Grossman, James. *James Fenimore Cooper*. New York: William Sloane Associates, 1949.

Long, Robert Emmet. *James Fenimore Cooper*. New York: Continuum Publishing Co., 1990.

Neider, Charles. *The Comic Mark Twain Reader*. Garden City, New York: Doubleday & Co., 1977.

Phillips, Mary E. *James Fenimore Cooper*. New York: John Lane Company, 1913.

Railton, Stephen. *Fenimore Cooper: A Study of His Life and Imagination*. Princeton: Princeton University Press, 1978.

War of 1812

1811
▼
Battle of Tippecanoe fought Nov. 7, later regarded as first battle of war.

1812
▼
President James Madison officially declares war on June 18.

1813
▼
Tecumseh loses Battle of the Thames on Oct. 5.

1813
▼
Battle of Lake Erie won by Commodore **Oliver Hazard Perry** on Sept. 10.

1813-1814
▼
General **Andrew Jackson** battles Creek Indians.

1814
▼
British burn Washington City on Aug. 24; precious items are saved by **Dolley Payne Madison.**

1814
▼
Peacemakers sign Treaty of Ghent on Dec. 24.

1815
▼
United States Congress ratifies Treaty of Ghent, which ends war.

1814-1815
▼
Jackson fights final battle of New Orleans on Jan. 8, 1815.

WAR OF 1812

Officially the War of 1812 began June 18, 1812, and ended on February 17, 1815, with the approval of the Treaty of Ghent. The war was declared by the Americans against the British, and Indian tribes joined the fighting on both sides. There were various battle fronts: the American North, South, and Old Northwest, Canada, and the Atlantic Ocean and Great Lakes.

President James Madison declared war for several reasons. Britain had been impressing America's sailors, forcing them into service in her Royal Navy. Perhaps 10,000 sailors fell victim to this practice in the early 1800s. Britain had also blockaded American ports, crippling shipping, and had broken promises to remove her forts from the American frontier. In fact, Britain seemed to be ignoring American independence. Another war, many Americans felt, would confirm it, and win guarantees for the safety of the new country's vessels at sea. America fought also for territory, hoping to drive the British out of Canada and the Spanish out of Florida.

Indians joined the war to further their own ends. White settlers had been steadily moving onto Indian lands. To resist them, warriors, in need of firepower and manpower, shrewdly linked their cause with that of the British. The Shawnee chief **Tecumseh** assembled members of sixty nations into a remarkable Indian army, the largest ever formed on the continent. Other warriors decided they would benefit more by supporting the Americans. Chief Black

Hoof, who led the majority of the Shawnee, opposed the British and Tecumseh.

America began the war with a feeble army run by aging, rusty generals and almost no navy. During Thomas Jefferson's presidency, the number of regular soldiers and sailors had been reduced to limit the power of the central government. There were few roads on which troops could travel and horses, weapons, and other supplies were limited. The country was unprepared for war. America would have to build roads, vessels, and a stronger military as she fought. She had no choice but to call on untrained volunteers and state militia units to increase her fighting force. Some states, such as Massachusetts and Connecticut, refused to cooperate. This was an unpopular war in New England, where citizens entertained the idea of seceding from the Union.

British War Goals vs. American War Goals	
Keep control of Canada	Win guarantees on the seas
Make Michigan an Indian state	Gain Indian lands
Win New Orleans	Win Canada and Spanish Florida

America scrambled for materiel and men as it fought. The navy struggled at sea and in the Great Lakes, fighting with little success until **Oliver Hazard Perry** won the Battle of Lake Erie. William Henry Harrison followed up this victory with another on land. Proud of these successes, Americans became more united in supporting the war. The remainder of the conflict saw more defeats and victories. British forces marched on Washington City to burn it down, but not before the First Lady, **Dolley Payne Madison,** saved the republic's most precious papers from falling into enemy hands.

On December 24, 1814, the United States and England concluded a peace treaty. The Treaty of Ghent brought an end to thirty-two months of fighting, restoring prewar conditions. News of the peace agreement did not reach America until February. Meanwhile, **Andrew Jackson** fought the Battle of New Orleans, commanding an assortment of units that included whites, African Americans, and Indians. They managed to halt the British attempt to capture this part of the American South. The episode turned into a smashing victory for the Americans, but it was only one battle in a close war.

Militarily speaking, the War of 1812 ended without a victor. No exchanges of territory were made in the treaty, and there were no guarantees of American rights on the seas. The long months of bloody fighting had claimed thousands of lives. Was the War of 1812, then, fought to no purpose?

Americans of the time considered the fight worthwhile. True, they had not won the war, but neither had they lost it. Mighty England had been unable to crush their newborn country, which was still struggling to get on its feet.

At first, distracted by their war against French emperor Napoleon Bonaparte, the British had aimed only to hold onto Canada and to support Indians in their battles against the Americans. Later, after defeating Napoleon, Britain sent her finest soldiers to America and adopted grander goals for herself in this war. Still, Americans managed to hold their own against the British on land, at sea, and on the Great Lakes. The American frontier quieted down, too, after Tecumseh's army dissolved.

Americans Killed and Wounded

Officially, 528,000 soldiers and sailors fought in the War of 1812. 2,260 were killed and 4,505 were wounded. The death toll, though, is much higher, since servicemen died daily from diseases and hundreds of untallied Indians perished in the war. While a total of less than 100,000 Indians fought in the war, nearly 900 Creek were estimated killed in the Battle of Horseshoe Bend alone.

Never had there been a question in the minds of the War Hawks, the citizens who favored declaring war, that this was a necessary fight. Others had objected, but by war's end most Americans came to regard the War of 1812 as a second war for independence and to view themselves as its winner. There were no visible gains, but the United States had proven to Britain and the world that it was, in fact, a nation to be respected.

Oliver Hazard Perry

1785-1819

Personal Background

Early years. Born August 23, 1785, in Washington County, Rhode Island, Oliver Hazard Perry was the oldest in a family of five boys and three girls. His father, Christopher Raymond Perry, served in both the army and navy during the Revolution. When Oliver was twelve, his father left home with his mother to oversee the construction of a ship for the infant navy, giving Oliver control of the family. The boy had other ideas. In a letter he beseeched his father to take him into the navy. Convinced by his son's earnestness, his father took Oliver on his ship, insisting that he meanwhile study seamanship, French, Spanish, and Latin. "If you want to become a Navy officer," his father said, "you had better become a good one" (Dillon, p. 5).

Training. President Thomas Jefferson (1801-1809) believed a strong army and navy would encourage attack, so he reduced the country's forces. Consequently, the older Perry lost his commission; Oliver, however, was chosen to remain on duty. He was given small gunboats—floating artillery units—to oversee in New York. There he met James Lawrence, who later commanded the warship *Chesapeake.* In 1807 the British blasted the unprepared *Chesapeake,* forcing it to surrender. Perry vowed never to let such unpreparedness defeat him.

▲ Oliver Hazard Perry

Event: War of 1812, Battle of Lake Erie.
Role: Stationed on a forsaken peninsula on Lake Erie, Oliver Hazard Perry orchestrated the "impossible" task of building an American fleet. The twenty-eight-year-old navy commodore led an attack on British warships to wrest command of the lake and regain the Northwest for America. His victory in the Battle of Lake Erie, his major wartime role, made possible the Battle of the Thames, in which Perry played a minor part.

In 1809, at age twenty-four, Perry took charge of the *Revenge,* a swift schooner with fourteen cannons. It was part of an ocean squadron of nine warships and a few smaller vessels that made up the whole American fighting fleet at this time. On one occasion, off the Georgia coast, Englishmen boarded the *Revenge* to search for deserters. Perry turned them away. He harbored no Britishers, he said, and would not allow "interference of any foreigner, whatever, with the American jurisdiction" (Dillon, p. 33). In 1811 Perry's pilot unintentionally wrecked the *Revenge,* and Perry lost his command.

A depressed Perry, now twenty-six, took a year's leave from the navy. Busying himself with his studies and family affairs, he married Elizabeth Champlin Mason, a striking twenty-year-old whom he had loved for four years.

Participation: Battle of Lake Erie

Military preparedness. Receiving news that General William Henry Harrison had defeated the British-supported Indians at Tippecanoe (see **Tecumseh**), Perry foresaw war. He rushed to the capital to ask the government for a warship, but there were none to be had. Instead Perry was ordered to Newport, Rhode Island, to command a gunboat flotilla. He cursed his country's unpreparedness for war.

By 1812 the United States had at home three midsized sailing warships, and a few more fighting ships at sea. Against this handful of fighting vessels, Britain's Royal Navy had 640 warships, some of them in North American waters. For years they had kept the American coast under a semi-blockade, halting and searching merchant and U.S. naval ships and forcing, or impressing, American sailors into British service, accusing them of being deserters from the Royal Navy. Some were, but most were not. Still, the captive sailors had to serve on British ships. By 1812 Britain had forced 6,000 Americans into service for its navy.

President James Madison declared war against Britain on June 18, 1812. America's army and navy were in sad shape at the time:

6,700 ill-trained, poorly equipped men in small detachments from New York to the Detroit wilderness. Leading them were veterans of the Revolutionary War, old in body and spirit. Still Madison, without complete support, had declared war for several reasons: the British were impressing American sailors into service on their vessels and were seizing cargo from American ships. Also, the United States wanted control of the Northwest Territory, which the Indians refused to give up and the British refused to leave, even after losing the Revolutionary War.

Though at war with France at the time, the British felt confident of winning against the United States. Their sailing vessels ruled the seas and would play a major role in fighting this war. Their newspaper, *Evening Star,* bragged that they had little to fear from "a few fir-built frigates, manned by a handful of ... outlaws" (Dillon, p. 49). Not only the ships but also American sailors and soldiers were belittled. Perry, convinced that the survival of his country was at stake, would prove them wrong.

Newport command. Assigned to command a Newport, Rhode Island, flotilla of gunboats, Perry put together a fighting team. He was ever anxious for command of a seaworthy warship, but meanwhile took pains to drill his men. The flotilla began with 12 gunboats and 200 men. Splitting the fleet in half for war games, Perry polished his sailors' ability to handle small and large arms; in the process he established a close relationship with the men.

A muscular, robust man with curly locks, Perry stood five-feet eight-inches tall. A hard worker, careful planner, and master of detail, Perry proved to be demanding of himself and his men, a quality he shared with another military leader of the war (see **Andrew Jackson**). He stood somewhat aloof and had a hot temper, which he mostly kept under check. Perry won the loyalty of his men; his voice inspired obedience.

Perry sharpened the skills of his Newport men until they deserved more than the gunboats to which they were assigned. Waiting around frustrated Perry to no end. He wanted and repeatedly requested sea command, but none came. Then the Americans surrendered Detroit. It dawned on Perry that the war in the Northwest might depend on naval success in the Great Lakes. Meanwhile,

Madison had made some decisions: the Americans must regain the Northwest, reinvade Canada, and seize control of Lake Erie. Encouraged by an old naval crony, Perry requested the Erie duty.

Lake Erie command. In charge of naval forces on the Great Lakes was Commodore Isaac Chauncey, a strong planner but certainly not a man of action, as Perry would soon discover. Under him was Commodore Jesse Elliott, a reasonably strong naval commander who had already achieved a small victory on Lake Erie. He had captured a small British warship, the *Caledonia,* and a couple of small cannons in a nighttime attack against the enemy. Elliott refused, however, to take charge of the feverish building program about to begin at Presque Isle on Lake Erie, and would later do his best to wreck Perry's efforts.

Madison named Perry the new commander for Lake Erie. His task was to build and launch the American squadron, including two 300-ton brigs, before the ice broke over the lake in June, when the British fleet would surely attack. Also, General William Henry Harrison, who commanded American land forces, needed Perry's naval support to regain territory. If the Americans got control of Lake Erie, they would cut off the supply route to the enemy and narrow its path of retreat. Since the British had control of the lake when Perry arrived, he had to transport all materials for building and outfitting the boats over 120 to 400 miles of difficult land. He had the materials transported from little towns like Buffalo, New York (100 dwellings), and from Pittsburgh, Pennsylvania (a metropolis of 6,000). The tiny town of Erie, Pennsylvania, consisted of a smattering of homes on a high bank above the lake and had a population of 400. Erie had no industry, just sawmills, a tannery, and a smith; however, there was plenty of food, such as venison, turkeys, pigeons, and fish. Given these conditions, Perry set out to build six new vessels while the enemy cruised off the harbor spying on his progress. He had few men to help him; his repeated requests to Chauncey seemed to fall on deaf ears.

Perry followed 150 of his well-trained sailors to Lake Ontario, where Chauncey awaited him. On his way he stopped at home and discussed his assignment with his father, who convinced him to take along his younger brother Alex. Perry headed for Lake

Ontario in February on sleigh with Alex and a black servant, Hannibal Collins. Chauncey sent Perry on to Lake Erie after a month but kept his 150 trained seamen on Lake Ontario. Perry took only his brother, Hannibal, and a few men. They stopped in Buffalo, where an innkeeper warned that the British meant to attack the base at Erie, 93 miles away, before the Americans could build and launch their vessels.

With builder Noah Brown, Perry embarked on a race against time. They had only green timber on hand. Perry had to depend on slow road-and-river transportation for every other supply. He requested men from Chauncey, cannons from Buffalo, canvas from Philadelphia, men from Chauncey, more cannons from Pittsburgh, men from Chauncey, guns from Buffalo, men from Chauncey, scrap iron from Pittsburgh, and men from Chauncey. In fact, his main problem became Chauncey, who neither replied to his letters nor sent him men. Desperate, Perry persuaded nearby Meadville to lend him 1,000 militia men. They marched and countermarched on shore to fool the British into believing there was a large force at Erie. It was an old tactic, used by other military leaders of the day.

Perry showed himself to be a master of organization. He scrambled to meet his own needs. Afraid the large cannons would not arrive in time from Buffalo, he hauled in smaller ones from Pittsburgh. He had every nearby home, smith, and farm searched for iron, fusing the scraps together to make bolts for the cannons. Perry restored an old fort and built two new ones for protection. He stationed the main body of militia by the shipyard. To guard against British spies, nearby innkeepers were alerted to notify him of strangers. Fever raged through the area, causing nearly half of his 100 or so seamen to fall ill. Perry kept the healthy ones working on morning and night shifts, maintaining strict discipline all the while. Some men complained of the strictness but all seemed to have high regard for Perry as an honest and considerate leader.

The shortage of ammunition and men, especially officers and seasoned sailors, kept Perry anxious. Not only Chauncey but also Elliott ignored his requests for men. Finally Elliott sent forty seamen under Acting Lieutenant Thomas Holdup (who later changed his last name to Stevens). They were a sorry bunch. Elliott had purposely sent the worst of the lot. He sent few sailors; most were landsmen.

Fort George campaign. With his requests for men still unanswered, Perry finally heard from Chauncey, who requested Perry's help in a campaign against the British stronghold of Fort George on Lake Ontario. Chauncey appointed Perry to direct the landing of the troops. Perry agreed to the request, hoping he could get Chauncey to meet some of his needs at last.

The attack on Fort George, combining naval and land forces, turned out to be finely planned and fought. Several hundred large boats, filled with soldiers, horses, and artillery, advanced over the lake in grand form. Perry landed the troops. From their vessels, the sailors got ready to shoot but stopped for fear of injuring their own soldiers. Seeing this, Perry boarded the *Hamilton* and opened fire at the soldiers on land, prompting some Britishers to retreat. Without enough troops, the British finally withdrew from Fort George altogether, blowing up their supply of ammunition to prevent it from falling into American hands. The Americans had won. Furthermore, Perry got Chauncey to agree that 680 men were needed on Lake Erie, though Chauncey never did send them.

Battle preparations. Perry and many of his men were sick with fever after the Fort George campaign, suffering chills, malaria, and the like. His men took heart, though, boasting of "Perry's luck" when their commodore managed to sail five small vessels past the British. They traveled 100 miles up Lake Erie protected by a thick fog.

Perry's fleet was coming together. Off Lake Erie on Presque Isle, the two largest vessels, the brigs, were nearly complete. Noah Brown had made do with whatever materials he could lay his hands on: planks of white and black oak, decks of white pinewood, the seams caulked with lead. Often wood that was part of a tree at dawn had become a plank by sunset. Progress was not fast enough, though, for Perry or for Harrison.

Harrison beseeched Perry to sail up the lake and fight the enemy to support the land forces. Perry, eager to help, had to decline for lack of men. Of the 680 sailors needed, he now had little more than 100 and many were bedridden with illness. Perry learned during this time that his old friend James Lawrence died in a fight on the open seas, crying, "Don't give up the ship!" To honor

Lawrence, Perry had his own men wear black armbands for three weeks and made a blue battle flag lettered in white with the captain's dying words.

The War Department began focusing on Perry's attack, deciding that the key to the Northwest lay in destroying the British squadron on Lake Erie. Only then would the Army of the Northwest be free to recapture the Michigan Territory and invade Canada. Perry was directed to launch his ships as soon as possible. As much as he ached to follow the order, there were two obstacles: 1) He had too few men. How could a squadron fight without sailors to man the guns? 2) He could not get the vessels into deep water. They had to cross a bar, a ridge with four feet of shallow water, before entering the lake. The brigs needed at least nine feet of water to move forward.

At his wits end for lack of men, Perry went over Chauncey's head and wrote Secretary of the Navy William Jones. Jones prodded Chauncey into giving Perry more men. Meanwhile, white men and black men who lived in the area joined as volunteers.

The British, under Commodore Robert Barclay, were now blockading Presque Isle. On July 31 "Perry's luck" gave the Americans the opening they needed. Barclay suddenly withdrew the blockade. Tired of waiting, one story goes, he accepted a town's invitation to a banquet. More probably, he left to resupply his ships, gambling that his absence would tempt Perry to move forward. If this was his plan, it paid off. Perry now had 300 men, less than half the force agreed upon, but in the face of repeated requests from General Harrison, Perry would wait no longer. He took advantage of Barclay's absence, working feverishly to get his vessels over the bar.

Perry had named his two brigs the *Lawrence* and the *Niagara*. For three sleepless nights, he and his men used their strategy for propelling the two vessels over the bar. Brown had built camels, large barges with one side shaped to fit closely under a brig's hull. They lowered the camels on either side of a brig, which had been emptied to reduce its weight, and secured them to the ship through the gunports. The camels lifted the brig, moving foot by foot until it slid into deep water, whereupon the cannons were remounted. Perry managed to get the *Lawrence* into deep water, but the *Nia-*

gara was still on the bar when the enemy reappeared. Since the boats were not yet ready, he bluffed Barclay. Perry sent two of the fleet's smaller boats, already in deep water, to open fire on the British as a distraction, having a sailor on the *Lawrence* beat a drum as if his side were ready for battle. Barclay, totally unprepared for Perry's getting his fleet over the bar, was hoodwinked, and retired to Fort Malden for a time. Readying himself for battle, Perry then alerted Harrison:

> The squadron is not much more than half-manned but as I see no prospect of receiving reinforcements I have determined to commence my operations. Will send an express to you the moment the issue of our contest with the enemy is known. (Dillon, p. 110)

Battle of Lake Erie. At the last minute, Perry received news that Elliott would join him with eighty-nine experienced seamen. His force still lacked seasoned officers, though Perry had done his best training his landsmen to load and fire cannons in naval combat. Elliott took command of the *Niagara* while Perry, still in charge of the entire campaign, took command of the *Lawrence*. In the end, Elliott kept all the seasoned sailors to himself. Perry, overjoyed at finally getting some experienced seamen for the fleet, let this pass.

Planning the campaign, Perry drummed into his sailors that they would win only by closing in quickly. Their short-range guns needed to come as close to the target as 300 feet. Perry then met with Harrison, who provided more seamen, giving the Americans 490 against 502 Britishers. At Harrison's suggestion Perry based his fleet at Put-in-Bay, in the southwest corner of Lake Erie 30 miles from Fort Malden, the British headquarters in the Northwest. The contest pitted Perry and Harrison against the English commanders Barclay, on the lake, and Henry Proctor, on land. Proctor was running short of food for the hundreds of Indian families depending on him, and Barclay's sailors were eating the last of their rations. It was fight or starve. Barclay fought.

Perry's plan was for the *Lawrence* and the *Niagara*—each had twenty cannons—to close in rapidly on the large enemy vessels while the smaller ships took on the others at longer range. Each vessel had a specific enemy to attack. The Americans had the advantage in number of craft, the British, in number of cannons.

American Vessels vs.	British Vessels
Lawrence (20 cannons)	*Detroit* (19 cannons)
Niagara (20 cannons)	*Queen Charlotte* (17 cannons)
Ariel (4 cannons)	*Lady Prevost* (13 cannons)
Caledonia (3 cannons)	*Hunter* (10 cannons)
Scorpion (2 cannons)	*Chippeway* (1 cannon)
Somers (2 cannons)	*Little Belt* (3 cannons)
Tigress (1 cannon)	
Porcupine (3 cannons)	
Trippe (1 cannon)	

The battle broke out September 10, 1813, at 11:45 a.m., and reached a spectacular finish at 3:00 p.m.

Just before battle, Perry examined each cannon, making a joke or two and leaving the gun's crew with some encouraging words. He recognized some of the recent additions as his former sailors and greeted them warmly. When they saluted, he responded, "I need not say anything to you. You know how to beat those fellows" (Dillon, p. 132). Dressed not in brass buttons and braid, but like a common sailor, Perry guarded against his uniform drawing enemy fire. He also tore his wife's letters to shreds to prevent their ever falling into enemy's hands. This was, he knew, the most important day of his life.

Playing "Rule Britannia," the *Detroit* fired first. Perry's plan quickly fell apart. Unaccountably, the *Niagara,* with Elliott in charge, hung back instead of fighting the British vessel *Queen Charlotte* as it was supposed to do. Three British vessels, the *Detroit, Queen Charlotte,* and *Hunter,* closed in on the *Lawrence,* bombarding it with cannon fire. The destruction went on for two hours, with the small but courageous *Caledonia* trying to help Perry's large brig as best it could. Thirty-five cannons blasted the *Lawrence* at once, bombarding it to shreds, killing twenty-two Americans and wounding sixty-two more. Meanwhile, the *Lawrence* never stopped firing back on the British, but, one by one, its cannons were crippled by enemy fire, and its rigging and canvas shot to pieces too. Still Elliott failed to bring the *Niagara* to the rescue.

Perry, carrying out the motto on his blue-and-white flag ("Don't give up the ship"), created a makeshift gun crew consisting of himself, an aide, and the chaplain. They fired until their cannon also was disabled. Through the whole disaster, Perry remained focused, flinching only when he thought his brother had been shot. (The shot, it turned out, missed the young man.) Still the *Niagara,* headed by Elliot, hung back; Perry decided to bring her into action himself. He and a few men boarded a small boat while enemy fire hissed and fell around him.

At 2:45, Perry reached the *Niagara.* He boarded and took charge of the vessel himself, altering its course by a right angle, bringing the *Niagara* directly down on the enemy. Fortune worked to his advantage (was it Perry's luck?) as the *Queen Charlotte* accidently plowed into the *Detroit,* giving him time to sail into the center of the British ships and to fire from all his cannons on both sides of the *Niagara* at once while his sharpshooters picked off anyone they saw. In just fifteen minutes, the British surrendered. From near defeat, Perry had risen to smash five enemy vessels of the strongest naval power in the world. He quickly scribbled a note to General Harrison: "We have met the enemy, and they are ours. Two ships, two brigs, one schooner and a sloop" (Dillon, p. 153).

Perry turned the *Lawrence,* now a wreck, into a hospital ship. He showed deep concern for the wounded on both sides. Perry reboarded the *Lawrence* to help his own men face surgery, bringing them fresh food and rigging the deck into a sick bay for

> ## Crossing the T
>
> There is a strategy in naval combat called "crossing the T." This happens when one vessel crosses at right angles to the bow (front) of another and can fire down the entire length of the enemy's vessel while the enemy can shoot back only from its bow. In the Battle of Lake Erie, Perry twice croosed the T. He led the *Niagara* at right angles across the bows of the two largest British ships, his cannon on one side raking both these vessels from bow to stern and on the other side blasting the smaller enemy vessels.

their comfort. His foe Barclay had been twice wounded. Checking on him, Perry and the Britisher began a lasting friendship. In his battle report, Barclay credited the victory to Perry's changing vessels in midbattle when any other commander would have, by then, honorably surrendered. Perry, in his report did not blame Elliott for keeping the *Niagara* out of action, a kindness he would later regret.

Perry in the Battle of the Thames. Having won Lake Erie,

Perry joined Harrison on land, becoming his aide for the rest of the campaign. Perry left the lake under Elliott's command.

The Americans marched to fight the Indians and British by the Thames River near Moraviantown. There were cavalry and infantry. The infantry met an obstacle when they reached the Thames River. They wondered how they would cross, for it was too deep for a foot soldier to wade and it appeared a horse could carry only one man across at a time. Suddenly Perry rode into the crowd, ordering an infantryman to mount behind him, and they crossed without difficulty. Others followed his example; 1,200 foot soldiers crossed the river in this way.

In the battle the American cavalry attacked first, a surprising tactic. British foot soldiers stood little chance against the mounted men. Proctor, their British leader, fled. The Indians put up a tougher fight but lost heart when their own leader, Chief Tecumseh (see **Tecumseh**), was killed. With Proctor gone and Tecumseh dead, the Americans had clearly won.

Aftermath

The nation rejoices. Victory at the Battle of the Thames was a direct result of Perry's victory on Lake Erie. The campaign ended with the Americans retaking the Northwest: Michigan, Indiana, Illinois, Wisconsin, and Minnesota. Perry, longing for time with his family, was transferred back to Newport, Rhode Island. All the way home, he encountered parades, dinners, and cheering crowds. The news of his victory electrified a nation, raising spirits and enthusiasm for the war, which until then had been unexciting.

Elliott vs. Perry. Congress awarded Perry and Elliott each 12,140 dollars in prize money. Before leaving Erie, Perry turned over command of the lake to Elliott. Afterward, the fleet broke down beyond recognition. Discipline collapsed, and so did the men's spirits. Sailors fought each other in drunken brawls, and the British torched five of the American vessels when Elliott was not looking. By April 1814 the fleet had foundered. One of its seamen was hanged and two more were shot by a firing squad, all for desertion. The reason for Elliott's failure to rescue the *Lawrence* during the Battle of Lake Erie finally surfaced: envy. He was jealous of Perry. Later, Elliott showed sorrow only for not having done more damage: "I only regret that I did not sacrifice the fleet when it was in my power to do so" (Dillon, p. 183).

The war ends. Back in Newport, Perry took command of the gunboats, then of the fighting ship the *Java* in Baltimore, Maryland. He saw more wartime action when the British invaded Washington. Ordered to harass the enemy with only one eighteen-pound cannon to use, Perry managed to damage a British ship before running out of ammunition. When the enemy reached Baltimore, a sleepless Perry rushed to fight there too. He later convinced the republic to let him build a few swift brigs to break through the British blockade on the Atlantic coast. Perry was in the process of building them at war's end.

Post-war service. After the war, Perry took the *Java* to the Mediterranean, but the craft proved unseaworthy. A disobedient captain, John Heath of the marines, goaded Perry into striking him. Both officers were courtmartialed, scolded in public, and reassigned to duty. To repair his reputation, Perry agreed to meet Heath in a duel. Perry intended not to shoot his pistol in the showdown. He had made up his mind in this way to atone for having allowed himself to act so poorly as to strike a fellow naval officer. Heath fired but missed, and the matter ended.

Assigned to the waters of Buenos Aires and Venezuela, Perry contracted yellow fever. He died at sea August 23, 1819, on his thirty-fourth birthday, leaving behind his wife and three children. Two years earlier the Rush-Bagot convention had outlawed armed vessels on the Great Lakes. Perry remains the only naval commander to have distinguished himself in fighting an armed battle there.

For More Information

Dillon, Richard. *We Have Met the Enemy: Oliver Hazard Perry, Wilderness Commodore.* New York: McGraw-Hill, 1978.

Dudley, William S., ed. *The Naval War of 1812: A Documentary History.* Vol. 1. Washington, D.C.: Naval Historical Center, 1985.

Elting, John R. *Amateurs, to Arms! A Military History of the War of 1812.* Chapel Hill, North Carolina: Algonquin Books, 1991.

Tecumseh

c. 1768-1813

Personal Background

Tecumseh, called Tckamthi by Shawnee Indians, was born in the 1760s, probably in 1768. The decade of his birth was somewhat of a golden era for the Shawnee. With a population that had grown to about 3,000, the Shawnee were gaining territory in southern Ohio. They lived in permanent villages for part of the year, several hundred inhabiting one village. Women would farm and gather wild foods while men hunted and fished. The rest of the year the Shawnee roamed in search of deer and elk. From their hunting grounds they traveled to trade animal furs at white men's posts and forts.

Training. Families of three to four children were standard in Shawnee society, but Tecumseh's family had nine. His mother, Methoastaske, married Puckeshinwa, a Shawnee chief. They had two sons and a daughter before Tecumseh. He had a younger brother, Lalawethika, a heavy, awkward youth who contrasted sharply with the athletic Tecumseh. Clumsy at sports and war games, Lalawethika blinded his right eye with an arrow. He would later play a key role in Tecumseh's life.

Around age twelve Tecumseh received his name, which translates to "He Who Waits as a Heavenly Panther or Shooting Star." In Shawnee society, names were given because of a deed performed

▲ Tecumseh

Event: War of 1812, Battle of the Thames.

Role: Tecumseh, a Shawnee chief, created a union of Indians in the old American Northwest. He formed, and in the Battle of the Thames led, the largest Indian army ever to fight on the continent. His actions helped delay the westward movement of white Americans for almost a decade.

or a character trait. Tecumseh's name was a tribute to the promise he showed of growing into a notable warrior. Already Tecumseh handled a bow and arrow with skill, as he did his favored weapon, the war club. He, like most Shawnee youth, learned to move silently through the forest and to communicate by using a whistling code. Making bird and animal sounds, the boys learned to contact each other without the enemy's knowing. Another art valued by the Indians, speechmaking, was taught by example. "It is better for the red men to die like warriors," a Shawnee named Cornstalk declared, "than to diminish away by inches" (Gilbert, p. 95). Tecumseh would live his life by this belief.

Deaths in the family. Among Cornstalk's followers were Black Hoof, Black Fish, Blue Jacket, and Tecumseh's father, Puckeshinwa. Puckeshinwa was killed by the Long Knives (white frontiersmen) during Pontiac's Rebellion in 1774. Dying in the arms of his eldest son, Cheesekau, the father made him promise never to surrender to the Long Knives and to raise his brothers as warriors. Tecumseh was six at the time. Black Fish adopted the six-year-old, but Cheesekau became Tecumseh's role model.

The Shawnee split into two groups in 1779. One group left for Missouri to escape the Long Knives and Tecumseh's mother joined them, taking along her youngest daughter. The rest of the family stayed behind in Black Fish's village. Tecumpease, the older sister, married a warrior and made room in her cabin for eleven-year-old Tecumseh. Twice that year whites attacked the village. In one attack they killed Black Fish, Tecumseh's foster father.

In 1787, Cheesekau took Tecumseh on a three-year hunt. Four other Shawnee youths came along. Nineteen at the time, Tecumseh stood five-feet ten-inches tall. He had grown into a strapping warrior with hazel eyes and a warm smile. During the first year of the hunt, the Shawnee joined some other Indians, the Chicamuauga, in a war party. One day Cheesekau had a vision: He would die in the fighting, at noon, shot in the head by the Long Knives. The others urged him to stay behind, but Cheesekau refused. To do so would be the act of a coward.

Cheesekau's vision came true. He was shot to death in the fighting at noon, as predicted. To avenge his brother's death, Tecumseh killed and scalped three white men. For the next two years Tecumseh roamed the south with Cherokee and Creek Indians, joining them in raids against the Long Knives.

Then came the Battle of Fallen Timbers in 1794. Blue Jacket commanded an army of more than 1,000 warriors from several Indian nations. Tecumseh led a party of Shawnee into action. When enemy guns flushed out his warriors from behind some logs, the twenty-six-year-old Tecumseh made a second stand in a dense thicket. There his oldest living brother, Sauwauseekau, died fighting the Long Knives, as Tecumseh's father, foster father, and eldest brother had before him. The Indians lost. Defeated at Fallen Timbers, twelve Indian nations signed the Greenville Treaty. It was a forced exchange: Indian land for American money. Tecumseh was the only leader who refused to sign any treaty, a decision that won the approval of other like-minded Indians.

Chief Tecumseh. After Fallen Timbers, Tecumseh chose to practice the old life-style rather than adopt white ways. He became chief in a village of 100 or so Shawnee. They hunted. They raised corn. But their old habits grew harder and harder to maintain with a million whites cluttering up the frontier.

Tecumseh's Family	
Mother	Methoastaske
Father	Puckeshinwa
Children	Cheesekau
	Tecumpease
	Sauwauseekau
	Tecumseh
	Lalawethika (the prophet, one of three triplets)
	Four other children

During these years, Tecumseh married Mamate, who bore him a son, Pachetha. It is unclear whether or not his wife died, but Pachetha was given to Tecumpease, Tecumseh's older sister, to raise. For the next five years, Tecumseh kept company with an attractive Indian woman. The relationship, his last long-term one, ended in 1807. Much has been made of a romance between Tecumseh and a white frontierswoman, Rebecca Galloway. Yet there is no evidence of such a relationship, and it probably never happened. In either case, after 1807 Tecumseh devoted himself wholeheartedly to the Indian cause.

Participation—War of 1812

Conflicting viewpoints. Though they had lost the Revolutionary War, the British kept their forts in the American Northwest, which at the time stretched from the Great Lakes Region south to the Ohio and Mississippi rivers. The few British who lived in the Northwest continued, as before, to profit from the fur trade and to deal with the sixty Indian nations in the region. But there was one major difference: the Americans now controlled the area. The British viewed the Indians as key to overturning this new balance of power. White Americans, on the other hand, saw the Indians as a defeated group, whose lands were lost when its British allies lost the Revolution. The American victors planned to buy Indian lands, then parcel them out to white frontiersmen.

But the Indians considered themselves undefeated. More often than not they had won frontier battles in the Revolution. Moreover, the Indians found the very idea of owning land strange. They believed that the Great Spirit had provided this land for his Indian children to use. Selling parcels of it made no sense. "God gave us this country," explained the Shawnee chief Kekewepellethe. "We do not understand measuring out the land. It is all ours" (Gilbert, p. 115). Again and again, Indians argued that a chief had no right to sign away territory they all owned.

Conflicts broke out among Indian groups, complicating the issue. The Iroquois in the East claimed that they had defeated and therefore controlled the territory of Indian nations in the Ohio Valley, including the Shawnee. With this in mind, the Iroquois sold the Shawnee hunting grounds to the United States as early as 1768, in the Treaty of Fort Stanwix. The Shawnee, of course, dismissed the idea that the Iroquois were their landlords. So the whites, the Shawnee warned, had better stay off their land. But the whites paid little heed. They would advance by force if necessary, and the Shawnee, in turn, would respond with force. Thus the tug-of-war between Indians and whites over the Northwest began in the 1760s, the decade Tecumseh was born. The fighting continued for almost fifty years, interrupted every so often by treaties and uneasy peace. It finally climaxed in the full-fledged War of 1812.

Speechmaking. Tecumseh stirred up frontier life in the prewar years. Through his speeches, he won Indians to his cause, and he met with white generals. Most other Shawnee—led by Black Hoof—were attempting to live in harmony with the whites. They dismissed Tecumseh as just another troublemaker. Whites, however, saw him as a serious threat. His arch enemy, U.S. general William Henry Harrison, warned that Tecumseh was a genius, the type of individual who could start a revolution. He was a "bold, active, sensible man," declared Harrison, "daring in the extreme and capable of any undertaking" (Gilbert, p. 192).

Tecumseh's followers continued to live in the forested villages and hunting camps of their youth. Into this old scheme, however, Tecumseh introduced one new ingredient: a union of Indian peoples, a federation of the sixty tribes between the Great Lakes and Gulf of Mexico. Only together, he argued, could they withstand the Long Knives. From 1803 into the war period, Tecumseh traveled widely, delivering stirring speeches to white and to Indian audiences. He blamed whites for breaking promises and cheating the Indians and generally failing to practice the values they preached. He also reminded them that their people had murdered the Shawnee chief Moluntha in front of the American flag. He urged the Indians to join the union he had begun to build. Traveling to different villages of the Cherokee, Creek, Delaware, Wyandot, Potawatomi, and more, Tecumseh left them with a harsh warning:

> Brothers—The white men are not friends to the Indians: at first they only asked for land sufficient for a wigwam; now, nothing will satisfy them but the whole of our hunting grounds.
>
> Accursed be the race that has seized our country and made women of our warriors! Our fathers, from their tombs, reproach us as slaves and cowards
>
> Do they not even now kick and strike us as they do their black-faces [slaves]? How long will it be before they will tie us to a post and whip us and make us work for them in their corn fields as they do them? (Gilbert, p. 207)

Tecumseh's heated words won followers. He usually tailored his speeches to the listeners, but his message remained the same. If the Indian nations failed to join forces, they would surely be defeated, group by group. Tecumseh was not above using dramatics to achieve his aims. He spoke in war paint. Once on a trip south, when some of the older Creek Indians disapproved of his words, an annoyed Tecumseh threatened to stamp his foot and make the earth shake. (He had heard a prediction that there would be an earthquake.) What the older Creek must have thought when, with Tecumseh already gone from their region, the earth did indeed shake! Even so, Tecumseh's success in the South was limited. Some of the young Creeks were the only ones to join the cause.

The Indian army. Still, the number of rebels mounted. As early as 1807, about 1,500 Indians from a mix of nations had arrived in Tecumseh's village. They sorely taxed the food supply. Soon Tecumseh had to turn to the British to help feed everyone. Still, the recruits were welcome. Several of them would become Tecumseh's main lieutenants: Shabbona, an Ottawa Indian; Roundhead, a Wyandot Indian; Billy Caldwell, a mixed blood; and Andrew Clark, who was white.

Whites on the frontier grew fearful. The very idea of an Indian union upset Harrison, who was now governor of the Indian territory. Like the sharpest of political leaders, Tecumseh answered his fears with a comparison: The Indians were just following the example set by the "United" States.

Indian-American relations. There was a weak attempt at peace talks between the Indians and white Americans. In August 1810 and July 1811, forty-two-year-old Tecumseh visited Harrison at Vincennes in what is now Indiana. He brought along several hundred followers, leaving them a short distance away from the official meeting. At Tecumseh's insistence, the Americans moved the meeting to a grove of trees. The leaders sat on the grass to talk. The conference grew heated: Tecumseh argued that recent land treaties were unlawful, made by chiefs who had no right to sell. Harrison objected. At a second meeting, Harrison warned that if there was war, the Indians would suffer. Unruffled, Tecumseh replied that whether or not war broke out depended on the Americans. All those Indians visible in the distance came not to make war but to prevent further trespasses on Indian land.

Battle of Tippecanoe. During Tecumseh's travels, the union back home fell apart. Tecumseh had left it in charge of his younger brother Lalawethika. The clumsy child had grown into a teenager who drank heavily. Later, he stopped drinking and became a prophet, or medicine man. He then had a conversation with the

▲ Tenskwatawa

Indian god, the Great Spirit, he claimed. Taking a new name, Tenskwatawa ("the Open Door"), the prophet won recruits to Tecumseh's army with advice from the Great Spirit. According to the prophet, the Indians must 1) get rid of white influences, mainly alcohol; 2) stop trying to acquire possessions; and 3) return to community, not individual, ownership of the land. Tecumseh, it seems, did not believe in Tenskwatawa's powers. He saw that others did, however, and used his younger brother to win followers.

229

Knowing the time was not ripe for battle, Tecumseh had warned his brother to avoid war with Harrison. The prophet did not listen. He had a vision, he claimed, that the Indians would defeat Harrison. So, before dawn on November 7, 1811, Tenskwatawa sent some warriors off to kill Harrison and his officers. Harrison escaped, barely. Close hand-to-hand combat followed, with soldiers chasing warriors to a nearby swamp. The soldiers burned the Indians' village and food supplies.

Called the Battle of Tippecanoe, the fighting ended in a draw. There was no clear victor, but, in effect, the Americans won because the battle showed that this union of Indians was beatable. Also, many Indians lost faith in the prophet. He had promised victory, but they had failed. So the union of different Indian tribes began to collapse. Later, the Americans came to regard the Battle of Tippecanoe as the first real struggle in the War of 1812.

British-Indian relations. After the battle, Tenskwatawa dropped out of action. Tecumseh and his loyal lieutenants became the heart of the Indian movement. They tried to salvage the union. From Tecumseh's point of view, united Indian resistance was still the only honorable course of action. "Will we wait to be destroyed … without making an effort worthy of our race?" asked Tecumseh in disbelief. "War or extermination is now our only choice" (Gilbert, p. 214).

After Tippecanoe, Tecumseh presented himself as a war chief seeking allies rather than as a head of a federation. In this way, he managed to patch together the faltering union of Indian nations. He then staged a scene to fool the Americans. In front of Harrison's men, an Indian named Isadore Chaine pretended to scold Tecumseh for being a troublemaker. Chaine then arranged a private meeting with Tecumseh, supposedly to continue the scolding. Once the two were alone, however, Chaine gave him a black wampum belt from the British, a sign that war was about to break out. Tecumseh should come to Fort Malden, British headquarters, for guns.

Tecumseh joined the British against a common enemy yet remained an independent leader fighting for his own purposes. The conflict, in his eyes, was between Indians and Long Knives over land and way of life. Recognizing the enemy's strength, Tecumseh adjusted his goal. He insisted not on getting back his people's old territory but on setting up an independent Indian state in Michigan. In hindsight, there was little chance of achieving even this goal. The arithmetic was against Tecumseh: less than 100,000 Indians against one million whites. Outnumbered and out-supplied, the Indians could not replace their losses quickly enough. This was far from clear at the time, however. Whites were frightened. Aided by the British, the Indians seemed a fearful foe. Long Knives envisioned swarms of savages descending on their families.

Detroit. A cry went up in the Northwest to conquer Canada. It was the only way, clamored the Long Knives, to quash the Indians and end the threat they posed on the frontier. The American government appointed Major General William Hull to lead its army. Meanwhile, Tecumseh and his followers joined the British at Fort Malden in Canada. There the warrior had the good fortune to meet his match in a British commander, Major General Isaac Brock. Several inches above six feet tall and forty-three years old, Brock was a man of action with great respect for Tecumseh's military mind. He supported the idea of an Indian nation in Michigan—fair payment, it seemed, for Indian aid in the war. Some Americans protested the partnership, arguing that it was improper for the British to use Indians as allies in the war. Brock dismissed the protesters with some rough advice: "If their warfare ... is more terror to the enemy ... let him retrace his steps" (Gilbert, p. 280). The British commander proceeded to make military decisions with Tecumseh. Together they moved on Detroit.

The American commander, Hull, advanced northward to capture Fort Malden. Because of false rumors, Hull operated under the notion that thousands of warriors lay waiting to pounce on the Americans. This was far from true, but Tecumseh and his warriors played on Hull's fears, noisily attacking American supply units bound for Hull's troops. Tecumseh suffered a leg wound in these skirmishes. Frightened, Hull fell back to Fort Detroit. Brock and Tecumseh planned an attack on the fort. Using his knife on elm bark, Tecumseh carved a map of Detroit—the fort and village—for Brock. The two commanders arranged their troops.

Brock's 600 soldiers and Tecumseh's 700 warriors opened fire on the 1,500 American soldiers inside the fort. A British cannonball hit Hull's quarters right away, just missing his daughter and killing some officers. Hull promptly ran a white bedsheet up the flagpole. Without fighting, he had surrendered the 2,000-strong army of the American Northwest. The credit, it turned out, belonged to the Indians. Hull panicked at the thought of what they might do to the women and children. Afterward, Tecumseh and Brock rode proudly into the fort. Tecumseh, always a plain dresser, wore buckskins and a wide red sash he had received from Brock. Later Tecumseh passed on the sash to his fellow warrior Roundhead for fighting more honorably than himself. The American army court-martialed Hull for his actions, then sentenced him to be shot. President James Madison canceled the sentence due to past service. But Hull was relieved of duty. William Henry Harrison took charge of America's army in the Northwest.

Fort Meigs. Given the success at Detroit, Tecumseh sent runners west to attract more Indians to the army. The Potowatomi meanwhile captured Fort Dearborn (now Chicago). By summer's end in 1812, the British and Indians controlled most of the Old Northwest. Their alliance was effective. Then on October 13, Isaac Brock was killed, and a much weaker British leader, Henry Proctor, took command. Tecumseh's spirits fell. There would be no straight talk from Proctor, and little direction. Around the same time, Tecumseh's family joined him, his brother Tenskwatawa, his sister Tecumpease, and his thirteen-year-old son, Pachetha.

Tecumseh continued to recruit Indians until, by April 1813, he had an army of nearly 1,500. They set out with 500 British soldiers to capture Fort Meigs on Lake Erie. Twice they attacked but failed. Tecumseh's old foe, Harrison, was defending the fort, with 1,200 men already there and 1,200 on their way. For three days British cannon bombarded Fort Meigs. It withstood the fire. Meanwhile, extra American soldiers arrived. At first they chased the Indians through some fallen timbers but the warriors turned, killing about 100 Americans and capturing 500 more. A few warriors began to butcher the unarmed American prisoners. Lashing his horse to the scene, Tecumseh chased the butchers away. Forty prisoners had been killed, but Tecumseh saved the rest. He had promised the British that his warriors would not commit torture. Such acts, he believed, rotted a man's soul.

Next Tecumseh made probably the greatest military mistake

of his career: a second attempt to take Fort Meigs. He now led an army of 2,500, the largest Indian fighting unit ever assembled in North American history. Reluctantly, Proctor agreed to let 500 British soldiers join this second attack. Harrison had strengthened his position by then, with men and with cannons. In hopes of drawing the men out of the fort, Tecumseh staged a fake battle in the woods against some make-believe Americans. Harrison stayed put, so the Indians abandoned the attack. Meanwhile, Proctor withheld news from them about British defeat at the Battle of Lake Erie (see **Oliver Hazard Perry**).

Proctor decided his forces should retreat from battle altogether. Meanwhile, Harrison marched north to pit his American army against the shrinking mix of British troops and Indian warriors. Discouraged by Proctor's attitude and by limited military successes, some of the warriors left the fight too. Tecumseh's army was reduced by more than half.

Battle of the Thames. Once he heard the news of the defeat at Lake Erie, Tecumseh scolded Proctor for withholding the truth. Then the Indian leader insisted on making a last stand:

> Listen, father! The Americans have not yet defeated us by land; ... we therefore wish to remain here, and fight.... You have got the arms and ammunition which our great father [English king] sent for his red children. If you have any idea of going away, give them to us, and you may go in welcome; for us, our lives are in the hands of the Great Spirit. We are determined to defend our lands, and if it is his will, we wish to leave our bones upon them. (Gilbert, p. 310)

There were British who agreed with Tecumseh. Finally Proctor consented to a last stand near Moraviantown on the Thames River.

Tecumseh suspected his life was nearing its end. Yet he seemed to enjoy himself in these last days. He had been trained to match wits with the enemy, and he welcomed the opportunity to do so once again. Tecumseh agreed to shield the British so they could retreat to Moraviantown before fighting. During this retreat, some Americans opened fire, wounding Tecumseh in the arm. Still, he and his warriors held them off, screening the retreat of the Indian families too.

Tecumseh caught up with the British the next day at noon. Now, in the final hour, Proctor had decided at last to rely on Tecumseh's advice and asked him where the Indians should fight. Tecumseh pointed to a brush-filled ridge between two swamps. The British were stationed nearby in two thin lines, 200 yards apart, in open woods. Tecumseh had 600 warriors and Proctor had an additional 600 British soldiers. Together this force faced Harrison's advancing 3,000 Americans. Proctor asked Tecumseh to survey the British troops. Tecumseh considered the soldiers. The men, he suggested, were too thickly arranged. Their lives would be wasted to no advantage. Striding down the line of soldiers, Tecumseh pressed the hands of the British officers to cheer them. He advised Proctor to encourage the men around the cannon particularly. Surely they would be the target of fierce attack.

Tecumseh returned to the Indian fighting ground. For two hours his warriors awaited the Americans. Suddenly, the sound of a bullet shot through the air. Tecumseh grabbed his side. It was a false alarm—he had not been hit. But, as with his brother Cheesekau so many years before, this seemed to foreshadow Tecumseh's death. The others urged him not to fight. But like Cheesekau, Tecumseh insisted on going into battle.

There are various stories about exactly how Tecumseh fell. One of his lieutenants, Shabbona, said a wounded American officer (possibly Robert Johnson) shot Tecumseh. Tangled in some horse harnesses at the time, the officer fired his gun in self-defense as Tecumseh was about to lower his hatchet. Some Kentuckians, it is said, scalped the fallen chief and cut off strips of his skin to use for sharpening razors. But Black Hawk claimed that the Kentuckians scalped the wrong body, that the Indians had dragged off Tecumseh for burial. In any case, Tecumseh's death brought an end to the fighting. Among those who mourned his passing were white Americans. They remembered his swiftness in saving their soldiers from torture. Some resolved to name their children after him.

Aftermath

Consequences of defeat. The Americans won, and many Indians gave up hope. "On seeing Tecumseh fall," Shabbona explained,

"I went off as fast as I could, and have been a good American ever since" (Gilbert, p. 324). The Battle of the Thames, on October 5, 1813, marked the end of Indian resistance in the Old Northwest.

The Battle of Lake Erie had made possible the Battle of the Thames. Together, they resulted in the first campaign won by the Americans in the War of 1812. The tide of war had turned. Not only did the Americans recover land in the Northwest, they also broke the power of the hostile Indians on the frontier. A few Indians went on fighting in Canada, but as paid soldiers without a cause. Others returned to Michigan, where Harrison forced them to accept final defeat by making them sign a second Greenville Treaty. Tecumseh's family—Tenskwatawa, Tecumpease, and Pachetha—stayed in Canada for the next ten years. Pachetha died in Kansas in 1840. His youngest son, Wapameepto ("Gives Light as He Walks"), is said to have inherited some of his grandfather Tecumseh's strengths. After growing older, he moved to Northern Mexico, refusing to adopt the ways of whites.

The dream of Michigan becoming an Indian state died with Tecumseh, but the war continued. Moving south, the banner of Indian resistance changed hands. It was picked up by the Red Sticks, the young Creek who had been stirred by Tecumseh's words. In the end they too were defeated (see **Andrew Jackson**) at Horseshoe Bend, the last major Indian battle east of the Mississippi River.

Thereafter, Tecumseh's memory was recalled by William Henry Harrison and others to advance their own careers. But more directly, Tecumseh influenced the outcome of the war itself. Historians suggest that the foresighted Indian probably kept the United States boundary from being pushed farther north. The cost in lives and money of the fifteen-month fight against Tecumseh had greatly reduced America's thirst for Canada.

For More Information

Elting, John R. *Amateurs, To Arms! A Military History of the War of 1812.* Chapel Hill, North Carolina: Algonguin Books, 1991.

Gilbert, Bil. *God Gave Us This Country: Tecumseh and the First American Civil War.* New York: Atheneum, 1989.

Handlin, Oscar. *Tecumseh and the Quest for Indian Leadership.* Boston: Little, Brown, 1984.

Dolley Payne Madison

1768-1849

Personal Background

Early years. The eldest daughter in a family of nine children, Dolley was born to John and Mary Payne, Quakers of English and Scottish descent. Dolley passed her childhood quietly in the Paynes' Virginia country home. In the late 1700s, society frowned on learned women, which suited Dolley fine, as she demonstrated little thirst for book learning. She was educated in the basics of reading and writing, though, and writing, especially, would later serve her well. Her talents lay rather in her zest for life, her tact, her warm personality, and her wholehearted devotion to the two men she would marry, Quaker lawyer John Todd, Jr., and James Madison (see **James Madison**).

First marriage. Dolley's father, who came to be against owning slaves, freed the ones on his plantation and moved the family to Philadelphia, Pennsylvania, when Dolley was fifteen. There his starch making business failed and he fell into financial ruin and ill-health. Deciding never to marry, Dolley refused lawyer John Todd's first proposal, then, at her father's request, reconsidered. She finally did marry him at age nineteen.

The couple had two sons, Payne and William. When an epidemic of yellow fever broke out in Philadelphia three years into their marriage, her husband and newborn son, William, fell victim.

▲ **Dolley Payne Madison**

Event: War of 1812, the burning of Washington City.

Role: Dolley Payne Madison, wife of the fourth U.S. president, James Madison, wielded great behind-the-scenes influence as First Lady. Among other achievements, she fostered communication between leaders with opposing viewpoints. Dolley believed she had a share in the presidency and a responsibility to advance her husband's career. Her most notable wartime acts occurred on August 24, 1814, when she saved valuable government documents before the British burned Washington City.

As the feverish John Todd lay dying, Dolley flung herself into his arms, heedless of the danger to herself. She survived her own struggle against the illness, left with only her older son, Payne.

Second marriage. Meanwhile, Dolley's mother, in order to support herself, had opened a boarding house for congressmen. Dolley moved in with Payne, showering her affection on her remaining son. Her grief-stricken moments were numbered, though. A young, wealthy, spirited widow, Dolley caught the eye of many young men in town. James Madison, a forty-three-year-old bachelor and the main author of the Constitution, noticed Dolley while walking through town one day. Dolley was twenty-six at the time. Attracted, Madison asked Aaron Burr, a frequent visitor at the boarding house, to introduce him that evening.

Dolley, dressed in mulberry satin, quickly won the heart of the "great little Madison," as he was called. He was seventeen years her senior and had been disappointed in love already by a young woman who called off their engagement abruptly. Fortunately, Madison found happiness with Dolley. Despite her stern Quaker upbringing, the woman had a fun-loving nature and a keen interest in family matters.

On September 15, 1794, four months after their first meeting, the couple entered a marriage that would last forty-two years and would be blessed with a deep, ongoing love and friendship. It was said that Madison could hardly stand to have Dolley out of his sight. He was a thoughtful, quiet man; she, an outgoing woman who loved the company of people. The couple remained childless but deeply involved in each other's lives throughout their marriage. Madison developed a fondness for Dolley's son, Payne, though the boy behaved in upsetting ways as time passed. Since his father's death, he had slept in his mother's bed and continued to do so after the marriage. He eventually moved away to school and grew up to dress fancily, drink, and gamble. Twice in prison for owing money, Payne built up debts that would cost his stepfather $40,000.

White House hostess. Because Madison was Episcopalian and not Quaker, Dolley was disowned by the Society of Quakers when she married him. She cast aside her plain dress and embraced the larger world. Taking in her sixteen-year-old sister

Anna, Dolley, who was just ten years older, raised her like a daughter. Later, the sisters maintained an ongoing correspondence that documents much of what would occur in the following years. Madison's niece Nelly joined the Madison household too. After Madison left Congress in 1797, the group lived on his family's estate, Montpelier, in Virginia. They moved back to Washington in 1801, when President Thomas Jefferson appointed Madison secretary of state.

Dolley developed her own personal friendship with Jefferson, who had long been her husband's closest friend. Jefferson persuaded her to reign as hostess of the President's House. In need of a woman to perform social duties, the president, a widower, turned to the wife of the highest-ranking cabinet member to entertain the women invited to dinners. Thereafter, people would affectionately call her "Queen Dolley." She would play hostess for the next sixteen years—through two terms of Jefferson's and two terms of Madison's presidencies. Warm-hearted and fun-loving, she rose to the occasion with relish.

To advance her husband's career, Dolley became politically aware and active. She learned much from her educated and experienced husband, encouraging him to share state details with her. "I wish you would indulge me with some information respecting the ... disagreement with England, which is so generally expected," she wrote him on November 1, 1805. "I am extremely anxious to hear ... what is going forward in the Cabinet" (Madison, p. 60).

Her genuine friendliness gave Dolley an advantage in relating to important statesman. She conversed easily on a multitude of subjects with key figures, meeting everyone from steamboat inventor Robert Fulton to several American Indian chiefs. Dolley had a talent, counted as invaluable in political circles, for never forgetting a name or face or an incident in someone's personal history. When told that everybody loves Mrs. Madison, she replied quite matter-of-factly, "Mrs. Madison loves everybody" (Anthony, p. 83).

Critics. But Dolley did have her critics. Some pointed to her less-than-respectable habits: her enthusiasm for card games and the racetrack, her lifelong use of tobacco snuff in public, and her delight in fashionable French clothing—flimsy, high-waisted, and low-cut gowns, elaborate hairstyles, and turbans. (Particularly noted for her turbans, Dolley wore some spectacular creations with foot-long feathers.) Her other vices included rich food, especially ice cream in warm pastry shells, and she had an ample figure to prove it. "Her soul is as big as ever," commented one wry observer, "and her body has not decreased" (Anthony, p. 85). Generally, Dolley paid little attention to her critics. She appeared to be quite comfortable with herself.

First Lady. After Madison won the election for president in 1809, Dolley's politicking continued. One evening each week she held a public reception open to statesman on both sides of issues. Called "Mrs. Madison's Crush" or simply "Wednesday Night," it gave statesmen access to the president and opportunities for informal discussion. People voiced their ideas quite freely at these receptions, a type of lobbyist's open house. Dolley would appear in queenly costume, joking and greeting the guests near the overloaded buffet tables. By then, the President's House contained a suite of public rooms: the state dining room on whose walls hung pictures of past presidents (Washington, Adams, Jefferson); Dolley's parlor, with sunflower-yellow sofas and drapes, a piano and a guitar, and a miniature portrait of Dolley; and a drawing room with red velvet curtains and cushions. At political dinners (for thirty or so guests), Madison would place Dolley at the head of the table. Next to her would be a key statesman, who voiced his views and would, in turn, be persuaded by Dolley to the president's position. Dolley also held "dove parties" for statesmen's wives to learn whatever she could about their husbands' thoughts.

Daily activities. Typically, Dolley rose early, took callers and wrote letters until noon, then returned visits in the afternoons, riding through Washington's dirt streets in a coach with a driver on the box and a footman on the platform behind. Social duties permitting, the presidential couple ate and read together in the evening. Madison would share Cabinet conversations, congressional reports, and military maneuvers with Dolley, who proved a willing listener. On her own, Dolley grilled others for information about her husband's political oppo-

---

A Rule for Presidents and First Ladies

Quoting Jemmy, as everyone called her husband, Dolley said about high office, "Be always on your guard that you become not the slave of the public nor the martyr to your friends." (Anthony, p. 97)

---

nents—she considered an election a race between married couples rather than just individuals. Like other leaders of the time (see **Andrew Jackson**), she cultivated helpful friendships. Dolley shared snuff with Henry Clay, for example, a War Hawk.

Favoring open conflict with England, the War Hawks were crucial to Madison's reelection in 1812. There was much controversy over whether to fight a war that year. New England, whose shipping and factories would suffer if war broke out, objected loudly to the possibility. The federal government was just getting on its feet at the time; the states still wielded great power. The governors of the New England states would, in fact, ignore federal calls to send state militia to battle during the war. Massachusetts would even advise its citizens to resist the war effort. Meanwhile, the War Hawks argued that Britain was impressing American sailors (kidnapping them and forcing them to go to war on their side) and stirring up Indians in the Old Northwest to halt the growth of the new nation. Despite the naysayers, Madison came to agree with the War Hawks. On June 18, 1812, he declared war.

Participation—War of 1812

Wartime responsibilities. Dolley followed each development leading to war as closely as anyone in the Department of the Navy. Though brought up in a religion whose members refused to engage in any battle, the one-time Quaker declared, "I have always been an advocate for fighting when assailed" (Anthony, p. 88).

Dolley was forty-four when war was declared in 1812. Until 1814, the daily routine would proceed as usual at the President's House with few outward signs of war. Dolley continued her Wednesday night receptions to keep spirits high and the lines of communication open. Those who attended included military leaders such as William Henry Harrison, a favorite of Dolley's. Of course, the president's duties escalated during wartime.

In 1813, when Madison's assistant Ned Coles fell ill, Dolley herself assumed Coles' tasks. Then the president lay dangerously ill with a fever for a month, and Dolley ignored all other tasks and steadfastly nursed him backed to health. An army doctor prescribed horseback riding before breakfast once Madison recovered. This he did when the family retired to his Virginia home in August to escape the Washington heat. But the following August, of 1814, would find the Madisons caught in Washington, facing more "heat" than just the weather.

British attack. Rumors smoldered that the British intended to burn Washington in retaliation for America's 1813 burning of the British capital in Canada, York, in present-day Ontario. While Americans were aware of the rumor, many did not believe it. Moreover, the American spy network did not piece together the British plan: to launch an all-out attack on Plattsburg in up state New York while distracting the enemy with a relatively unimportant attack on Washington City. The orders were to burn certain public buildings. Of course, the Madisons would be captured if found at the President's House, but reports were at least an hour or two ahead of the enemy's approach, enough time for the Madisons to flee.

Washington City at the time was only a village, with a population of perhaps 8,000 and several public buildings scattered here and there. High society consisted mostly of the official families in Washington and nearby Georgetown. The residents, including Dolley, kept slaves. Some of these "city folk" would remain in Washington and bear witness to the events about to occur.

There were townspeople who objected to the idea of Madison's leaving as the British approached. They threatened to stop him from leaving the President's House, feeling it was more proper for him to fall with it. One long-haired woman drove up to the house, loosened her locks, and swore to use them for hanging Madison if he fled. In command of the British, General Robert Ross and Admiral George Cockburn would lead the troops into Washington. Cockburn, it was rumored, threatened to parade Dolley through the streets of London. But Dolley wasn't concerned for herself, at least not until the final moments. Her worry over her husband's fate kept her in Washington until the end.

The attack began August 23, 1814. The president was off at Bladensburg, Maryland, a nearby battlefield, acting as commander in chief. Meanwhile, panic rose by the hour among Washingtonians. Crowds of fleeing women and children loaded down with baggage pressed onto the wooden bridge leading over the Potomac River and out of the city. They fled in numbers that made the bridge as dangerous as the enemy. "By nightfall the roads west of the city were choked with wagons laden with furniture and other valuables that would fit into buckboards and buggies" (Rutland, p. 160). Later, the bridge over the Potomac would be burned to prevent the enemy from using it.

Battle of Bladensburg. Pitifully few steps were taken to defend Washington City according to critics of the day. Madison, like President Jefferson before him, had operated on the belief that the militia, not a regularly trained army, could provide the soundest, most cost-effective defense for the new nation. Accordingly, a notice was posted on August 23, 1814, that all able-bodied citizens and free men of color should meet at 6:00 a.m. the following day near Bladensburg to construct a barricade to defend Washington. The government would provide the shovels, spades, and pick-axes. If a man could not attend, he was to send a substitute. Only about 100 soldiers were stationed on the north side of the President's House, behind a cannon mounted at the gate. Many more soldiers fought at the Battle of Bladensburg, which finally broke out on August 24. But, poorly trained, most of them fled.

The fighting at Bladensburg took a short three hours. British admiral Cochrane had ordered General Ross to abandon the attack. But Ross ignored this change in orders and followed the original command to capture the city, destroy its public buildings, and cause general panic. Altogether 6,000 American militiamen and sailors were pitted against slightly over 4,000 experienced British soldiers. The odds were in the Americans' favor, but they had no idea this was the case. Rather, they focused on the fact that untried American militiamen were pitted against skillful British soldiers who had just conquered French emperor Napoleon Bonaparte in Europe. Madison tried to strengthen his forces by ordering sailors to join the militia at Bladensburg. Still, some 2,000 Americans retreated before the battle even started. Most of the militia ran helter-skelter into the woods.

In the end, the battle was a disaster for the Americans. Only ten to twelve troops actually died while about sixty-four British were killed, but the British gave the impression of being much stronger than they were. Thus, General William Winder ordered the American forces to retreat, leaving the road to the city of Washington totally undefended. The battle had lasted from 1:00 p.m. to 4:00 p.m. Menacingly, the British advanced on Washington while the Americans retreated in the distance and injured soldiers moaned on the battlefield.

Dolley Madison's flight. During the day, Madison sent Dolley several messages. An early one was calm: "The reports as to the enemy have varied every hour. The last and probably truest information is that they are not very strong … and of course that they are not in a condition to strike at Washington" (Rutland, p. 160).

The final message, delivered by a free black man known as James Smith, ordered Dolley to flee. Ever the correspondent, she had been writing her sister of events as they occurred: "Three o'clock.—Will you believe it, my sister? We have had a battle, or skirmish, near Bladensburg, and here I am still, within sound of the cannon" (Madison, p. 110).

Since sunrise Dolley had turned her binoculars on the crowds, racked with concern for her husband and disappointed in her search for him, eyeing only groups of military and panic-stricken citizens wandering in all directions. Dolley had already made certain that important documents—the Declaration of Independence, the Constitution, and treaties—were packed in coarse linen bags readied for flight. They were taken to a vacant stone house in Leesburg, Virginia, thirty-five miles outside Washington. Most of the Madisons' private property had to be sacrificed, but Dolley did manage to grab some silverware, the red velvet curtains from the drawing room, the miniature of herself from the parlor, and George Washington's portrait by Gilbert Stuart from the state dining room. The large, framed painting proved impossible to take down from the wall quickly, so the canvas was detached from the frame, then given to two gentlemen for safekeeping. Her husband had promised to save the portrait if the house was burned and Dolley, in her most memorable act, insisted on keeping the promise for him.

True Confession

Dolley confessed that as the British approached she was free from fear, and willing to remain in the Castle. "If I could have had a cannon through every window, but alas! those who should have placed them there, fled before me, and my whole heart mourned for my country!" (Moore, p. 107)

▲ Saving the Declaration of Independence

Fear finally got the better of Dolley. "I lived a lifetime in those last moments," she remembered, "waiting for Madison's return" (Madison, p. 109). With her carriage loaded with public and the little private property she could carry, Dolley finally fled the city at 3:30 p.m. Searching for Madison, she came upon him and Secretary of State James Monroe an hour or so later near one of the bridges. Madison had sent the remnant of the army to Baltimore, Maryland. Now preoccupied with that city's defense, he made plans to meet Dolley later.

Destruction by fire. At 7:30 that evening the British reached Washington. They restrained themselves to some degree, sparing private property but torching public buildings, including the Capitol, the President's House, and government offices. They spent twenty-eight hours in the city, leaving before planned because of two strange disasters and the fear that American soldiers would attack any moment. The first evening the British were wild in their destruction of the public buildings. Major General Ross is said to have mounted the Speaker of the House's chair in the capitol building, which at the time was only two wings connected by a temporary wooden structure. He mockingly posed the question, "Shall this harbor of Yankee democracy be burned?" whereupon his troops responded "Aye." Then came destruction by fire.

On reaching the President's House, the British ransacked it, finding little of value except some penciled notes from Madison to Dolley when he was with the troops. They took an old hat as a memento of Madison and, more crudely, a cushion that brought to mind "Mrs. Madison's seat." Having expected Madison and some officers for dinner after the battle, Dolley had set the table for forty or so guests. The British, according to fifteen-year-old Paul Jennings, the president's black servant who witnessed the scene, washed down joints of meat with an assortment of wines before burning the building. Outside, fifty men marched down the street, carrying long poles with balls of wildfire (flammable material). On command, they broke the windows, threw in their wildfire, and burned down the house. Other buildings were spared. American citizens still in the city convinced the British not to burn a building if doing so would endanger the surrounding homes. Private residences were plundered, but mainly by American ruffians who took advantage of the chaos for their own gain.

Two calamities put an early halt to the British attack. A tremendous hurricane stormed through Washington on August 15, covering the city in a blanket of darkness, unleashing a flood of rain and tearing off rooftops. The disaster lasted two hours, during which time many homes that had been spared by the British were blown apart. Buried beneath the ruins were some thirty British soldiers and as many Washingtonians. A second disaster was brought on by an officer who pitched his torch into a dry well, thinking it was a safe place to extinguish it. At the bottom of the well were weapons and munitions, probably dating back to the Revolutionary War. There was an instant, tremendous explosion that flung debris far and wide and wounded nearly one hundred British soldiers, who were taken in their now bloody red uniforms to a makeshift hospital in a house near the Capitol.

Battle at Baltimore. Meanwhile, Dolley headed for a tavern in Great Falls, Virginia, where she and her husband had arranged to meet. Not everyone in the country had been in favor of this war or the president's handling of it. The tavern keeper's wife refused to serve Dolley because the president had her husband out fighting. Other hecklers seconded the refusal. While the storm raged, Dolley, finally given shelter, spent an anxious night awaiting Madison. He appeared the next day. Warned that the enemy had discovered their hiding place, Madison advised Dolley to put on a disguise and escape farther into the country. Dressed as a farm woman, she went back on the road. Madison, meanwhile, caught up with the Baltimore-bound American troops. He discussed strategy and then headed back for Washington.

Frightened by the two disasters and supposing that American soldiers would descend on Washington at any moment, the British fled secretly in the night. They left August 25, 1814, driving some sixty head of cattle before them.

The British soldiers' next destination was Baltimore, a city four times the size of Washington with a population of 40,000. Baltimore had seen to its own defense. Forewarned about the British, the citizens built earthworks, or embankments made of dirt, to protect the city. British general Ross and Admiral Cockburn meanwhile wasted time trying to convince their superior, Admiral Cochrane, that they should in fact attack Baltimore. Eight days passed, allowing more than 12,200 American soldiers—including 3,200 from Washington—to collect at Baltimore.

On September 12, the British finally attacked the city. They were met by the Americans, who opened fire on the advancing British, killing General Ross in the first few moments. The sharpshooters surprised the British with their accuracy. Unable to get close enough to do damage, cannons on the British boats bombed the Americans to little purpose. Few hit their targets, bursting in mid-air. This inspired Francis Scott Key, an American gunner on another vessel, to write The *Star Spangled Banner,* which became the national anthem. The lyric includes the passage: "The Rockets red glare, the bombs bursting in air, gave proof through the night, that the flag was still there." Defeated at Baltimore, the British fell back to the island of Jamaica and prepared to attack New Orleans, Louisiana (see **Andrew Jackson**).

Aftermath

Effect of the attack on the capital. Why had the British bothered to attack Washington City and then pull out? In Europe the fall of a capital spelled final defeat. That this was not the case in the United States was due to the fact that the national government was still struggling for power. The states, then in control of day-to-day living, wielded more power than the central government. So nobody considered surrender just because Washington fell.

In the end the attacks on Washington and Baltimore had given the Americans a victory. It was surprising news to the English back home, who were highly embarrassed at reports of how their soldiers had acted in Washington City—such wildness, they believed, was not proper behavior for Englishmen.

The Madisons' return. The President's House was a charred hulk now, so the Madisons occupied the Octagon House, where the French Minister had once lived. Dolley, now fiercely anti-British, resumed her Wednesday night receptions.

The original President's House had taken ten years to build. A newly built structure would be finished in three years. Dolley had mourned the loss of the "Castle" for a few months, but soon found new cause for celebration. Jubilant over the American victory at New Orleans, she lit up the Octagon House with scores of candles. Her husband held a reception for General Andrew Jackson, at which Dolley was as honored as the war hero. As always, she did not receive total applause, however. Critics had long frowned on her use of slaves to hold candles at the presidential receptions. Now the Madisons were criticized for having fled Washington during the British attack, though the couple was also applauded for their speedy return and resumption of government life.

The Madisons moved once more before retiring to their Montpelier home in 1817, after James Monroe became President. They rarely left Montpelier for the next twenty years, the world coming to their doorstep. It was not unusual for the Madisons to entertain thirty guests at once there. After Madison died in 1836, Dolley moved back to Washington for the final twelve years of her life. Plunged into debt, largely by the misdeeds of her son, she sold her husband's papers to Congress: notes on the Constitutional Convention for $30,000 in 1837 and his correspondence for $25,000 in 1848. After settling her debts, Dolley was left with about $29,000. Her niece Anna lived with her until Dolley's death of apoplexy in 1849 at age eighty one. In her will Dolley, who always cherished the company of loved ones, rewarded the loyal Anna with $10,000. Her son Payne contested the will and lost.

For More Information

Anthony, Carl Sferrazza. *First Ladies: The Saga of the Presidents' Wives and Their Power, 1789-1961.* New York: William Morrow, 1990.

Arnett, Ethel Stephens. *Mrs. James Madison: The Incomparable Dolley.* Greensboro, North Carolina: Piedmont Press, 1972.

Madison, Dolley. *Memoirs and Letters of Dolly Madison.* New York: Houghton Mifflin, 1886.

Moore, Virginia. *The Madisons: A Biography.* New York: McGraw-Hill, 1979.

Rutland, Robert Allen. *The Presidency of James Madison.* Lawrence, Kansas: University Press of Kansas, 1990.

Seale, William. *The President's House.* Washington, D.C.: White House Historical Association, 1986.

Andrew Jackson

1767-1845

Personal Background

Early war experience. Born in a backwoods settlement in Waxhaw, South Carolina, Andrew Jackson came from Irish stock. His parents had emigrated from northern Ireland in 1765, and his father died a few days before Andrew's birth. Andrew grew into a tall, thin, sandy-haired, moody young boy. His mother, Elizabeth Hutchinson Jackson, taught her sons, by example, to always back up their beliefs with action.

The American Revolution exploded onto Andrew's home ground, claiming the life of his older brother Hugh in 1779. A year later the British staged a surprise attack on the Americans, who surrendered and then were butchered, giving young Andrew first-hand experience with the cruelties of war. The two remaining Jackson boys, sixteen-year-old Robert and thirteen-year-old Andrew, enlisted in the backwoods cavalry. Already a quick rider well acquainted with the backwoods roads, Andrew became a mounted messenger.

In 1781 the British captured both brothers. While he was a prisoner, Andrew was ordered by a British officer to wipe his boots. When Andrew refused, the officer raised his sword and slashed at the boy's head and arm, which he had thrown up for protection. Robert, just as uncooperative, received a gash on his head. Later,

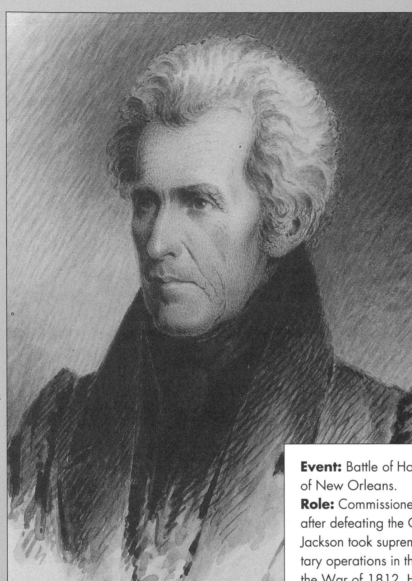

▲ **Andrew Jackson**

Event: Battle of Horseshoe Bend; Battle of New Orleans.

Role: Commissioned as major general after defeating the Creek Nation, Andrew Jackson took supreme command of military operations in the Southwest during the War of 1812. His victory at New Orleans (after the peace treaty that officially ended the war was signed) launched him to immediate fame and, in 1828, to the presidency. Even today, historians view the Battle of New Orleans not as wasted effort but as reason enough for having fought the entire war.

when the boys caught smallpox, their mother persuaded the British to release them. Andrew walked the forty miles home barefoot and coatless. Two days after they arrived, his brother Robert died. Then his mother left home to nurse the sick in Charleston, and she also died. Andrew, at fourteen, was alone in the world. He developed a hatred for the British during these days, which would remain with him. He would remember, too, his mother's last words when disputes arose in his personal life: "Never ... sue ... for slander [insults] ... settle them cases yourself" (Davis, p. 7).

Law. Jackson lived with friends and relatives for the next few years, becoming a saddler's apprentice and a schoolteacher. Mostly, though, he indulged his taste for worldly pleasures: horse racing, gambling, cockfighting, and some drinking. He began to adopt the airs of a South Carolina gentleman. Shortly thereafter, a grandfather in Ireland left the orphan a small fortune, most of which he lost in merrymaking and betting on horse races. At age seventeen, he took the little money he had left and, after casting around for a profession, shrewdly decided to study law in North Carolina, a profitable trade in those times. After two-and-a-half years of training (and continuing to indulge his more scandalous tastes), Jackson was admitted to the bar on September 26, 1787. Soon afterward he set out for Tennessee with a fellow law student, John McNairy, who became a judge and appointed Jackson a prosecuting attorney. Jackson, throughout his career, seemed to make useful friendships with people he genuinely liked and who were successful in their own right.

Romance. Of course, the hot-tempered Jackson made his share of enemies too. He settled in Nashville, Tennessee, then a stockaded village of log cabins. The young lawyer found lodging with a widow whose daughter, Rachel Donelson, had at seventeen married Lewis Robards. Robards, it seems, was an insanely jealous husband, and Rachel had returned home to Nashville to escape the miserable marriage. There she met Jackson and the two were attracted to each other. Meanwhile, Robards had applied and received permission for a divorce. Both Rachel and Jackson believed the divorce was granted, so in 1791 they married. To Rachel's horror, she discovered two years later that the divorce had never been finalized. She was guilty of bigamy or being married to two people at the same time. The enraged Jackson, as fierce in his love for Rachel as he was in every other aspect of his life, felt responsible for the disgrace. Robards finally did get the divorce, on the grounds now of adultery. "I expected him to kill me," moaned Rachel, "but this is worse" (Davis, p. 24). Knowing they were innocent, Jackson saw no need to remarry but did so in 1794 for Rachel's sake. The scandal would later resurface in his public life when political enemies would use it against him.

Politics. Meanwhile, Jackson had set himself up as a gentleman of the frontier. He rode the circuit (that is, traveled from court to court to practice law in the district), planted cotton, raced horses, and made notable friends, such as Governor William Blount of North Carolina. When Tennessee became a state in 1796, Jackson helped frame the constitution. That same year he was elected to the United States House of Representatives, followed by a stint in the United States Senate in 1797. Jackson made an unfavorable impression in Congress. "His passions are terrible," Thomas Jefferson observed. "He could never speak on account of the rashness of his feelings. I have seen him attempt it frequently, and as often choke with rage" (Davis, p. 41). As major general of the Tennessee militia in 1802, Jackson held a post second only to the governorship.

Duels. In business, Jackson experienced successes and setbacks. He bought and sold thousands of acres of land. Jackson owned slaves and several small plantations. The Hermitage, outside Nashville, became his permanent home. There he lived as a cotton planter, running a nearby boatyard and a store, where he traded cotton and animal pelts from his area for factory articles from the East. Jackson in one business venture agreed to build boats for Aaron Burr, not hearing the rumors of his treachery against the United States. This too would later be used against him by his political enemies.

Business reverses made Jackson turn to horse racing to restore his fortunes. His plan paid. He bought a stallion, Truxton, for 1,500 dollars, spent four to five months training him, won a 5,000 dollar race against a gelding, then purchased the gelding and won another 5,000 dollar race with it. A third race brought trouble. Truxton was pitted against a horse owned in part by Charles Dickinson, a twenty-seven-year-old ace with a shotgun. Dickinson, it seems, made some insulting remarks about Rachel in public. Jackson, thirty-nine at the time, won the horse race, then challenged Dickinson to a duel, remembering perhaps his mother's advice that the law has no remedy for an insult.

Jackson planned his strategy. He would let Dickinson, the better shot, fire first and wait to fire back. That way the bullet that entered Jackson's body—he was sure of being hit—would not upset his aim at Dickinson. Dickinson raised his pistol and fired; a cloud of dust rose from Jackson's chest but he remained standing. In horror, Dickinson, thinking he had missed Jackson, waited for the return bullet. Jackson squeezed the trigger; it failed; he recocked the gun and fired again, killing Dickinson.

In Jackson's mind, he had deliberately killed a man who was bent on killing him. Jackson started to leave, and the physician at the scene suddenly noticed his blood-filled shoe. Dickinson's bullet had lodged in his chest, missing Jackson's heart by an inch or so, too close to operate. Jackson would simply have to live with it. The duel revealed two truths about his personality: He preferred action to words and had an almost superhuman will to achieve his goals—"I'd have hit him," declared Jackson, "if he'd shot me through the brain" (Davis, p. 49). Citizens of Nashville were outraged by what seemed to be the cold-blooded killing of Dickinson. Jackson's reputation was in sore need of repair. His future actions would do the job.

Participation: War of 1812

As early as 1805, Jackson spoke of the British seizures of American ships and sailors on the high seas. "We must fight England again before long," he predicted. "I only hope we'll go to war before I'm too old to fight" (Davis, p. 47). In 1812, six days before President James Madison declared war, he sent out express riders to alert the country. Billy Phillips, a jockey who once rode Jackson's stallion Truxton, galloped southwest, screaming that war had erupted with England. Later, Phillips joined Jackson's troops.

Relationship with the troops. Soon after war was declared, America's General William Hull surrendered Detroit (see **Tecumseh**) to the British. A shocked Jackson beseeched the War Department to let him recapture it. The government did not respond, but Jackson's old friend, Governor Blount, put him to work as commander of the Tennessee volunteers. From this small beginning, the inexperienced but self-confident Jackson blossomed into probably the finest military leader in the war. He used sound military strategy and developed a tender, almost fatherlike relationship with the troops, who feared him for his temper, loved him for sharing their hardships, and laughed with affection behind his back at his dysentery (a disease causing pain, fever, and severe diarrhea). Jackson was forty-six now. Trudging for miles alongside untrained volunteers before the country even had roads would have defeated a less determined man.

Jackson had his own private pains to endure on top of every other obstacle. Aside from the bullet near his heart, a new one had lodged in his shoulder during another gunfight. Three weeks after the fight, his arm in a sling, the general was on his way to crush the Creek Indians.

Jackson versus the Creek Nation. Like most Westerners, Jackson viewed the Indians as bitter enemies. They were perceived as cruel childlike people who cheated, broke promises, murdered innocent settlers, and had to be forced into behaving. His view would change somewhat as the years passed and individual Indians touched Jackson's life and heart. However, his hunger for the United States to get hold of Indian lands never faded.

From October 1813 through March 1814, Jackson led a campaign against the Creek Indians of the Southwest, who owned some 50 million acres of land. Inspired by the Indian leader Tecumseh, a band of hostile Creeks, called the Red Sticks, had been formed to fight whites who moved onto Creek territory. Leading the Red Sticks was Chief Red Eagle, a mixed-blood, who was known also as William Views.

About a hundred miles north of Pensacola, Florida, some white settlers attacked a party of Red Sticks. The Indians escaped, then took revenge by attacking Fort Mims, which held a few hundred whites, mixed-bloods, and black slaves. Children were seized by the legs and killed by batting their heads against the stockade. Women were murdered and scalped. Chief Red Eagle tried to stop the savagery, but the Indians turned on him with their war clubs, threatening his life. In the end only twelve of the white population survived; most of the blacks were spared to serve as slaves to the Indians.

Meanwhile, Jackson's troops had not yet seen major action. Supplies were a constant problem. "There is an enemy I dread much more than I do the hostile Creek," admitted Jackson, his mind filled with the faces of hungry men, "that meagre-monster 'Famine'" (Davis, p. 79).

Still weak from the gunfight, Jackson set out to punish the Red Sticks for the attack at Fort Mims. "I march and before we return, if the general government will only hands off—we will give peace in Israel [the Promised Land]" (Davis, p. 78). Jackson struck several times, fighting and (unlike other generals in this war) repeatedly winning skirmishes at places such as Tallushatchee, Talladega, and, finally, Horseshoe Bend.

Chief Red Eagle had 7,000 warriors, but they were spread out in smaller fighting units. Jackson had 2,500 men and 1,300 horses. His strategy called for always outnumbering the enemy he attacked. Commanding two of his divisions were John Coffee and William Carroll. Jackson sent Coffee and a thousand horsemen to destroy the Creek town of Tallushatchee.

Once there, Coffee encircled the village, and the Creeks charged out, but, outnumbered, they were driven back to their village. They fought to the last man, with the whites slaughtering the warriors in their own doors. "We shot them like dogs," Davy Crockett recalled (Davis, p. 80). Jackson's army killed 186 braves and took 84 women and children prisoners. A Creek baby was pulled from his dead mother's arms and taken to camp. No one wanted him, so the general named the boy Lincoyer and adopted him. Childless, Jackson and his wife had already adopted her nephew, Andrew Jackson, Jr., as their own. (Lincoyer, lived, rather unhappily, at Jackson's home until age sixteen, when he caught tuberculosis and died).

Mutiny. More skirmishes followed. Meanwhile, the army continued to suffer miserable conditions, especially Jackson, cursed not only with piercing hunger but also with dysentery. One day, a half-starved soldier begged the general for anything to eat, and Jackson took a handful of acorns from his pocket. They were all he had, declared the general as he offered them to the starving soldier. Endearing him to his men, this tale of kindness spread throughout the camp. Affectionately, his troops coined a nickname for him— Old Hickory. The general was tough as hickory wood.

In spite of their affection for Jackson, the men rebelled at the miserable conditions. The unit of volunteers got ready to mutiny. But Jackson would not stand for mutiny, not in his outfit. With militia soldiers at his back, he blocked the volunteers' path. Then the militia decided to mutiny, and Jackson blocked their path with the volunteers at his back. He snatched a musket with his one good arm and swore he would shoot the first man in his outfit to mutiny. The rebels backed off.

One rainy day John Woods, not yet eighteen, was standing guard. He received permission to leave his post for a few moments, then left to gulp down some breakfast in his tent. Another officer, thinking Woods was shirking his duty, ordered him to pick up trash around the camp—immediately. The young man refused; he seized a gun and swore to shoot anyone who laid a hand on him. Someone cried, "Mutiny!" Jackson had said the next one to mutiny would be shot, and he aimed to keep his word. Tried by a court of five officers, Woods was sentenced to death. Jackson could have canceled the sentence; he spent two sleepless nights weighing Woods's life against the safety of the army and the need to teach the militia they absolutely must follow the rules of war. Woods was executed by firing squad before the entire camp. Afterwards, Jackson's men became a strictly obedient striking force.

Mutiny's Reward

After John Woods, six more militiamen committed mutiny during the campaign against the Creek Indians. They were sentenced to death. After winning the Battle of New Orleans, Jackson approved the sentence.

Battle of Horseshoe Bend. The campaign climaxed March 27, 1814, at Horseshoe Bend. Jackson had artillery there—a six-pound and a three-pound cannon—and about 2,500 men. His forces advanced against Chief Red Eagle and 1,000 warriors, plus 500 women and children. The Creek had skillfully defended themselves, building a zigzag breastwork, or fence, of logs with port-holes for the warriors to fire through on the advancing line of sol-diers. Jackson, surprised to see the clever barricade, said with con-fidence, "They've penned themselves up for slaughter" (Davis, p. 90). He opened fire, shooting his cannons for two hours before ordering a charge on the Indians. His soldiers ran to the wall and fired through its portholes—soldiers and Indians exchanged shots, muzzle to muzzle.

Finally, a commander tried to rush over the works, dying in the attempt. He was followed successfully by Sam Houston, who scaled the wall. Others followed. The killing grew savage, the Indi-ans continuing to fight against all odds, with bows and arrows, tom-ahawks, knives, and muskets. The slaughter continued for hours. When Jackson asked for their surrender, the Indians shot the mes-senger. Jackson finally ordered the underbrush—the Indians' last defense—set on fire. It was a clever move. The Creeks darted out to escape the fire, at which point the soldiers shot as many as they could hit. Still the Indians resisted. At dawn, Jackson's men rounded up the last sixteen warriors. They refused to surrender, so the soldiers killed them. Altogether, close to 900 warriors perished at the Bend; the tips of their noses were cut off to get an accurate count. Most of the 500 squaws and children became prisoners. Red Eagle had escaped but later appeared before Jackson, who had ordered him caught and chained, of his own free will. Dressed in tattered breeches and moccasins, Red Eagle addressed Jackson:

> "I am not afraid of you or of any man ... kill me if you like ... I come to beg you to send for the women and children of the Creek Nation, starving in the woods ... I am done fighting. The Red Sticks are almost all killed. If I could fight any longer I would not be here. But please send for the women and children. They never did any harm. Now you can kill me if you like." (Davis, pp. 91-92)

Jackson was impressed. Red Eagle had marched calmly through a campful of soldiers bent on butchering him. Here was a brave leader, a great leader. After the war Red Eagle would become an Alabama planter, and the friendship that began that day would con-tinue in visits between Red Eagle and Old Hickory.

With their fighting force crushed, the Creek had no choice but to sue for peace. Jackson decided to punish the whole Creek Nation, even the peaceful chiefs. The Creek, by the Treaty of Fort Jackson, had to turn over 23 million acres of land, stop all communication with the British and Spanish, allow roads to pass through Creek territory, and surrender any of their warriors who had fought against the whites.

Jackson, some said, had overstepped his rightful power. Without consulting Congress, he set down the terms of the treaty. Yet his success at Horseshoe Bend brought him a promotion to major general, the highest rank in the U.S. army. The British, meanwhile, were preparing to invade the American Southwest to establish a British government there.

Jackson versus the British. Old Hickory invaded Florida first. Spain owned the area at the time and was officially neutral in this war. But Jackson believed, correctly, that the British spy system in America was centered in Florida. He intended to destroy the headquarters and punish the Spanish for failing to remain neutral. So, without approval from President James Madison, he launched a surprise attack. The attack succeeded, the Spaniards surrendered, and Jackson left for New Orleans.

While Jackson himself had an excellent spy system, he was unaware of exactly where the British would strike first. The most sensible route was through Mobile, Alabama, so he defended it heavily, then returned to New Orleans. Full of bayous, creeks, and soggy ground, New Orleans offered the worst possible terrain for battle. Jackson was about to face enormous odds. Departing from Jamaica, the British had some 8,000 veteran soldiers against perhaps 3,000 of Jackson's untried troops. The British also had twice as much artillery power. Moreover, New Orleans was a hotbed of disharmony at the time. The city, located within the Louisiana Territory, had become part of the United States only a generation earlier, and its citizens—Spanish, French, Creole, and Choctaw Indians—did not yet feel American.

City of New Orleans. Tall and gaunt, Jackson arrived in the city wearing an old blue Spanish cloak and mud-spattered boots. His hair was iron grey; his vision, keen; his complexion, sickly yellow. He slipped easily into the role of leader, calling on the citizens

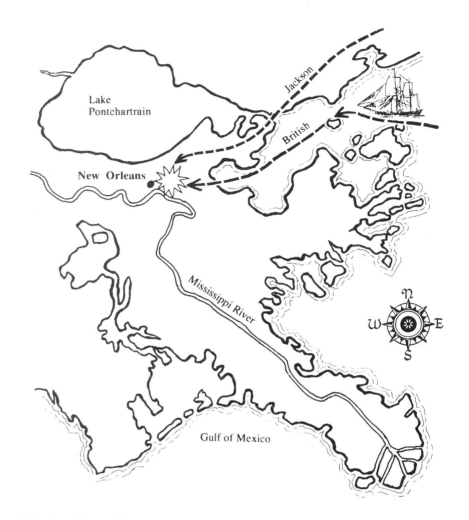

▲ Battle of New Orleans

to help him drive the enemy into the sea or die in the attempt, to help him bring honor to the city. Cleverly he strengthened their shaky ties to the nation by promising them not only their safety, "but victory over the insolent enemy who insulted you by an affected doubt of your attachment to the constitution of your country" (Remini, p. 258). To Jackson, morale was essential to winning battles. He would continue to build it throughout his defense of New Orleans.

His troops were a mix of peoples and colors. Jackson summoned his experienced fighters, John Coffee and William Carroll, to New Orleans. He set down strict rules in the city too, declaring martial law. The curfew, beginning December 16, 1814, was nine o'clock; no one could leave or enter the city without Jackson's written permission. He ordered bands to play *Yankee Doodle* and the *Marseillaise* to raise spirits and troops. On December 18, he called for a review of the battalions. Among them were city militia, free black men, and pirates.

Jackson had at first resisted help from the pirates, the Baratarians, but their leader, Jean Laffite, had offered his services—his shot, his cannon, his 1,000 men—in return for a general pardon for them for laws they had broken. Jackson consented. He needed both the men and the firepower. "The enemy is near ...," Jackson told the men, "but the brave are united; and if he finds us contending among ourselves, it will be for the prize of valour and the rewards of fame" (Remini, p. 259). The soldiers straightened with pride—Jacksons' words ignited their spirit.

Battle of New Orleans. The enemies fought four times: December 23, 1814; December 28, 1814; January 1, 1815; and January 8, 1815. The British advanced over Lake Borgne on forty-five boats loaded with sailors, marines, muskets, and cannons. They overpowered the handful of five American gunboats on that lake. The Americans who were taken prisoner all swore that Jackson's army was four times as large as it really was, frightening the enemy. The British approached more cautiously than planned, moving their troops to Pea Island—a tiny, insect-ridden island on the Mississippi. The men's spirits flagged. Finally, the British troops were ferried down a reed-filled swamp to the mainland.

On December 23, they took over the Villeré plantation and made it their headquarters. As they approached, Major Gabriel Villeré was smoking on the porch. The British caught him, but he leaped out a window, racing to alert Jackson in New Orleans, which

> ## Jackson and the Baratarian Pirates
>
> The pirates of Barataria Bay, a lagoon off southeast Louisiana, normally attacked British and Spanish ships. They operated off islands in the area, storing their pirated goods in forty warehouses and smuggling them into New Orleans for sale. Before the Battle of New Orleans, the pirates offered Jackson their cannon and soldier power if they would be pardoned for past offenses. The general hesitated to accept their services but, by the end of the battle, said "I wish I had fifty such guns ... with five hundred such devils at their butts." (Remini 1977, p. 139)

was just twelve miles away. "By the Eternal, they shall not sleep on our soil," Jackson promised (Remini, p. 263). It was 1:30 p.m. At 7:30 that evening Jackson stunned the British with an attack, begun by red, white, and blue signal fire shot into the air from one of the two American warships. The fight stopped at 9:30 due to heavy fog. There was no clear winner, but the Americans had answered a surprise invasion with a surprise counterattack, frightening the British into staying where they were for the time being.

The next day, December 24, Jackson ordered a defense line built along the Rodriguez Canal. His troops and 2,000 slaves worked in relays, enlarging the four-foot-deep, eight-foot-wide canal. They formed a barricade, hauling in firmer soil from higher elevations, laboring for four days and nights without pause. Jackson helped, sleeping little and eating only rice due to his indigestion. Food for the others was plentiful. New Orleans had responded to the general's call for unity with wagonloads of cornmeal, sweet potatoes, and other freshly grown foodstuffs. By Christmas Day, the barricade was already 8-feet high, 12-feet thick, and 1,800-feet long; it stretched from the river to a swamp.

Behind the finished barricade stood eight cannon and 4,000 soldiers. They fought in battalions: the city militia, freemen of color, Carroll's sharpshooters, Coffee's cavalry, and more. The fighting force, by the end of the battle (January 8), totaled 5,000 against the 8,000 British troops.

British spirits continued to slide as engagements on December 28 and January 1 brought no victory. Defeating the Americans was not going to be as easy as they had thought. General Sir Edward Pakenham, the British commander, had his naval cannon dragged onto the soggy land for the final attack. Meanwhile, people in New Orleans got cold feet. City lawmakers spoke of surrendering. Jackson was furious. If such talk continued, he advised Governor Claiborne, it was time to blow the legislature up. He later apologized, but his words reflected his habitual use of heated language and his determination to win. Jackson, if need be, would have burned the city to keep the British from laying their hands on it. His concern was for the safety of the Promised Land, the nation.

Commander Pakenham decided to storm the American barricade. Trapped between a river and a swamp, the British had no other choice. It was the key moment in their attempt to seize New Orleans and the American Southwest. Pakenham's troops advanced bravely, but column after column was mercilessly mowed down by American firepower. They became open targets, marching in amazing discipline to probable death. The slaughter was frightful. American cannons went off, then held their fire so the riflemen could see to shoot. "They're near enough now, gentlemen," Jackson commanded. "Fire when ready" (Davis, p. 140). Behind the barricade, the riflemen shot in rotation. The first line fired, then stepped back to reload while the second line fired, then the third, and so on without pause. Carroll's sharpshooters seemed to hit every mark. Jackson, passing a pirate, asked him in surprise why he was not firing his cannon. The pirate explained that his ammunition was faulty, so Jackson railed at Governor Claiborne, "If you don't send powder and balls instantly, I'll chop off your head and have it rammed in one of those guns!" (Davis, p. 132). The ammunition came.

Jackson moved up to higher ground to survey the field. Although he could not see that far, the British were winning on the west side of the Mississippi River. On the main front, though, Jackson saw that the ground was covered with their dead and wounded, heaped one atop the other in red or green-gray uniforms. Nine hundred plaid-trousered Scottish Highlanders advanced toward the breastwork to the tune of bagpipes playing the regimental charge (the *Monymusk*), but American firepower mowed them down too. Then Pakenham himself fought, was hit, and died.

The British retreated. Their killed and wounded numbered 2,037; the Americans, 45. Jackson walked down the American line, congratulating each battalion for its bravery and skill. Nervous about another possible British attack, he insisted on keeping the curfew and martial law in New Orleans until news of the peace treaty at Ghent reached him March 13, 1815.

Aftermath

There was grim business to take care of after the victory. Though the American death toll was slight, the troops became sickly. Over 500 soldiers died of fevers within two weeks after the victory at New Orleans. '

Jackson's career. Jackson was fined for misbehavior by a New Orleans judge, Dominick Hall, who decided the general had taken too much power into his own hands when he kept up martial law in New Orleans (and had Judge Hall arrested for trying to cancel it). Yet Jackson was hailed a hero in both New Orleans and Washington. Later, in 1818, the War Department called on him to defeat the Seminole Indians in Florida. In 1821, after Spain gave up this territory to the United States, Jackson accepted an appointment as Florida's first governor. In 1828, he was elected president. Jackson served for two terms and then retired to the Hermitage in 1837. His wife had died of a heart attack before his first inauguration. Gossip about their illegal marriage, spread by Jackson's enemies during his campaign, is said to have weakened her. Rachel was buried in the white gown she had planned to wear at the ceremony when her husband took office.

Final days. Jackson suffered financial losses due to the mismanagement of his affairs by his adopted son Andrew. In 1844, Congress decided to refund him the 1,000 dollars Judge Hall had fined him at war's end. Jackson refused to take it unless the charges against him for misconduct in New Orleans were taken back. Congress agreed to this.

Jackson's health, for decades a concern, declined. Now seventy-eight, he suffered hemorrhages, a constant cough, and frequent headaches. Word spread that he was about to die, and visitors appeared at the Hermitage in droves. They entered a few at a time, seeing symbols of a lifetime in his home: his dueling pistols, swords, and a log with a spear in it, memento of the Creek campaign. One of his slaves, Hannah, refused to leave the room at the end. He addressed them all: "My dear children, and friends and servants, I hope and trust to meet you all in heaven, both white and black. Both white and black" (Davis, p. 385).

Jackson had a religious side, despite all his heated language. He, in fact, regarded his victory at New Orleans as a heavenly miracle and afterward had asked the city's abbé to hold a thanksgiving service. Endeared to the city by this gesture, Jackson viewed himself as only an instrument in an astonishing victory, which had proved to the world that the United States was indeed a power to take seriously.

For More Information

Bassett, John Spencer, ed. *Correspondence of Andrew Jackson.* Vol. 1. Washington, D.C.: Carnegie Institution, 1926.

Davis, Burke. *Old Hickory: A Life of Andrew Jackson.* New York: The Dial Press, 1977.

Owsley, Frank Lawrence, Jr. *Struggle for the Gulf Borderlands: The Creek War and the Battle of New Orleans, 1812-1815.* Gainesville: University of Florida Press, 1981.

Remini, Robert V. *Andrew Jackson and the Course of American Empire, 1767-1821.* New York: Harper and Row, 1977.

Bibliography

Bakeless, J. *Lewis and Clark*. New York: Morrow, 1947.

Carter, Paul A. *Revolt Against Destiny: An Intellectual History of the United States.* New York: Columbia University Press, 1989.

Coit, M. *The Growing Years*. Volume 3 of *Life History of the United States*. New York: Time, 1974.

Fuller, George W. *A History of the Pacific Northwest*. New York: Alfred A. Knopf, 1952.

George, Carol V. R. *Segregated Sabbaths: Richard Allen and the Rise of Independent Black Churches, 1760-1840*. New York: Oxford University Press, 1973.

Horsman, George. *Expansion and American Indian Policy*. New York: St. Martin's Press, 1967.

Irving, Washington. *The Complete Tales of Washington Irving*. Edited by Charles Neider. Garden City, New York: Doubleday, 1975.

Josephy, A. M., Jr., editor. *American Heritage Book of Indians*. New York: American Heritage, 1971.

Lopez, Claude-Anne, and Eugenia W. Herbert. *The Private Franklin: The Man and His Family*. New York: W. W. Norton & Company, 1975.

Lyman, William Denison. *The Columbia River*. New York: G. P. Putnam and Sons, 1911.

Lynd, S. *Class Conflict, Slavery, and the United States Constitution*. Chicago: Greenwood Press, 1967.

Minot, George R. *History of the Insurrections in Massachusetts in the Year 1786 and the Rebellion Consequent Thereafter*. Salem, New Hampshire: Ayres Publishing Company, 1900.

Mitchell, Broadus. *Alexander Hamilton: The Revolutionary Years*. New York: Crowell, 1970.

Monaghan, E. Jennifer. *A Common Heritage: Noah Webster's Blue-Back Speller*. Hamden, Connecticut: Archon Books, 1983.

Morgan, Murray. *The Columbia*. Seattle: Superior Publishing Co., 1949.

Remini, Robert V. *The Revolutionary Age of Andrew Jackson*. New York: HarperCollins, 1976.

Rossiter, Clinton. *1787: The Grand Convention*. New York: Macmillan, 1966.

Schafer, Joseph. *A History of the Pacific Northwest*. New York: Macmillan, 1926.

Singletary, Otis A. *The Mexican-American War, 1846-1848*. Chicago: University of Chicago Press, 1974.

Skinner, Constance L. *Adventurers of Oregon*. New Haven, Connecticut: Yale University Press, 1921.

Taylor, Robert J. *Western Massachusetts in the Revolution*. Millwood, New York: Kraus, 1954.

BIBLIOGRAPHY

Warfel, Harry R. *Noah Webster: Schoolmaster to America.* New York: Macmillan, 1936.

Whitney, D. C. *American Presidents: Biographies of the Chief Executives From Washington Through Carter.* Garden City, New York: Doubleday, 1979.

Wise, W. *Alexander Hamilton.* New York: Putnam, 1963.

Index

Boldface indicates profiles.

PROFILES IN AMERICAN HISTORY

Significant Events and the People

Who Shaped Them

Volume 5: *Reconstruction to the Spanish American War*

Reconstruction
Andrew Johnson, Thaddeus Stevens

Indians and Government Policy
George A. Custer, Carl Schurz, Chief Joseph

Labor Movement
John D. Rockefeller, Henry George, George Pullman, Samuel Gompers, Thomas Watson

Struggle for Civil Rights
Ida B. Wells, Booker T. Washington, W.E.B. DuBois

Realism in American Literature
Mark Twain, Helen Hunt Jackson, Stephen Crane

Social Reform
Elizabeth Cady Stanton, Josephine Shaw Lowell , Frances Willard

Spanish American War
William McKinley, William Randolph Hearst, Theodore Roosevelt

Volume 6: *Chinese Exclusion to the Women's Rights Movement*

Immigration
Yung Wing, Bartolomeo Vanzetti, Abraham Cahan

Social Welfare
Jane Addams, Herbert Croly, Louis Brandeis, Upton Sinclair, Ida Tarbell

World War I
Woodrow Wilson, John Pershing, Oliver Wendell Holmes

Industrial Growth
Henry Ford, John L. Lewis

Scopes Trial
Clarence Darrow, William Jennings Bryan

Harlem Renaissance
Marcus Garvey, James Weldon Johnson, Zora Neale Hurston

Women's Rights and Roles
Charlotte Perkins Gilman, Margaret Sanger